PHILLIPSBURG LIBRARY

6748 9100 033 061 1

D0629733

BY THE SAME AUTHOR

Minturno to the Apennines

*The Language of Natural Description in
Eighteenth Century Poetry*

On A Mask Presented at Ludlow-Castle

On the Poetry of Spenser and the Form of Romances

Dante, Michelangelo and Milton

The Art of Shakespeare

Milton and the Italian Cities

SHAKESPEARE:
THE EARLY WRITINGS

Shakespeare:
The Early Writings

JOHN ARTHOS

WITHDRAWN
Phillipsburg Free Public Library

ROWMAN AND LITTLEFIELD
TOTOWA, N.J.

All rights reserved
First published in the United States 1972
by Rowman and Littlefield, Totowa, New Jersey

ISBN 0-87471-109-6

*Printed in Great Britain
by W & J Mackay Limited, Chatham*

822.33
Ar787

To the memory of
my father and mother

To the memory of
my father and mother

CONTENTS

PREFACE

In the first few years of his career—say, before 1595—Shakespeare wrote history plays and comedies, two splendidly finished
poems of a currently fashionable kind, and a number of sonnets.
The precise dates of these writings cannot be fixed although our
knowledge is good enough to enable us to place them in those
years and in reasonable order. Yet it must always astonish us that
in his very beginnings Shakespeare should have been drawn to
such different undertakings. With no certain identification to go
by, a playgoer and reader of 1595 might have been pardoned if
he refused to believe these were the works of one man.

We shall never know enough to take in the complexity of this
great and various mind, this young giant simultaneously bringing
forth works of such, one might say, antithetical character as *The
Comedy of Errors*, *Henry VI*, and *Lucrece*. Nevertheless, we cannot fail to try to discover what is common in all of this, what the
springs of life are in this variety, what likenesses and commonnesses there are in such different enterprises. We shall always be
drawn to discover the character of Shakespeare's greatness even
in the apparently disparate. In this book I am accordingly
following one more approach in this absorbing undertaking. The
life of Shakespeare's mind is such that it is always offering us
revelations, and almost any fact we might have thought simply
self-explanatory again and again shows itself to be continually
rich and strange as well. In attempting to look at some, if not all,
of the writings of these first years I have been led to consider
once again what Shakespeare was doing with some of his source

material, to weigh his place in certain traditions, to study the significance of certain conventions. Sometimes this has required rather sustained investigations into matters of background, and although these may be of interest in themselves, I hope they will not detract from the main matter, the attempt to discover something of unifying direction in this magnificent variety.

Grants from the Rackham School of Graduate Studies of the University of Michigan have made it possible for me to carry this study forward, and I wish also to express my appreciation for the hospitality of the American Academy in Rome where I was able to do much of the writing.

INTRODUCTION

Society among the English began with a few obligations, in the service lords undertook for their dependents, in the loyalty with which their servants repaid them, and in fair dealing when transferring property and in honouring bequests. By these bonds men were tied to each other and in time the habits and institutions that grew in following these obligations wove more and more complex relationships. We who have profited by these original bindings have learned that it is not only a society that has become possible through them, it is the inner life of each individual that has also been able to flourish. Doing what loyalty and honesty dictate, each man understands that what he owes to others has become what he owes to himself. Kent without a lord to serve and obey would have been only another unrooted warrior. In loyalty he protects Lear and in that loyalty he finds the measure of truth and falseness in the world, the touchstone of his own worth and of the worth of life itself.

What is true for Kent is true for us in responding as we do to him. He is our touchstone for judging what is good and evil in those distant times, and it appears that honesty such as his is even the instrument for measuring the worth of love. With a lord to serve who has protected him, Kent finds himself bound in affection as in obligation; in his attachment he has discovered the grounds of service and the substance of reflection and judgment. Through undistracted loyalty to a master who deserved loyalty he has come to recognize the degrees of falling off, in daughters and in such as Oswald, to recognize and to reject every falsification of loyalty and honesty and affection. Divining falseness as instantaneously as Prince Pericles he also can say, 'Good sooth, I care not for you.' At the end, deprived of the master and the mistress who have deserved trust he must say, 'all is cheerless, dark, and deadly.' These rudimentary relationships are the central matter of *King Lear* and they underlie as well the attachments and negotiations and confusions of the processions of men and women who come upon the stage from the beginning to the end of Shakespeare's work.

When Christianity came to Britain it brought an increase in obligations and it invested those and the others with a certain charm. Simply in the nature of successes in war and adventure and exploration populations grew and obligations increased, and in the nature of those successes religion served their glorification, in ceremony, in refinement, and in cultivating the idea of the sacred everywhere. Certainly a variety of pagan religions together with the most stirring reverberations from the invasions of the Romans brought wonder and beauty to the sense of community, but Christianity brought its own colours, its own understanding of the sacramental, astonishingly subtle intellection, to shine in the poetry of *Beowulf* and in all the intricacies of the growing civilization. Sooner or later England came to know Christian feudalism, monarchy, a universal church, and yet with so much that was imported so little was displaced. The vitality and authority of those earliest acceptances of obligation, those acknowledgements so deeply rooted they became as it were acknowledgements of what was purely and simply English, kept, as we may judge by unlimited evidence—by *Lear*, for example— an authority more deeply resistant to subversion than even Christian faith. From another point of view one would say that the matrix of English culture lay in the requirements of humanity itself.

But there was of course also the barbaric, to resist Romanization and Christianity alike. The institutions of blood—of guilt and revenge—may have been dissipated in time, here and there they may have disappeared, but the appeal to the brutal, the exercise of ferocity, the dedication to one ancient code or another, much, in short, of the most ancient kinds of dedication, would continue to persist whatever the appeal of civilization. The ancient habits of appetite and aggression, the rooting of courage, comradeship and alliances in war, continued to demonstrate their authority.

It has been said that Shakespeare is the most English of English writers, and in the history plays especially where he lays so much before us that we recognize as the very stuff of English life, we think we see something of the character of the poet too as an Englishman. As for the life he shows us we judge it to be English—rather than Christian, say, or more generally pagan— from so many simply physical qualities, in the descriptions of the countryside, in the naming of rivers and forests and farms, all those features of the particular lands that were fought over and traversed and loved, where the naming of the thing is inseparable from the love of it and of its history. The work of the poet may be thought of as English too from a certain insularity, the matter-of-fact acceptance of English life as self-sufficient in its own merely local terms, so that even in the distant Britain of Lear, the Wales of Glendower, the Scotland of Macbeth there is no significant sign of the presence of pagan gods or pagan cults, there are no inhabitants of the land except men, Britishers. There are of course the witches, the fairies and elves, and spirits from the vasty deeps of Wales. There is folklore aplenty, but it is given to us as fanciful and unbelieved in, or when almost believed in we recognize its creatures as diminutive Englishmen, Puck and Ariel being minims of Pistol and Bardolph and Bottom. Nor are there imported deities from Rome or Scandinavia or Ireland to haunt belief, however much they enrich the poetry.

This imaginative particularizing paradoxically provides the very means of opening up vistas upon the most general and even universal of conceptions. As Ruskin put it, the profundity of Shakespeare depended upon the strength of his attachment to Stratford. The attention to the native and the local led into the the exploration of what has been spoken of as the irreducibly human. If some of these figures of his imagination aspire to citizenship in the world, they will always remain Englishmen, we shall never mistake them for, let us say, Athenians. It is as if by virtue of all the traces of a particular nativity they are on the way to becoming disencumbered of what Lear would call the superfluous.

Finally, I think it is necessary to accept the greatest tragedies as representations of life in which we are led to try to think of men as divorced of all the endowments of religion and Christianity and of the idea of the state. Romans or Italians or Englishmen to begin with, we are led to try to think of them finally as unaccommodated men. It is not otherwise in the histories and comedies when the references are extended beyond the circumstantial.

The plays accordingly thrive upon contrasts. In the phrase 'side-piercing sight' in *Lear* as in the image of 'cherubim upon the sightless couriers of the air' in *Macbeth*, Shakespeare points towards the two possibilities, the idea of the unity of mankind in the embrace of Christianity set against the idea of isolated endurance. The contrast is as moving philosophically as it is dramatically, for it brings to bear all that the humanism and the scepticism of the times can bring to bear in weighing all belief. So it is that we take the cultivated young courtiers of the comedies quite as much as the English monarchs and the Roman generals as men ultimately falling back on what Kent has to fall back on, those most primitive bonds, or else discovering another hope entirely.

So Shakespeare gives the barbaric its full play, the barbaric splendour and filthiness. Or he goes to Rome and he takes Livy and Tacitus and Plutarch and Caesar and re-creates the life of another pagan society, he even has the sense of the slime of the Nile and of the life in the slime, and it is as if this English playwright were able to conceive of a world that had never been touched by the messages of Saint Paul and Saint Augustine and Saint Alban, he could as freely represent the life of pre-Christian Rome as of Britain, he would indeed contrast those two worlds

4

as much as he would contrast barbarism and Christianity. It is not only that he has the power of seeing Rome as Livy did, he will test the adequacy of that way of seeing.

When we try to take in the range of feeling and thought that Shakespeare presents us with and the depths of the greatest work, we find ourselves weighing what he presents as if unillumined by anything other than the common understanding of men who live according to the obligations they owe each other and to themselves although they know they are acted upon by powers who are independent of them—nature, fate, capricious spirits. They live with the known and the unknown, and even when like Henry VI they call upon Christ we see them exactly as we see those who do not. Shakespeare gives us an at once profligate and spare representation of the variety of experience, profligate in offering to include all potentiality, and spare in refusing to appropriate the miracles Christianity attests to and that medieval writers would not have thought of excluding. But he lets us know what it is he is excluding and in such a way that it provides a criticism of all that he is bringing before us. We are able, we think, to see the world of Lear and Macbeth as pagans would see it, and at the next instant as Christians might. The plays become at once a pagan criticism of the Christian view of life and death and happiness and suffering and a Christian criticism of pagan views. We have it both ways and we are able to have it so, because, to begin with, all is so faithful to uninstructed sense.

It would never be true to say that Shakespeare approaches drama without preconceptions, for one thing his moral sense is so unwavering. But there is a need to weigh the importance of the attitudes in him that contemporary humanism and scepticism have influenced, for he plainly owes much to the interplay and the cross-lighting of humanist thought everywhere in the Renaissance. Only infrequently does Shakespeare set up the polar contrast in clearly philosophical terms, it is generally enough for him through imaginative and dramatic effects to relate the experiences of Elizabethans to those told of in ancient

5

stories, to create through imaginative sympathy the conviction of a common character to the experience of ancient Greeks and Romans and Britishers and modern Englishmen and Italians. As always the form art takes leads thought on as it serves it. This recognition helps us in studying these early works as we think of them in the light of the later accomplishments. We see in the earliest comedies and histories not only that he is discovering the forms he will need later, we see that the forms themselves are leading into the speculation and understanding that will be his as one of the wisest of men.

In *The Comedy of Errors* Shakespeare was using as his model Plautus' *Menaechmi*, a work that had been imitated before him, as were others of Plautus, in Italy and Spain and France.[1] In this possibly the first of his complete dramatic workings, Shakespeare had adapted a play that as much as any other single one had initiated the transformation of comedy in Europe, the kindler of all those productions and translations and imitations that were to use the ancient style as the clue to a new one.

On the face of it, then, *The Comedy of Errors* presents itself as a work forwarding humanist interests, although, of course, not as a learned elaboration. It is in the vernacular in almost every sense and as rich with the tone of contemporary English life as humour could make it. Above all else, it is meant to delight, not as a re-creation but as entertainment. Its effects are manifold, but the most elementary feature—its plotting, an imbroglio—dominates our attention and gives us our greatest pleasure, and, as it turns out, this way of composing drama is to remain at the heart of Shakespeare's dramatic imaginings throughout his career. It will remain a living force in his mind in composing his greatest tragedies and it will be a means of instructing him in the transformation of histories. As a dramatic pattern it will have much charm for him, he will ring changes on it many years later. It will become embedded in works of the most variegated richness.

So it is, I think, that we may turn to this and the other early writings, looking at them somewhat closely, for their own sakes of course always, but with the further purpose of seeing how they illustrate what Italians might call Shakespeare's *vasta cultura*, the mind so profoundly and richly engaged in embodying what came before it that it might seem, in Dryden's words, that Shakespeare was naturally learned, everything became his own, and had the air of being nature's as well.

NOTE

1 Still one of our finest sources for the study of the importance of ancient comedy to Shakespeare is Cornelia C. Coulter's 'The Plautine Tradition in Shakespeare' (*Journal of English and Germanic Philology*, XIX [1920], 66–83). A more general but also excellent early work is M. W. Wallace's *The Birth of Hercules. With an Introduction on the Influence of Plautus on the Dramatic Literature of England in the Sixteenth Century*, Chicago, 1903. Professor T. W. Baldwin's researches are as valuable as they are extensive, in his *Shakespeare's Five-Act Structure*, and *On the Compositional Genetics of The Comedy of Errors*, Urbana, 1965. Recently Mr. Richard Hosley has made a remarkably suggestive contribution in his 'The Formal Influence of Plautus and Terence', in *Stratford-upon-Avon Studies*, 9 (1966).

There is a useful brief survey of the history of the *Menaechmi* by Ulisse Fresco, *La Fortuna dei Menecmi di Plauto nel Secolo XVI*, Camerino, 1903.

Plautus and *The Comedy of Errors*

The fixed setting of Roman comedy—a piazza, an intersection of streets, a couple of doorways—focuses the goings and comings, the sudden departures, the retirements within doors as the plays take up the affairs of a group of people in a city or a port. The meetings and confrontations are frequent and often hurried. The pursuits, the expulsions, the chases and concealments are always being interrupted, and it is then that there is time for words, when the audience learns what the excitement is all about. Because almost everything happens in the public streets the audience is as it were licensed to be in on it all.

Scholars still do not know how generally the Romans made use of masks in comedy. There is considerable opinion that Plautus did not demand them. Music, however, permeated the performances, and the verses of Plautus were all either declaimed to music or sung. Even in the sixteenth century printed editions gave some indication of the requirements of musical accompaniment and singing although, of course, there was no tradition to preserve anything like the original manner of performance. At any rate, the wonderful high spirits of these plays with their vivid language and their hilarious activity plainly call for jigging and dancing and all manner of movement to accord with music as well as with the entire conception.

As the classical forms came to supplant indigenous comic compositions in the Renaissance, sometimes assimilating medieval traditions, sometimes submitting to wholly different ideas of comic purpose, they united with other forms of expression—

with the *ballet de cour*, the *ballet comique*, the *opera buffa*, masque and anti-masque, triumphs and pageants and skits from the *commedie dell' arte*. The productions of Calderon and Shakespeare and Molière would variously combine music and dancing and poetry and they would never merely recreate the patterns of Roman comedy. In *The Comedy of Errors* Shakespeare would divine more than a little of Plautus' controlling conception, and in the present century a production of Shakespeare's play as a ballet and the translation of it into *The Boys from Syracuse* suggest that a fundamental factor in the Roman conception of comedy was inherent in Shakespeare's re-working of it.[1] The formalized street-scenes, the varied verse forms, the rapid changes of pace, the lyricism of many of the speeches, the occasions for pantomime in the innumerable confusions of identity represent something of the form as well as of the spirit of the ancient practice. But the plot itself, and the comic stuff, these became quite other things as it all turned out. Plautus is the source of the plot and the plotting, he fixes the manner of the progress of the play, but the representation of young men in the streets of Roman and Greek cities soon enough involves something other than the matter the ancient audiences were accustomed to regard.

Classical scholars for many years have done increasing honour to Plautus, and in Italy especially they have learned to recognize qualities in his writing that are too often overlooked when we think of his use to Shakespeare. For in Plautus' way of doing things there is much more than plot and contrivance and rough humour and farce. At the heart of many of the comedies there are beautiful and poetical conceptions. The laughter itself is often rich not only with thought but with wonder as well, and I think it is quite certain that this meant as much to Shakespeare in his exploitation as the plot and the management of the episodes. Accordingly I think it useful to develop an idea of the character of Plautus' accomplishment generally in order to help assess the character of the limited part of his work that Shakespeare clearly drew on, for in this way we may see better that it was not

9

only a plot and a set of conventions Shakespeare was taking over, he had got the spirit of Plautus' comedy in its richness and complexity.

Plautus customarily begins his plays in headlong exuberance. A prologue will list the preposterous causes of hilarity and confusion and then the play goes to work. In the *Asinaria* a slave undertakes to goad his master with outrageous humour: 'As you hope to have your only son healthy and sound, sir, after you're dead and gone yourself, I beg you, sir, by your white hair, and by the one you fear so—your wife—if you tell me a lie today may she outlive you by years and years, yes sir, but before then may you live long, too, live a living death with her beside you.' (I, 16–22)

The master enjoys the teasing for the fun it is, taking up the idea that the slave is indeed a conjurer who has just this power to contrive so horrendous a future, and in much fear he swears he will treat as truthfully with the slave as with himself. Underlying the interchange is Plautus' ridicule of a man who is so foolish he believes the gods would never go this far in tormenting a mortal.

Outrageous and preposterous as the thoughts are, the incidents are more so. As the Argument lists them, the intricacies of the plot are baffling enough although in the representation we manage to keep them straight. The heart of the matter is that a young man hopes to purchase the daughter of a procuress for his own. He loves her deeply but he lacks the purchase price. His father can get it for him only if he can succeed in cheating his wife, who holds the purse-strings. The two of them do this by tricking an ass-dealer who has come to pay the wife some money he owes her, but the father agrees to turn the money over to the son only on condition that he himself enjoy the girl for a day before the boy has her. The bargain completed, all three are sitting down to a banquet to celebrate the coup when the old man's wife, informed of what has been going on, bursts in, abuses the old man and drives him out. The lovers are left to themselves.

The main result of course is that the lovers have won, and they have escaped a certain shame. Some rascalities have succeeded, others have been thwarted. A certain defilement has been prevented, and in the prospect of happiness decency is being honoured. The boisterous humour is all the stronger for the triumph over meanness, and there is also the suggestion of an idyll to diminish what otherwise might remain oppressive in the thought of the old man's trickery. Even so, I think there is nothing in this play of the acid of a Renaissance production such as the *Mandragola*. In the happiness that 'The Company of the Comedians' contemplates in the Epilogue there is nothing cynical or bitter as they ask for our tolerance of such mischief: 'If this old fellow, unknown to his wife, has been in any way indulging his own inclinations, he has been doing nothing new or wonderful, or otherwise than others are in the habit of doing. There is no one so severely minded, or of so fixed a nature but that he will enjoy himself when he has the chance. Now if you in the audience want to come to the aid of this old man so that he will not be punished, we think it can be arranged if you will give us your applause.'

Everywhere there is laughter over this harmless wishing for the death of a wife, over the devices necessary for the gaining of a love, over cheating that is less than disastrous, over the lust of the old, over the temper of a wife, over the immorality that is more in thought than in action—where the wife is not abandoned, where the father does not lie with the girl, and where the indignities the young lovers are forced to—the girl embracing the slave who has brought the trick off, the young man forced like an ass to carry the servant on his back—are left as mere jokes because there has been so little malice in the teasing.

Plautus is as exuberant in his speech as in his contrivance—not even Mercutio could take more pleasure in language than Megadorus does in the *Aulularia*: 'Wherever you go nowadays you see more wagons in front of a city mansion than you can find around a farmyard. That's a perfectly glorious sight, though, compared with the time when the tradesmen come for their money. The cleanser, the ladies' tailor, the jeweller, the woolen worker—they're all hanging around. And there are the dealers in flounces and underclothes and bridal veils, in violet dyes and yellow dyes, or muffs, or balsam scented foot-gear; and then the lingerie people drop in on you, along with shoemakers and squatting cobblers and slipper and sandal merchants and dealers in mallow dyes; and the belt makers flock around, and the girdle makers along with 'em. And now you may think you've got them all paid off. Then up come weavers and lace men and cabinet-makers—hundreds of 'em—who plant themselves like jailers in your halls and want you to settle up. You bring 'em in and square accounts. "All paid off now, anyway," you may be thinking, when in march the fellows who do the saffron dyeing—some damned pest or other, anyhow, eternally after something.' (505–22 [Paul Nixon])

And indeed the fun runs as high as it does, the flirtation with fantasy is as provocative as it is because the mocking is based on both feeling and thought, the situations as much as the lines are at once calculated and imaginative. All is presented as if it were to be taken in at first glance, and yet all is dense with assumptions and implications about the nature of social life, about destiny, about the rascality as well as the righteousness of the gods, a marvellous energy is in all of it. These amusing persons belong to a world in which causes and consequences are serious enough. Humans are sometimes moving towards a state of goodness they only rarely speak of. Sometimes the gods play tricks on humans, and sometimes even the humans know it is a game. The world of Plautus' imagination is partly the Rome he knows, and partly it is the beauty and wonder of a limitless fancy.

As for his Rome, the main point about this is that it is an old man's bailiwick which the young men mean to take over, and young and old are at once exploiting and protecting themselves against slaves. Male strength and male power, particularly in the free, is the basis of virtue and health and wit.

But there is also another important strain in Plautus' dramas that will encourage not only Shakespeare but many others to some of the most significant modifications of the ancient comedy. When in the late seventeenth century Madame Dacier translated the *Rudens* as *Le Naufrage Délicieux*, and Bonnell Thornton in the eighteenth called his delightful verse translation *The Shipwreck*, both were emphasizing the romantic interest of the play. The *Rudens* is perhaps the most romantic of Plautus' work, and when we see here how far such an interest carries him we may come to believe the romantic appeal is inherent in his idea of comedy itself.

In this play Terence and the Greek romances have led him to move his embattled masters and slaves away from the city streets —at least much of the time—to the sea shore, and like *The Tempest* the play commences with a storm. Thornton describes the opening scene in this way: 'At the further end of the stage is a prospect of the sea, intersected by many rocks and cliffs, which project considerably forward upon the stage. On one side of the stage is represented the city of *Cyrene* at a distance; on the other, the temple of *Venus*, with a sort of court before it, surrounded by a wall breast high, and in the middle of this court is an altar. Adjoining to the temple, on the same side, is *Daemones*' house, with some scattered cottages at a distance.'[2]

It is in the third scene that the likeness with *The Tempest* is most striking. A master and his servant are watching the storm from the shore. A ship has foundered, and they see two women in a small boat miraculously hurled by the surges away from the rocks on to the beach. One of the women was washed overboard but fortunately she came to rest upon a spit from which she could wade to dry land. The other also arrived safely. As one of the women later tells it—

> Seeing the ship borne full upon a rock,
> I hasten'd to untie the rope that held her;
> And while the rest were wrapt in wild dismay,
> Our boat was sever'd from them by the storm,
> Which drove us to the right; and in this wise,
> Poor helpless souls, tost by the winds and waves,

We pass'd the live-long night; till on the morn
The wind scarce bore us to the shore quite spent—
(II, iv, 46–53)

In scene after scene someone harks back to the storm that has brought these two and still others from the ship to the place before Venus' Temple and by this means Plautus keeps reminding us of the occasion of it all, for the fact is that the storm has been created through a divine agency—somewhat as Prospero's was—an instrument of divinity has brought it all about, and for a like reason. Arcturus, who speaks the Prologue—'a fair and splendid star' (l. 4) by night, by day like other stars—dwells with mortals. He is one of 'God's spies', mingling with men, sending back to Jove reports of those who had been virtuous and had deserved rewards, and reports of those whose wrong-doing called for punishment:

> *Jove*, supreme sovereign of Gods and men,
> Spreads us throughout all nations several ways,
> To mark the people's actions, learn their manners,
> Their piety and faith, that so each man
> May find reward according to his virtues.
> Those, who suborn false witnesses to gain
> A villainous suit in law, who shuffle off
> Due payments by false swearing, we return
> Their names in writing to high *Jove*: each day
> He is inform'd of those that call for vengeance,
> And seek their own perdition by their crimes. . . .
> Yet wicked men
> Fondly imagine they can *Jove* appease
> With gifts and sacrifice; and thus they lose
> Their labour and their cost: for no petition
> Is acceptable to him from bad men.
> He that is good and just, will sooner find
> Grace from above, in praying to the Gods,
> Than will the wicked. Therefore I advise you,

> You that are just and good, who pass your days
> In piety and virtue, persevere,
> That so you may rejoice from all your doings.

(Ll. 10-20, 27-37)

In the performance of such tasks Arcturus discovered that a certain girl-merchant was plotting to transport these young women into slavery, and one of them in particular he knew to be deserving Jove's protection:

> I, seeing that the girl was borne away,
> Brought her relief, and ruin to her owner.
> I rais'd a hurricane, and stir'd the billows:
> For I *Arcturus* am, of all the signs,
> Most turbulent. . . . (Ll. 80-4)

Where so much is wonderful, the introduction of the idea of providence and of divine justice seems natural, and Palaestra, the maiden who is being saved, may plead to Venus for protection and her prayer will be granted:

> Gentle *Venus*!
> Thus lowly on our knees, and bath'd in tears
> Embracing this your altar, we beseech you,
> Guard and receive us into your protection:
> Avenge you on those miscreants, who dare slight
> Your temple, and permit us to approach
> Your altar, who last night by *Neptune's* power
> Were cast away: O hold us not in scorn,
> Nor think it done amiss, that thus we come
> Less seemingly accoutered than we ought.

(III, iii, 36-45)

As affecting as anything in the play is the quality of the appeals the women make to Venus, an idea they have of a character of tenderness in the goddess and of the holiness of her sanctuary. In the customary man's world of Plautus' there is here the intromission of a more moving religiousness than, for example there is in Venus' Temple in *Hero and Leander*, there is much more the air and climate of Delphos in *The Winter's Tale*, the climate delicate, the air most pure, the celestial habits and the reverence of the grave wearers—

> —I'll do now what the Priestess order'd me;
> I'll beg some water here at the next house.
> She told me if I ask'd it in her name,
> They'd give it me forthwith. I never saw
> A worthier old woman, more deserving
> Favour from Gods and men. How courteously,
> And with what gentle breeding she receiv'd us
> Trembling in want, wet, cast-away, half-dead,—
> And treated us as though we were her children!
>
> (II, v, 1–9)

In the end the play will substantiate her faith, and more, and not only Venus, Arcturus, and Jove, but mortals will uphold right and law, and will see implacably to the punishment of the wicked: goodness in slaves as well as masters will work to bring evil to judgment and to punishment.

In all the work of Plautus the *vis comique*, the satire, and the obscene are in harmony with a truly marvellous humanity. The sufferings that masters inflict upon slaves is understood as suffering. The loss of liberty is known for what it is. There is no callousness that Plautus does not recognize as callousness. The slave mentality is the occasion for many jokes, yet there is hardly ever, perhaps never, a suggestion that men are slaves by nature. In *The Captives* the slave Stalagmus, who caused all the trouble originally when he kidnapped and sold his master's small son, will say after years of servitude and deceit—

> A fine slave! I ne'er was, nor ever shall be;—
> Hope not to make me so. (V, iii, 4–5)

Plautus retains the ancient romantic affirmation that the free-born, taken into slavery, preserve something of the manner and generosity of free men always. So, in the same play, Tyndarus, brought up from childhood as a slave, yet honours truth and loyalty unquestioningly, to the point of his own sacrifice:

> Against your will, why should I wish to live?
> My loss of life will be a loss to you.
> There is no evil I need dread in death,
> When death is over. Were I to survive
> To th'utmost age of man, my space of time
> To bear the hardships, which you threat me with,
> Would yet be short.—Then fare you well,—be happy,
> Though you deserve another language from me.
>
> (III, v, 95–102)

Plautus is very like Shakespeare in this, he is never small-minded. The tone of magnanimity never falters whatever wickedness and poverty of spirit come into view. What is as wonderful as anything is the splendour that accrues to the religiousness, quite as genuine I think as the humanity, but of course it is in effect made more spectacular by the romantic impetus and context. *The Winter's Tale* and *The Tempest* and the masques and operas of the seventeenth century will call for representations of divinity upon the stage of one might think unmatchable magnificence, but I judge that Plautus is inferior neither to Shakespeare nor Monteverdi in the sense of glory. And it is glory accompanied by his sense of what is due to humanity and by something like reverence for virtue. Shakespeare in his beautiful appeal to 'heart-felt repentance and a clear life ensuing' is not more instinctive with such reverence than Plautus—

> There is indeed
> A God, that hears and sees whate'er we do:—
> As you respect me, so will He respect
> Your lost son.—To the well-deserving, good

17

Will happen, to the ill-deserving, ill.
(*The Captives*, II, ii, 94–8)

The tenderness of a father's love of his sons is equal to anything in Shakespeare, nor is there anything to surpass the friendship he records between master and slave:

> Say, I'm well;
> And tell him, boldly tell him, that our souls
> Were link'd in perfect harmony together;
> That nothing you have ever done amiss,
> Nor have I ever been your enemy;
> That in our sore affliction you maintain'd
> Your duty to your master, nor once swerv'd
> From your fidelity, in no one deed
> Deserted me in time of my distress.
> When that my father is inform'd of this,
> And learns, how well your heart has been inclin'd
> Both to his son and to himself, he'll never
> Prove such a niggard, but in gratitude
> He will reward you with your liberty;
> And I, if I return, with all my power
> Will urge him the more readily to do it.
> For by your aid, your courtesy, your courage,
> Wisdom and prudence, you have been the means
> Of my return to Ælis. . . . (II, iii, 54–72)

The *Menaechmi*, perhaps the earliest of Plautus' surviving plays, is as intricate as an imbroglio can very well be, a succession of scenes in which almost every possible confusion is exploited when one identical twin, arriving unbeknownst in the city of his brother, finds himself mixed up in his brother's somewhat dubious affairs, and that brother in turn finds himself mistaken for the traveller. Yet the discriminations among the characters are fine and significant, and what in farce might be simply amusing discomfitures are here important to the maintenance of sympathy, for the discomfitures sometimes bring shock and pain, and precisely where morality and decency are offended. When the defeats and disappointments are no great matter—when, for example, the parasite is being deprived of the banquet he has built his hopes on—there is nothing to engage our feelings in anything but what ridicule excites. But when Menaechmus of Epidamnum, to escape his shrew of a wife, spitefully takes a robe of hers to his mistress; or when the other Menaechmus, initially carefree and even innocent, finds his visit to the city turning into a nightmare—our revulsions, our sympathies, and above all our imaginations are captured; suspense, pity, fear, and even wonder take hold of us, and the element of easy ridicule becomes but one of the many feelings absorbing us.

The care taken in the characterization is but one side of an interest in doing honour to humanity generally and so accords with the charm allowed the romantic aspirations and the wonder of the gods. We see something of this harmonizing of interests in the representation of the quality of the servant of Menaechmus of Syracuse, a man nearly as noble as the Tyndarus of *The Captives*. In the longest *canticum* of the play—a most elaborate metrical performance on Plautus' part—he expatiates upon servitude with such feeling and emotion that he brings alive an image of a particular servant and a particular master:

> 'Tis on all hands allow'd to be the proof
> Of a good servant, when he takes good care of,
> Looks after, thinks of, and disposes rightly
> His master's business. That, when he is absent,
> Things may go on as well, or even better
> Than when he's present. He whose heart is right,
> Will think his back of greater consequence
> Than is his gullet: Ay, and to his belly
> Prefer his legs. He ought to bear in mind
> The wages, servants good for nothing, idle,
> Or wicked, from their masters' hands receive;
> And these are, stripes and chains, the stocks, the mill,

Hard labour, cold and hunger. Such as these
Are the rewards of idleness. This evil
I'm terribly afraid of; therefore choose
Rather to do my duty, than neglect it.
Words I can bear, but stripes I hate. I rather
Like to eat that which has been ground by others,
Than grind myself what others are to eat.
I therefore execute my master's orders
Well; and with sober diligence I serve him:
This turns to my account—Let others act then
As best they think it for their interest,
I'll ever be that which I ought to be:
This fear I'll still retain, to keep me free
From fault; that wheresoe'er my master is,
I may be ready there to wait on him.
Those servants who have nothing done amiss,
Yet keep this fear, still make themselves of use
To their respective masters. But the servants
Who never live in fear of doing wrong,
Fear, when they've something done to merit punishment.
As for myself, I shan't live long in fear—
The time draws nigh, when master will reward me.
For all the pains I have been at to serve him.
I've serv'd him, so as to consult my back. (V, iv, 1–36)

When he is set free at the end of the play we are glad that we are seeing borne out what we have come to expect of the quality of his master. And it is in fact he who first begins to put the pieces of the puzzle together—

Ye gods! confirm the unexpected hope
Which I'm conceiving. (V, vii, 34–5)

But before then, when his master, increasingly confused by the attacks that have been made upon him—by his supposed wife, by her father, by a physician, by his brother's servant, and by the parasite—accused right and left of madness, thinks that madness might indeed be his salvation, he feigns it in order to frighten off his persecutors. The ruse succeeds, and in effecting it he brings a wild and wonderful imagining into the play—vivid, flamboyant, spacious—a lyrical beauty it had not shown before this:

> *Apollo*! fast thou pour'st thy great behests—
> Now thou command'st me, harness my wild steeds,
> Fierce and untam'd; and now to mount my car
> And crush in pieces this *Getulian* lion,
> This stinking, toothless beast.—Now do I mount,
> And now I shake the reins—I take the lash;
> Now fly, my steeds, and let your sounding hoofs
> Tell your swift course—Shew in the turn your speed. . . .
> Again, *Apollo*! thou again command'st me
> To rush upon yon fellow that stands there,
> And murder him. But who is this, that by
> My fluttering tresses plucks me from my car,
> The dire commands revoking of *Apollo*?
>
> (IV, iv, 152-9, 161-5)

The contrast with the sober confusion of Menaechmus of Epidamnum could hardly be greater:

> What I've to-day experienc'd
> In many instances is most extraordinary.
> Some of them say, that I am not the man
> I am, and shut me out of doors. And here
> A man insists upon't, he is my servant—
> And I just now have given him his freedom.
> He talks of bringing money to me strait;
> Which if he does, I'll tell him he has liberty
> To go from me whene'er it suits him best.
> My father-in-law and the physicians say
> I am mad. 'Tis strange what this should be;
> It seems to me no other than a dream. (V, v, 73-84)

In the *Menaechmi*, in the jockeying with dreams and madness, there is nothing of the poignancy of the thought of real madness that hovers over the confusions of *Amphitryon* and especially over the servant Sosia in that play, driven from pillar to post unmercifully by Mercury; nor I think is there anything like the sense of pain we share with Hegio in *The Captives*, who believes a servant has destroyed his last hope of retrieving a son. Nor as in *The Shipwreck* is there the pathos and loneliness of a youth whose betrothed has been stolen from him, although Menaechmus of Syracuse is in bad straits. The hints of such feelings in the *Menaechmi* may have been enough for Shakespeare for the emphasis he required in *The Comedy of Errors*, or the *Amphitryon* may have given him the lead, but, however that may be, for Plautus as for Shakespeare comedy such as theirs would always entertain sharp distress and pathos in the midst of the fun. The pain is set off against the charm of the idea of faithfulness in the affections, and that contrast Shakespeare will develop most beautifully.

The conditions of Roman society account for much in Plautus' ethics that is alien to Shakespeare, but even so it is surprising how much even in moral matters Plautus offers to Shakespeare that he can use in developing the humane interests of his comedy.

Plautus' play begins in an uproar. Menaechmus of Epidamnum, very angry, is simply putting his wife aside and going to his mistress in a huff. It is a man's world, and this is the point— it is every man's unassailable right to have his dinner as he likes it, when he likes it, where he likes. And afterwards he is content.

> Immortal Gods! is there a man on whom
> You've in one day bestow'd more good, or one
> Who less could hope for it? I've dined, I've drank,
> I've feasted with my mistress. (III, ii, 10–13)

Now and then the women display their energy and their charm, now and then they put almost insuperable difficulties in the way of a man's ambitions, but no one is ever permitted to doubt that the power of decision remains with the lords and masters. What is said elsewhere applies here:

> Should a master
> Commit unworthy actions, yet his slaves
> Must think them worthy ones.
>
> (*The Captives*, II, i, 9–11)

What happens in the *Menaechmi* happens in all the plays—fortune rains its blows everywhere sooner or later, and the moral is that the most important thing is to bear the blows well. The blows do not always come from the heavens—although births and deaths play their parts; chiefly they are the defeats and disappointments men suffer when someone else gets his way, or when the dice take the unwanted turn. And they are by and large the defeats that come not through the excesses or the misplacing of passions but in the matching of wits. Almost everyone is a good fellow or at least a likeable rascal, but there are very few holds barred in their encounters with each other. There is a continuous interplay of something like cynicism—everyone has the right to outwit the other, jailor and prisoner, slave owner and slave, father and son. As a jailor says to a slave in *The Captives*,

> Yet, by my troth! was there an opportunity [to escape],
> I would not be the man that should dissuade you.
>
> (II, i, 24–5)

Very much as criminals understand the universal disposition to criminality, and as liars count on others lying, there is in Plautus the perfectly clear understanding on all sides that perfidy is to be expected:

> I see through your design: because I trusted you,
> You would deceive me. (*Menaechmi*, IV, iii, 19–20)

SHAKESPEARE: THE EARLY WRITINGS

And again—

> It is too oft the way
> With most men;—when they're suing for a favour,
> While their obtaining it is yet in doubt,
> They are most courteous; but when once they've got it,
> They change their manners, and from just, become
> Dishonest and deceitful. (*The Captives*, II, i, 50–5)

This is the real key to Plautus' world:

> The greatest care
> Is scarce enough to guard against deceit;
> And the most cautious, even when he thinks
> He's most upon his guard, is often trick'd.
> (*The Captives*, II, ii, 6–9)

There is an inexhaustible vitality in the contrivance of deceit.

The dignity that is inherent in men is the dignity inherent in enmity. Each one owes respect to the other's power to conduct intrigues. One supposes in the other what one depends on in one-self, the strength to rally from any worsting and to begin the war all over again. If you win, you may do as you like, and slavery, or the idea of it, sets the terms for every undertaking. This is apparently true of the society the play is written to entertain and this is why the idea of slavery gives substance to the laughter. Out of the indefatigable determination to survive, the slaves devise every impudence. The masters, having discovered the means of enslaving, accept the impudence as a measure not only of their mastery, but of their dignity, their capacity to outwit. Cleverness is so rampant, intrigue is so much the air men breathe, that without wit power is almost useless.

Yet Plautus also counts on good feeling and good spirits in men as well as in their lust to be free. Again and again plays end in reconciliations—brother is restored to brother, son to father, wife to husband. When the father asks the suitor in the *Aulularia*—

24

> why
> D'ye ask my daughter for a wife?
the answer is—

> to serve you   ,
> And to promote my good through you and yours.
> (I, vi, 72–4)

There is mockery in this just as there is in the prologue the Household God speaks in introducing the play—

> She indeed
> Makes ev'ry day her constant supplications
> With frankincense, or wine, or something else. (28–30)

But here as everywhere the word *probus*—decent, upright—manages to preserve an integrity mockery does not erode. The role of the parasite in the plays sets off the decency and generosity of the better sort. The plays interest us in the affairs of not just anybody, but ones with whom we can feel sympathy on something like moral grounds, for vitality and power, as it turns out, have their Achilles' heels. The prologue to *The Captives* tells us that 'the capacities of men for evil are limited. And quite often people do good in spite of themselves.' This happens so frequently in fact that one must even suppose that Fortune, conscienceless though she is, helps not only those who use every trick in the book to help themselves, she teaches them how to keep on hoping for good, and this is the funniest thing of all. At the end of the *Menaechmi* when all his property is to be sold the Messenger announces—

> The auction of *Menaechmus* will begin
> The seventh of this month: when will be sold
> Slaves, household goods, farms, houses, and—et cetera.
> All may attend that will; and we sell all
> For ready money. Sell his wife besides,
> If any purchaser should offer. (V, vii, 146–51)

25

The cult of dominance ends in hilarity, not even Menaechmus dreaming that Fortune will allow his wife to be bought away from him. For the fact is none of these young men-about-town, none of these slave-holders, is malevolent, and Fortune generally allows herself to work together for the good of those who have meant reasonably well, providing they are men. Twins are restored to their father in the *Menaechmi*, brother to brother and son to father in *The Captives*; in the *Aulularia* a marriage is finally permitted against which almost insuperable obstacles had been contrived; in the *Asinaria* an old man is prevented from stealing his son's mistress. The charming epilogue to *The Captives* speaks of this as a play 'ubi boni meliores fiunt' (1034), where 'better' means better off, but 'good' also means decent and well disposed. We in the audience are enlisted in the service of such a meaning, for, as the epilogue asks us, 'You who wish virtue to be rewarded give us your applause.'

The happiness of re-union is the reward Plautus' comedies constantly look forward to; such is the reward for decency.

Kittredge in remarking on Shakespeare's indebtedness to the *Menaechmi*, observed that the important borrowings he was also making from the *Amphitryon* in *The Comedy of Errors*—especially at the beginning of the third act—brought a special sense of dignity to his play.[3] The point is important. *Amphitryon*, as Plautus thought of it, is a tragi-comedy, a kind of drama in which laughter and sympathy were mingled. Such a mingling is a staple of his comic writing, but in this one the nature of the mingling is profoundly affected by the importance given to ideas about divinity. Force, animality, even outrage are presented as comically as they are in plays where no gods are present, but this time the idea of the beauty of the immortal gods and the beauty of divine power transmutes even a trick.

This is, I suppose, the most brilliant of all the treatments of Jove's affair with the wife of Amphitryon. The action is resolved, we remember, with the marvellously burlesque consolation, that Alcmena will bring forth two infants in a single delivery— partly of course to save her trouble—one, sired by the general, the other by the god. Parent and foster-parent and audience and, one supposes, Jove himself are further delighted, exalted, even perhaps edified, that the one who is son of the god, no other than Hercules, hardly sees the light of day before he takes off after a couple of intruding serpents that in his burgeoning strength he immediately strangles.

Consolation, hilarity, impiety, nonsense—whatever it adds up to, it is all suddenly translated into something astonishing and affecting. It was prepared for by the companion's account of the circumstances of Alcmena's labour:

> When she found
> Herself in labour, she invok'd the Gods:—
> Then what a rumbling, grumbling, flashing, clashing,
> Straightway ensued! Suddenly, how quick,
> How terribly it thunder'd! All that stood
> Fell flat down at the noise: and then we heard
> Some one, I know not who, with mighty voice
> Cry out, '*Alcmena*, succour is at hand:
> Be not dismay'd: the heav'n's high ruler comes
> To you propitious and to yours. Arise,
> (Says he,) ye who have fallen through the terror
> And dread of me.'—I rose from where I lay,
> And such a brightness stream'd through all the house,
> Methought it was in flames. Then presently
> *Alcmena* call'd. . . . (V, i, 12–26)

It was further prepared for by the reconciliation of the husband and wife—even though there was mockery of that too—but in the words of Jove, blessing the pair he has so selfishly abused, there is such beauty that we either forget or else forgive the outrageousness of the legend and the condescensions of the gods. The benediction is worthy of a better god on a more worthy occasion, it has something sometimes spoken of as an unearthly charm:

> Be of good cheer, *Amphitryon*; I am come
> To comfort and assist you and your family.

27

Nothing have you to fear; then let alone
All soothsayers and diviners: I'll inform you
Of what is past, and what is yet to come,
Much better than they can, since I am *Jove*.
Know first of all, I have enjoy'd *Alcmena*,
Whence she was pregnant by me with a son:
You likewise left her pregnant, when you went
To th'army. At one birth two boys together
She has brought forth: the one, sprung from my loins,
Shall gain immortal glory by his deeds.
Restore *Alcmena* to your ancient love:
In nothing does she merit your reproaches:
She was compell'd by my resistless power,
To what she did.—I now return to heav'n. (V, ii, 1–16)[4]

A sense of dignity and a sense of glory, whether of glory lost or in the offing, are as important to *The Comedy of Errors*.

In Shapespeare's play we encounter at the outset what later we should recognize as the Shakespearean hall-mark, the idea of a social hierarchy, and at the top a minister of justice—the Duke, presiding over Syracuse, handing down a verdict. Plautus' play had commenced with a seafarer intruding upon a domestic scene where incidentally we learn about some legal business that is under way in the Forum. There follows almost nothing else that would give us anything like an idea of the complexity of the arrangements of society—an occasional oath, some talk about a contract, rather more about the various ties that laws and money weave, but the ties are barely the ties that bind and the society is no such ordered world as Shakespeare's. Here there is at the very beginning the idea of a social entity, of a city being preserved from pollution, of law being enforced at the top in the name of what is holy, and in the sense that is increasingly stressed of a stable social life.

That is the first, inescapable note that the play strikes. The next one is quite as inescapable, the note of the exotic and the

romantic. It is not merely in the strange pathos of the story of a
stranded old man, it is in the extravagance with which the circumstances of his fate are spoken of, the extremes of death and
joy, of danger and felicity, the references to heaven and death,
and through it all the note of yearning, the note traditional to
romances of the yearning for the absolute:

> For, ere the ships could meet by twice five leagues,
> We were encountered by a mighty rock,
> Which being violently borne upon
> Our helpful ship was splitted in the midst;
> So that, in this unjust divorce of us,
> Fortune had left to both of us alike,
> What to delight in, what to sorrow for.
> Her part, poor soul, seeming as burdened
> With lesser weight but not with lesser woe,
> Was carried with more speed before the wind;
> And in our sight they three were taken up
> By fishermen of Corinth, as we thought.
> At length another ship had seized on us,
> And, knowing whom it was their hap to save,
> Gave healthful welcome to their shipwracked guests,
> And would have reft the fishers of their prey,
> Had not their bark been very slow of sail;
> And therefore homeward did they bend their course.
> Thus have you heard me severed from my bliss,
> That by misfortunes was my life prolonged
> To tell sad stories of my own mishaps. (I, i, 100–20)

Everywhere there is the sense of the invaluable, and when that
is lost, of the irretrievable. As for the note of yearning—

> Five summers have I spent in farthest Greece,
> Roaming clean through the bounds of Asia,
> And, coasting homeward, came to Ephesus,
> Hopeless to find, yet loath to leave unsought,
> Or that, or any place that harbours men. (I, i, 132–6)

And there is another note that is perhaps even more impressive in its frequency, and more significant in its contrast with Plautus, the note of tenderness. In the second scene a merchant is commenting on the fate that is likely to be the old father's, yet even as a stranger he must express sorrow and pity:

> This very day a Syracusian merchant
> Is apprehended for arrival here,
> And, not being able to buy out his life,
> According to the statute of the town,
> Dies ere the weary sun set in the west. (I, ii, 3–7)

This note is elaborated on magnificently in the figure of speech that Plautus had given Shakespeare: in Plautus it had been simply witty and ironic—'I never saw one man so like another; water to water, nor milk to milk, is not liker than he is to you.' (1088–89) In Shakespeare this becomes an image of the ocean of mankind—

> I to the world am like a drop of water
> That in the ocean seeks another drop,
> Who, falling there to find his fellow forth,
> Unseen, inquisitive, confounds himself. (I, ii, 35–8)

But it is not merely an image of drops of water in a vast sea, and left at that, it is a sea of life, in which there is order and excellence:

> There's nothing situate under heaven's eye
> But hath his bound in earth, in sea, in sky.
> The beasts, the fishes, and the wingèd fowls
> Are their males' subjects and at their controls . . .

Thus it of course is picking up the theme of the superiority of the male from Plautus, but making it into a vaster principle—

Men, more divine, the masters of all these,
Lords of the wide world and wild watery seas,
Indued with intellectual sense and souls,
Of more preeminence than fish and fowls,
Are masters to their females, and their lords.
(II, i, 16–24)

Later Shakespeare takes up the same figure again, this time
to give us a view of the universe as a blessed thing, as if not
merely the principle of order but the idea of the spirit of holy
marriage pervaded it all. Adriana addresses the one she supposes
her husband, as Alcmena might have addressed Jupiter:

O, how comes it,
That thou art then estrangèd from thyself?
Thyself I call it, being strange to me,
That, undividable, incorporate,
And better than thy dear self's better part.
Ah, do not tear away thyself from me!
For know, my love, as easy mayst thou fall
A drop of water in the breaking gulf,
And take unmingled thence that drop again
Without addition or diminishing,
As take from me thyself, and not me too.
(II, ii, 121–31)

In Plautus everyone is always figuring out how to make terms
with fortune and from time to time someone suggests there may
be such a thing as justice, if not here then beyond the grave.
There is a kind of nagging notion that there ought to be justice,
that the world ought to be willing to be a nest for homing birds,
and there is even the notion sometimes that women might just
possibly make life a little more pleasant for men, but mostly all
there is to fall back upon is cash, and whatever ways power can
help a man preserve his liberty. But when Shakespeare's brothers
find each other, when the servants quarrel or exchange puns,

when wife or mistress rails, we know we are in the midst of a seamless world, in the ordering there is a pattern, and in the pattern is an informing life:

> The capon burns, the pig falls from the spit;
> The clock hath strucken twelve upon the bell;
> My mistress made it one upon my cheek.
> She is so hot, because the meat is cold;
> The meat is cold, because you come not home;
> You come not home because you have no stomach;
> You have no stomach, having broke your fast.
> But we that know what 'tis to fast and pray,
> Are penitent for your default today. (I, ii, 44–52)

The details of domestic life, the tempers of fretting women, the overlordship of a church's sytem of rewards and punishments, the individual sense of obligation and responsibility—these are always before us as part of a significant existence. But it is not only society that holds men, it is nature: the weary sun, the blessed light, the storming winds, are as intimately informed with a providential care:

> A league from Epidamnum had we sailed
> Before the always wind-obeying deep
> Gave any tragic instance of our harm.
> But longer did we not retain much hope;
> For what obscurèd light the heavens did grant
> Did but convey into our fearful minds
> A doubtful warrant of immediate death. (I, i, 62–8)

And again:

> At length the sun, gazing upon the earth,
> Dispersed those vapours that offended us;
> And, by the benefit of his wishèd light,
> The seas waxed calm. (I, i, 88–91)

In all this—in the personification of the sun, in the welcomed complicity of winds—

> the merry wind
> Blows fair from land— (IV, i, 90–1)

in the beneficence of the light, Shakespeare is evidently being held by a sense of the communion of man and nature, indeed of all physical things. And so while it is at least half fun, the figure Adriana uses in speaking of her husband exploits a metaphor that would have been alien to Plautus and that is part of the very texture of Shakespeare's play:

> Thou art an elm, my husband, I a vine,
> Whose weakness, married to thy stronger state,
> Makes me with thy strength to communicate.
> If aught possess thee from me, it is dross,
> Usurping ivy, briar, or idle moss,
> Who, for all want of pruning, with intrusion
> Infect thy sap and live on thy confusion. (II, ii, 175–81)

But there is more than the metaphor of communion.[5] There is the idea of magic. All creatures and all things are suspended in mutual attraction and repulsion, in a universe divinely ordered from the beginning:

> Some devils ask but the parings of one's nail,
> A rush, a hair, a drop of blood, a pin,
> A nut, a cherry-stone;
> But she, more covetous, would have a chain.
> (IV, iii, 72–5)

> this drudge, or diviner . . .
> told me what privy marks I had about me, as, the
> mark of my shoulder, the mole in my neck, the
> great wart on my left arm . . . (III, ii, 144–8)

33

It is also the world of sorcerers:

> There's none but witches do inhabit here,
> And therefore 'tis high time that I were hence.
> She that doth call me husband, even my soul
> Doth for a wife abhor. But her fair sister,
> Possest with such a gentle sovereign grace,
> Of such enchanting presence and discourse,
> Hath almost made me traitor to myself,
> But, lest myself be guilty to self-wrong,
> I'll stop mine ears against the mermaid's song.
>   (III, ii, 161–9)

Here is where one can see that this preposterous plot, this exaggeration of Plautus' imbroglio by a multiplication of twins and all the other compoundings, is merged in a kind of metaphysic. Character after character comes to think he is dreaming—as indeed Alcmena might have thought she was:

> Sure, these are but imaginary wiles,
> And Lapland sorcerers inhabit here. (IV, iii, 10–11)

> Am I in earth, in heaven, or in hell?
> Sleeping or waking? mad or well-advised?
> Known unto these, and to myself disguised?
> I'll say as they say, and persever so,
> And in this mist at all adventures go. (II, ii, 213–17)

> This fellow is distract, and so am I,
> And here we wander in illusions.
> Some blessèd power deliver us from hence!
>   (IV, iii, 41–3)

And so it is that the conception of the world of this play as preposterous and sorcerer-ridden and somehow all of a piece merges into the idea of life as a dream. This is brought to mind not only in the elaboration of the device of providing twin

34

masters with twin servants, and through the consequent confusions in the very idea of identity, it works itself out finally in
the reconciliation of Antipholus and Adriana and in the restoration of his long-lost wife to Aegeon. Reality outgoes the dream,
and what began as a play about a wanderer searching for what
might have been irretrievably lost is brought to a fulfilment happy
beyond expectation. The romantic conception underlying that
initial incident has sustained the entanglements of farce and in
the end has brought everything, the comic and the tragic alike,
to a single fulfilment.

There is even a likeness in all this to the world of *The
Tempest*, to the tyranny of Prospero over Caliban:

> I have served him from the hour of my nativity
> to this instant, and have nothing at his hands for
> my service but blows. When I am cold, he
> heats me with beating; when I am warm, he cools
> me with beating. I am waked with it when I sleep,
> raised with it when I sit, driven out of doors
> with it when I go from home, welcomed home with
> it when I return; (*The Comedy of Errors*, IV, iv, 30–7)

as well as of the felicity of the island under Prospero's sway:

> Faith, stay here this night, they will surely
> do us no harm. You saw they speak us fair,
> give us gold. Methinks they are such a gentle
> nation, that, but for the mountain of mad flesh
> that claims marriage of me, I could find in
> my heart to stay here still, and turn witch.
>   (IV, iv, 152–7)

I happen to believe that there are few writers in the world so
vigorous, with so soundly self-sustaining an imagination as
Plautus. He belongs with the most powerful minds of antiquity.
He has a view of the strength of human character which is itself

35

a support to whatever we may think about the capacities of humanity. And Shakespeare, I suppose, taken with his plays as school exercises, something the choirboys at Stratford or somewhere had put on, saw the *Menaechmi* as introducing his imagination into a view of the profligate extravagance of nature and of men, of the hidden meshes catching up the particulars of the world's existence, and, taken with the charm of its fun, he elaborated it, and yet found that he was also looking at life by his own light. He brought his own light to it—not that clear hard-edged Mediterranean brilliance of Plautus, but something richer, more golden, almost more oriental. Those wonderful words of Antipholus of Syracuse—

> Against my soul's pure truth why labour you
> To make it wander in an unknown field?—

express the idea of holiness that we can see has enchanted Shakespeare in his very beginnings. And it will never be exorcised.

> Against my soul's pure truth why labour you
> To make it wander in an unknown field?
> Are you a god? Would you create me new?
> Transform me then, and to your pow'r I'll yield.
>   (III, ii, 37–40)

> Sing, siren, for thyself, and I will dote;
> Spread o'er the silver waves thy golden hairs,
> And as a bed I'll take them, and there lie,
> And, in that glorious supposition, think
> He gains by death that hath such means to die.
>   (III, ii, 47–51)

And having gone so far Shakespeare did something still more extraordinary—he gave the idyllic a Christian cast.

At the end, when the Abbess speaks of the new life that lies before them all after their trials, she uses words of unmistakably

Christian reference. 'Thirty-three years have I but gone in travail,' she begins, putting herself in the role of a figure almost like Providence, responsible for the new life they are now to have, but in naming that particular number of years she introduces the unexpected suggestion of the life of Christ. And by another phrase she is now to use, 'gossips' feast', together with some other terms she seems to be speaking of the festivities traditionally accompanying baptisms:

> Thirty-three years have I but gone in travail
> Of you, my sons, and till this present hour
> My heavy burden ne'er delivered.
> The Duke, my husband, and my children both,
> And you the calendars of their nativity,
> Go to a gossips' feast, and joy with me
> After so long grief, such festivity (V, i, 401–7)

Evidently even in this high-spirited entertainment, with the romantic dreaming crowding in, Shakespeare was willing to let the ending happiness give rise to other suggestions, as if to say that in a play where confusion and dreams and the thought of madness add their jumble to the aspirations of love and to the fear of the loss of love, it was proper to bring in reminders of the faith of Christians, in particular glancing at the idea of rebirth in the course of life. I think we are to regard this as something more than mere extensions of the playing of a profligate imagination, for we can see that it picks up a suggestion inherent in that earlier phrase, 'that glorious supposition'. More than that, Christianity is itself in the very character of this proligacy, of the delight in God's bounty, the joy in celebrating the infinite variety of the world. It belongs with the character of the Gothic, medieval, English heritage, the wealth and beauty that is transfiguring the world of Plautus.[6]

It was long ago observed that the *Rudens* possessed a romantic tone that reminds us of *Pericles* and *The Winter's Tale*. J. W. Mackail noticed in the play itself 'the atmosphere of the *Odyssey*, of the fisher-idyll of Theocritus, of the hundreds of little poems in the Greek Anthology that bear clinging about their verses the faint murmur and odour of the sea'.[7] I do not know that Shakespeare had read the *Rudens*, but something of this same romantic character belongs to Plautus almost everywhere, although there is only a hint of it in the *Menaechmi*, notably in the brief comment on the father in the Prologue—

> Hopeless and helpless doth Aegeon wend,
> But to procrastinate his lifeless end— (I, i, 157–8)

whether this was the hint that Shakespeare took, or whether it was the beauty of the wonderful in the *Amphitryon*, or still something else, it is precisely the incident about the father's arrival in Ephesus that provided Shakespeare with the play's initiating circumstance and that gives it its initially romantic cast.

It all began as a pathetic story about a man who may lose his life because in searching for one of his twin sons who has been lost, he has come to a city where citizens of his country are forbidden to set foot. A stay of execution is granted him for a day, and what follows is a series of most unlikely happenings. When the day is over the lost son has been found and the father has been pardoned, but before any such fortunate conclusions could be contrived we have come to expect marvels and even splendour to cap the madness and the fun and the dreaming. The play exclaims at the end—'After so long grief, such festivity!'—as if indeed wonder had been brought to birth in the very process of nature.

The general technique of the play is of course the customary procedure of farce, the discomfiture of one poor devil after another, over and over again, to the point of dizziness. The masters are discomfited by the wrong servants, the servants by the wrong masters, the wife by the one she mistakenly supposes to be her husband. The succession of misunderstandings has led to nothing more unfortunate than an occasional beating, a particularly startled revilement, a partly unbelievable indignity, but as the day passes, tempers fray, the time of reprieve draws to an end, a sane man is about to be committed to an asylum, and in still other affairs suffering and ruin are on the point of taking over.

Still, the action has been so fast, the characters have so often been screaming louder than they are hurt, that on the whole we continue to charm ourselves with the idea that the distress goes hardly more than skin deep. And again there is such fun in the incongruities—a loving wife locking her husband out, the robbed instead of the robber being taken to the bailiff. In the incongruous penalties and incongruous plasters for them, our amusement approaches the point where all seems to dissolve in the kind of nonsense we must cherish, where, as the audience, we can tell ourselves we are superior to everything, even sanity. Which is in part to say the spirits of madness (at times almost too vividly in the saddle) and of illusion and delusion, the dreaming of fantastic fulfilments, the playing about with ideals of justice and revenge and love and wealth, are contributing not merely to the hilarity, they are contributing to the charm.

These romantic influences accord with the play's general defiance of the claims of realism and verisimilitude, and the impudence superbly authorized by Plautus. The preposterousness in the original is largely inherent in Plautus' elaborate manner of combining drama with musical effects, and while Shakespeare had not developed so complexly articulated a union of drama with music, nevertheless I think *The Comedy of Errors* owes something to this aspect of the *Menaechmi* and other Plautus plays, and obtains at least something of a like effect.

Plautus' plays are in verse, they are constructed in elaborate schemes of metrics, drawing upon various kinds of musical accompaniment, and they were to be sung or declaimed in various styles. All this wild cavorting and locking out of doors and invective is to music and it is being sung to. As Rostagni says, 'By virtue of the singing and the music such works raise themselves above the level of ordinary life into the sphere of intoxication, into the spheres of lyrical excitement and the exalted imagination. The varied metres and the music set the tone of the whole—they underly as well as determine the un-realistic nature of it all, emphasizing not the declarative nor the reflective but the exalted spirit of the work, they have the sound of the sparkling accompaniment of laughter, but not of that alone, for they speak to the heart as well as to the mind.'[8]

Professor Kittredge suggested that the remarkable metrical variety of *The Comedy of Errors* was probably an attempt of Shakespeare's to imitate the complex metres of Plautus in his devising of choruses and recitative and diverbium.[9] But I think also that the fundamental conception of Shakespeare's play as a doubling of what he found in his original was effected in aiming at a production governed by comparable musical principles. In *The Comedy of Errors* the imbroglio is only one aspect of the manipulating of the affairs of twin masters and twin servants, for in the manner in which the scenes are paired and contrasted a pattern is established for the progression of the play that over-laps the pattern of encounters and the consequences that follow from them. A quarrel between one master and one servant is followed by a scene in which we see the other master quarrelling with the same servant, whom he supposes to be his. The themes of the quarrels are the same and different. Much of the point of the humour in contrasting one argument with another is in the obvious likeness in the rhetoric that is developed. Thus the going back and forth establishes a rhythm for the play, and in the paral-lel encounters, the parallel dialogue, the parallel expulsions and beatings and chases, we are taken up with another movement than that of the plot in itself. There are parallels too in the love stories, in the mistakings and advances and reconciliations, so that I think we must say that all that contributes to this rhythm is integral to the conception of the work, probably not of such dominance as like devices would be in Plautus, where music and dancing would be part of it all, but nevertheless analogously.

The play moves beautifully. The imbroglio takes hold of our interest almost at once. We follow intently into the last possible confusion and yet it is not merely the untangling of the confusion we are hoping for, for soon enough the mix-ups reach the point where untangling seems impossible and our very despair for a solution becomes part of our amusement. What we do look forward to with such cheerful expectation, along with an almost exhausted hope that things will straighten themselves out, is a growing assurance of the presence of good and truth and decency, an assurance of the growth of good in this furious succession of misunderstandings against the light of that pathetic story of the separation of infants and parents at sea which we are being reminded of as the play nears its end.

We look forward to the righting of wrongs, to the restoration of happiness, to the effecting of justice or the tempering of justice, to the removal of the barriers to love. And here and there we are being led to suppose that love through devious and unplottable ways will achieve all the triumphs we can hope for, and more. So it seems to me that it is wise to speak of this play as in part harmonically ordered, and perhaps the analogy with some of the geometric dances of the time is as good as any. But whatever the analogy, the play has been moving towards an enrichening of the sense of the power of love and of the beauty of wonder through elaborate patterns of repetition and amplification. It does not do this of course with any such richness as the later romantic comedies, but something of that same loveliness is playing its part here.

NOTES

[1] Francesco Arnaldi, *Da Plauto a Terenzio*, Naples, 1948, I, 39, concludes that the *Menaechmi* is a transformation of comedy into the *opera buffa* on a scale not elsewhere in Plautus.

[2] *Comedies of Plautus, Translated into Familiar Blank Verse*, Vol. II, London, 1769, p. 272.

[3] G. L. Kittredge, *The Complete Works of Shakespeare*, Boston, 1936, p. 133.

4 '. . . il finale, pieno di prodigi e di panico, ha qualche cosa di tragico e di religioso insieme. Eppure l'impostazione e il tono generale del dramma sono profondamente comici' (Raffaele Perna, *L'Originalità di Plauto*, Bari, 1955, p. 303).

5 Mr. Harold Brooks extends this further than I care to: 'At the centre is relationship: relationship between human beings, depending on their right relationship to truth and universal law: to the cosmic reality behind appearance, and the cosmic order' ('Themes and Structure in "The Comedy of Errors",' *Stratford-upon-Avon Studies*, 3 [1961], p. 67).

6 I may anticipate here something to be developed later in this study, the idea of the character of the richness of the imagination as it was fostered by medieval culture. I am in this much obliged to M. Henri Foçillon:

'Cette notion d'un humanisme médiévale, telle qu'elle se dégage de l'étude des monuments, excède singulièrement, on le voit, toute définition qui voudrait la limiter à l'heritage plus ou moins précaire des cultures antiques. Il existe, certes, un humanisme des humanistes, mais il en existe un autre, plus large et, si l'on peut dire, plus authentique, parce qu'il demande infiniment moins à la tradition qu'à la vie. L'art du moyen âge nous fait connaître sa vaste conception de l'homme et de ses rapports avec l'univers. Il ne l'isole pas. Il le montre aux prises avec les exigences, les misères et les grandeurs de son destin. Il ne s'arrête pas à l'épanouissement de sa jeunesse, sauf quand il le couche sur la pierre des tombeaux. Il le prend à tout âge, dans toute condition, maniant l'outil, subissant les maux. L'aveugle des parties hautes de Reims proclame la gloire de la justice de Dieu et la gloire de la patience humaine. A la douceur des Évangiles, à la majesté de la théologie, cet humanisme figuré ajoute la puissance de sa sympathie pour tout ce qui respire, une compassion, une cordialité, une bonhomie formidable. Il embrasse le tout, il met l'homme au centre, et cette image de Dieu est toute humanité. Ce mot acquiert ici la plénitude de son sens. L'admirable humanité de la statuaire grecque est incomplète. Elle se meut dans l'impérissable, elle est une affirmation si catégorique de l'homme qu'elle le voue à une sorte de solitude. Le moyen âge le baigne de toutes parts dans le courant des êtres et des choses. Mais cette générosité n'est pas un ruissellement. Si près de la matière et de la chair, si captivé par toute aventure de la vie, si sensible, fût-ce au tendre repli d'une plante, cet art est esprit. Non seulement il honore les travaux de l'intelligence, non seulement il dédie la cathédrale de Laon aux arts libéraux, mais la règle qui préside à la repartition et à l'enchainement des figures, en d'autres termes le style même de leur plan ordonnateur prend sa source dans une haute pensée. L'ordre des symétries et des correspondances, la loi des membres, une sorte de musique des symboles organisent secrètement ces immenses encyclopédies de pierre. Sans doute nous avons là, je ne dis pas le témoignage d'un temps, mais, sous leur forme la plus complète et la mieux liée, l'histoire naturelle et l'histoire idéale de l'homme' (*Art D'Occident : Le Moyen Age Roman et Gothique*, Paris, 2nd ed., 1947, pp. 5–6).

7 *Latin Literature*, New York, n.d., p. 20.

8 Augusto Rostagni, *Storia della Letteratura Latina*, Turin, 1949, I, 131.

9 *The Complete Works of Shakespeare*, p. 134.

It is Professor B. A. Taladoire's thesis that in general it is wise to consider Plautus' plays as composed in 'movements' rather than in acts (*Essai sur le comique de Plaute*, Monaco, 1956, p. 87).

Italian Contributions

In taking a beginning from Plautus Shakespeare was participating in a movement that was transforming the writing of drama in Europe. The special influence of Plautus as of Terence upon a particular work is always of interest, but there is also the matter of probably as great consequence, their part in contributing to a new tradition. The Italian, Spanish, French and English playwrights as well as those in Germany and the Low Countries were making translations and adaptations of the ancients that would in the end lead to distinctly new kinds of writing. It is interesting to observe what is special to, say, Ariosto's divergences from the ancient models, and Shakespeare's, and it is also interesting to notice what in the midst of all the variations is leading to modes and conventions that will be at hand for Molière and Congreve.

There is a particular reason for bringing to bear upon a study of Shakespeare's work some notion of the new ways of writing comedy, for although it seems that he never again followed any single dramatic source so closely as he had the *Menaechmi*, he was almost always dependent upon sources and he was to draw upon Italian comedies—Ariosto's *Gli Suppositi*, for example, by way of Gascoigne for *The Taming of the Shrew*; *Gl'Ingannati*, perhaps directly, pretty certainly indirectly, for *Twelfth Night*; and others from time to time in combining a variety of suggestions. On occasion he may have had recourse to similar writings from France and Spain, but the Italian influence was clearly dominant for him as for his predecessors in England, Gascoigne and Udall and Lyly.

44

But as important as these were, he was to draw even more frequently upon Italian story-writers—Boccaccio, Bandello, Cinthio, Masuccio di Salerno—as the Italian playwrights themselves did, and for the same reasons. It was the nature and spirit of the *novella* as Boccaccio established it that more than any other single influence was to direct the imitation of classical drama into new ways. 'The fact is that our comic writers saw in the great testament of Ser Giovanni Boccadoro—as Lasca called Boccaccio—not only an exemplary repository of intrigues and of comic characters, but, however indistinctly, they saw the forms and even the scenic attributes of theatrical representation; they found in his writing the kernel of a lay-profane theatre. . . . One might be tempted to grant a real, not a metaphoric, value to the traditional definition of the *Decameron* as a human comedy. It was truly a theatre, this profane world of Boccaccio's, with all its variety of incident and plot, everything determined by human powers—by will and by fortune—recited for a noble brigade of young women and men not very unlike those crowds of actors and spectators at sixteenth-century productions, academic and private, created against a natural backdrop, idyllic but not fictitious, like the backgrounds of the great Renaissance paintings that provide a luminous perspective for the figures in the foreground, like actors coming forward upon a stage.'[1]

The Boccaccio tone and spirit, his secularity, would go farther with the Italians than with Shakespeare, and in them it would also be more in harmony with their traditional humour and their manner of satire. To follow in this direction as far as Machiavelli and Bruno were to would be possible, I think, only in countries in which classicism might be said to be at home. The limits of its appeal and use for Shakespeare were in part set by the character of the English but perhaps even more by the direction Shakespeare would follow in developing conceptions of the nature of love that would, in effect, counter the appeal of extreme secularity. Among the Italians there would also be those who would hold back from the extreme, but all, I think, understood that Boccaccio had shown the way to make ancient comedy over in

45

the spirit of the new age. Accordingly I think even a brief look at a few Italian comedies will throw light upon the ways in which Shakespeare met similar issues in developing his own modes.

Plautus' *Menaechmi* was performed at Ferrara in 1486. In succeeding years it was offered many times at various other places in Italy. It turned out to be one of the most popular and influential of Plautus' comedies as the revival of the ancient dramas progressed. First offered in the original, both his and Terence's plays (Terence was produced first in Florence, in the 1470s) were soon translated, adapted somewhat loosely, and then of course imitated.

Terence was first produced in England in 1510, Plautus in 1519. The *Menaechmi* was put on in Cardinal Wolsey's palace in 1528.

The transformation of comic writing now owed more to one, now more to the other of the ancients. In form and procedure their work was much alike but in substance and manner there were marked differences. Plautus' imbroglios and intrigues were high-spirited, sometimes magnificently imaginative, sometimes outrageously preposterous, highly lyrical, and in almost every sense more masculine. Terence made more of differences in manners, he expanded on incidents in which pathos was delicately represented, he displayed a generally finer temper. The structure of his works provided more encouragement for theorists in the new age who argued for the moral worth of comedy.

The French and the Spanish and later the English took up with the new ways and were glad enough to follow the Italians in their innovations, but until Lyly and Shakespeare it was the Italians who achieved the greatest successes and who continued to exert the greatest influence.

The key matter as in the ancients was the single scene, an open place—a piazza or a less extensive area where streets converged and a few houses had their doorways. The persons of the play met here, sometimes coming out of the houses or entering them. In the succession of exchanges they make the business of the play known to us, they conduct some of their affairs, and they inform us in various ways of what is happening at other places and behind doors. Problems of a personal and private rather than public character concern them—courtships are not going well, there are difficulties about dowries, impostors or frauds are up to devilment—and the plays proceed by letting us know what's afoot and presenting a series of encounters until finally the affairs are settled.

Fathers and sons, lovers and their beloved, go-betweens, parasites, tricksters, and every variety of servant confide in each other, trick each other, compound confusion, work at cross-purposes, fall into desperation before they find a clear road ahead of them. On the face of it the imbroglios and intrigues in the new plays are very much those of the ancient and except for the different roles that the women have—they come upon the stage in some modern versions, and their seduction rather than rape is a prime business—all at first glance might seem a close adaptation of the classic mode.

But there are differences of a very important kind. The vernacular brings with it not only the colour and character of contemporary Italian life, it also exploits relationships within society of a very different nature than that of the ancient Romans, with different institutions, and with different attitudes towards moral matters. Also, these plays are generally written in prose rather than in verse, and in every sense the lyrical inspiration of ancient comedy gives way to a celebration of the actual, even if exaggeration, satirical and otherwise, is present. There is a much greater wealth of incident, and there are commonly many more characters—Montaigne was to complain that the Italian comedies brought three or four stories into a play where the ancients were satisfied with one.[2] Most significantly of all, an idea, a pointed significance, controls the interest. There may be as much mockery in Plautus as in Ariosto, as coherent a criticism in Terence as in Machiavelli, but in the ancients intelligence only

47

serves the manipulation of the comic action, in the Italians the comedy again and again is in the point that is being made. The example of Boccaccio was irresistible.

Because it embodies a perfection of intellectuality not attained again until Molière, Machiavelli's *Mandragola* cannot be typical but in the character it possesses as a work designed to make a point it manifests the controlling disposition of the comedy of the century. The matters broached, the ideas tested, the actions undertaken, are ordered to advance a young man's ambition to conquer a woman of legendary virtue. We are to be left with the conclusion that virtuous women are like others, born for conquest. The special brilliance of the play is in the portrait of Lucrezia, as long as circumstances permit a simple peasant body faithful to conventional morals, but once her senses are stirred she becomes another self, animal and cunning.

In the elaborate preparations for her overthrow, in the intrigues laying the groundwork, nothing is put before us that is interesting or amusing merely in itself, although everything seems to be falling into place naturally, one might even say guilelessly. All the same we understand that every character, every joke, every comment is brought forward in order to establish the full complexity of the circumstances that will make the seduction inevitable; the most faithful attention is being paid to the complexities of human relationships so that the conclusion all is pointing to we shall accept as a conclusion life supports.

The art itself enchants. With Machiavelli as with Molière we are delighted to recognize the means by which we are being embroiled and led about by the nose. But the art, in the perfection of its discipline, is even so only serving the thought that makes the point of it all valid. The art charms, but in the end it is the authority of the thought that brings the point home. The foolish husband, the slippery friar, the mother-bawd, the cowlike wife, the lover so driven by passion he can only fear, not regret, that the woman is accessible to corruption—corruption is his word—all this that is so plainly contrived, contrived to be amusing and also horrible, comes to seem to be a paradigm of life as it is. The characters are as quick with life as they are with thought, the succession of incidents follows as surprises life could provide, and accordingly the conclusion we are compelled to entertain as one life would authorize. Yet we come back to our never-fading sense of the artifice of what is holding us, for the point the comedy is making is one that after all must be forced upon us, we do not take to it easily, any more easily than we take to the promise and satisfaction of comedy itself. We are being told that life properly understood is comic even when women are seduced and corrupted.

It is the same point applied to private matters that Machiavelli makes of public life, men are foxes or wolves, and women, like fortune, have no settled character at all. Because the intelligence in the play is so great, the meaning naturally escapes formulation, and the play is to be called neither cynical nor realistic, but with respect to any judgments we wish to form about the nature of the developing comedy it is important for us to recognize that the intent is to represent men as neither better nor worse than they are, but indeed as they are, in Florence, in that particular year. Realism is at the heart of it, and we take the comedy as seriously as we do because we are persuaded we are attending to what is as real as it is intelligible. The point it makes is too painful for laughter, as none ever is in Plautus, otherwise we might think it all-embracing.

The play of Shakespeare's that comes closest to this kind, *Timon of Athens*, should perhaps be called a comedy even though that term for Shakespeare seems almost improper for a play without a love story. The title itself of *The Taming of the Shrew* tells of an action that is controlled by an idea and a point. The comedies of the middle period—*All's Well that Ends Well* and *Measure for Measure*—are declaredly to be related to moral schemes. On the other hand, *The Comedy of Errors* is a stranger to such direction. I judge that *Love's Labour's Lost* and *The Two Gentlemen of Verona* in their exploitation of intellectuality are the first responses to the direction comedy was taking among the Italians. Not all the Italian comedies are in this respect so pure

49

as Machiavelli's, and perhaps only Bruno's *Candelaio* approaches the complexity of the thought of *The Two Gentlemen of Verona*. Shakespeare would never put a comedy so wholly to the service of intellectuality as in this strand of the history of Italian comedy, although like the Italians he saw the use for it that the Romans had not. But there is also this distinction to make, that while Shakespeare stopped short of putting comedy under the control of intellectuality, he put philosophy itself to the service of comedy.

The *Mandragola* dates from about 1513, preceded by Ariosto's *La Cassaria* in 1508 and *Gli Suppositi* in 1509. Dovizi da Bibbiena's *La Calandria* was apparently produced in 1513, and *Gl'Ingannati*, that directly or indirectly provided the basic plot of *Twelfth Night*, was produced by the Accademia degli Intronati of Siena in 1531. These are the landmarks, plays as committed to intellectuality as Machiavelli's, but they differ from his on several scores and most strikingly in developing interests that were most important to Shakespeare also and that he was to accommodate in not unlike ways. Ariosto and some others were not only ordering the ancient forms and ostensibly the ancient matter in the light of their critical and realistic motives, they exploited sensibility and sympathy as Machiavelli never could have. Boccaccio's spirit was still ascendant but these others would allow poetic and romantic interests to qualify profoundly the effects of realism. For them it seemed that comedy must not exclude a sense of happiness, it must express sympathy for the young and the loving deeply enough to counter the pitilessness of implacable criticism.

Not inferior in intelligence to Machiavelli, Ariosto creates a more vivid sense of the wealth and variousness of life. In some others the series of scenes are plainly directed by an idea, normally an idea of complication controlled by the resolution that is being planned for, but in Ariosto the governing connections derive quite as much from the complexities in the relationships between the characters. In *La Cassaria*—the example is typical—Lucrano, the ruffian, has a couple of young girl slaves he would like to sell, but if he can't he will put them out to day-work. He is prudent, astute, arrogant, and when in danger, demoralized and servile. He is accustomed to employ the most underhanded and ruthless means of exploitation. When he is himself worsted he cringes before a servant. In coping with him the young fellows who are out to get the girls for themselves are entangled not only in the complications of intrigue and duplicity, they are themselves taken off balance by surprises in the character of those they are coping with. All is as complexly conceived as it is felt, and every move that is made has consequences as un-expected as those we meet with in life. As in all Ariosto's come-dies there is what we recognize as the very stuff of the *Orlando Furioso*, the unending *intrecciamento*, and in the *Cassaria* the Shylock-like creature is carried along by the same unknowable currents that are carrying the others. Somehow, in the end, they will all be cast up on shore, fortune will always see to that in such a comedy, and for the young ones at least, it will all end happily, probably enough, but for all that, surprisingly.

The *Suppositi* is even richer with the sense of the fullness of life, and Gascoigne in his translation makes no effort to catch this. But he does make a great deal of what Ariosto gives him the grounds for, kindness and humanity, decency shining through all the folly, and a certain loveliness in the young.

Ariosto, however, holds to a view that Shakespeare no more than Gascoigne could entertain. The young fellows in his plays move heaven and earth to get the girls, there is no doubt about the strength and enthusiasm of their passions, but the protesta-tions of constancy, such as they are, say nothing about the marriage of minds and spirits, of the delight that soul affords to soul, of that stunning aspiration more romantic comedy makes so much of. No doubt these young slaves were originally gentlewomen, and in Ariosto they are certainly not the chattels of Plautus' plays, yet they are in fact chattels and their lovers mean to pur-chase them. We are to agree that this is moral, in spite of, or perhaps because of, the absence of romantic oaths. Ariosto is always smiling, sympathetic up to a point, detached after that point, wondering a little, and if not complacently yet unprotestingly in accord with the idea of the proprietary in matters of love as well as of passion. In this he remains true to the spirit of Boccaccio as Shakespeare never was to be.

And yet he is like Shakespeare and unlike Boccaccio in the gentleness and the respect for honour that justify the hopes for happiness his comedies allow. For all their joyous mockery these plays make remarkably little use of satire, just as they give us almost nothing of the raucousness of Plautus, or the happy grossness of the popular Italian drama, or the coarseness and libel and strength of Aretino and Bruno. When there is a plot involving slave-girls who pray to be bought by young men they can love, or when a well-born heiress is to be won through a trick and a disguise, whereby she is a mistress long before she can become a wife, there governs all the relations a certain almost high tone, and a note too about the right of sentiment to disregard the claims of caste. Even the monsters are treated rather gently, and the slave-merchant in the *Cassaria*, more fool than whore-master, is worsted with something less than slam-bang denunciations, and the Negromante himself is disposed of much less brutally than Shylock. As in Ariosto's satires, the Horatian manner counts for a great deal. So we may think that Terence meant more to him than Plautus, and despite the lead Roman comedy gave in drawing on the charm of the Greek romances, Ariosto does not make as much of this as either Plautus or Terence does. His wonderful distinction is that he is more humane than romantic.

He is of course modernizing, he is intent on what is Italian and contemporary, in his heroes and heroines as in his villains and buffoons; the critical intelligence shines as splendidly as the humanity, but the intellectuality was, so to speak, restrainable as it was not in Machiavelli and Bruno.

The thought is there inevitably, the multiplication of incidents and characters, plays with a dozen servants to complicate matters where two or three would have done for the ancients, entanglements enough to make a mess, but it would not be Ariosto if it turned out to be a mess, if everything did not in the end fall beautifully into place, as if the unravelling had been in all its neatness implicit in the confusion. As in the *Orlando Furioso* itself, and as in Shakespeare, there is the delight of the poet in detail for its own sake, in variety for the sense it gives of the endlessly fruitful.

The difference deserves to be underlined.

At the end of the second act of the *Cassaria* the slave-seller for nearly two hundred lines gives what at first appears to be a conventional speech setting forth some information the audience needs to know if we are to be able to keep the complications in the action clear in our minds. The speech is far longer than the immediate need requires, and in other hands it would be boring. But in fact the words are so full of meaning, they communicate so comprehensive a criticism of character as such and morals as such, that any audience attracted by thought at all could be persuaded to listen to such talk indefinitely.

The slave-seller is apparently serious as he speaks of himself as truly heedful of those he is selling, he expresses quite sensitive concern for them and likens himself to a bishop, as if his charge too had been given him by Christ—all this is as provocative as it is feeling and brilliant because there is a kind of beauty in his energy and restlessness, a fallen angel. The calculations of the man are joyless but Ariosto allows him a sense of the preciousness of what he's selling. He does not want just any purchaser for these young girls, and he mocks the spendthrift sons of cautious fathers so ardent in their desires, so careless in oaths he takes for granted from them, oaths that would never have been dreamed of by the young blades of Plautus and Terence but that he requires. Corrupt as he is, he knows nobility when he sees it. Perhaps no one but Ariosto could control such irony, showing even courtliness in him.

At first glance then, this might be an ancient lupanar or a Pandarus or a Lucio, whose depravity in the end is uninteresting, but Ariosto sees such life in his merchant that we see he is not

53

yet ready to judge that he is lost. In the complexity of such a conception the irony and the poetry are indistinguishable.

Cardinal Bibiena developed still another potentiality in the new comedy in his *Calandria*, one of the greatest successes of the period. In certain obvious matters it elaborates upon the romantic features of ancient comedy, in this respect surpassing the *Menaechmi* and many another. This tells also of twins separated, of a distraught father, of kidnappings and sea-voyages, of disguises and ultimate reunions and there is a double wedding at the end. More extensively than even *Il Negromante* it makes use of the supposed powers of magic, partly in a plot to bind lovers unchangeably to each other, partly to raise the possibility of changing an individual's sex. Accordingly magic not only provides charlatans with devices for their frauds it brings into the play the sense of truly mysterious powers.

A young girl, one of twins, lately arrived in Rome, disguises herself as a man and is pursued by the wife of a certain citizen who supposes her to be the twin brother. In his turn her husband is pursuing the girl's twin who has been disguised as a woman in order to gain access to the wife. A magician is brought in to complicate what one might think could be complicated no more. At one point a servant explains that his master-mistress is capable of serving lovers of both sexes, this after the pursuing woman, having won over one she supposes to be a lover, discovers 'him' to be a woman.

The main matter is in the fun. The ingenuity of the lovers as well as their naiveté, their inexhaustible persistence, their careless immorality, all is presented as if the audience were perfectly agreeable to conspiring with license, with unaffected grossness, and sometimes with lubricity. In *The Comedy of Errors* it is the confusion itself that amuses us most, in this it is the display of the intricacies lust and love devise. In the dismay there is very little opportunity for the sympathy Plautus and Shakespeare draw on in differing degrees although occasionally a cry opens up the possibility—'in che laberinto mi trovo io!'—'Io me stesso non conosco?' A servant becomes so confused she begins to think she is 'impazzata'. In Shakespeare such commonplaces led into an embracing conception, but there is nothing of that here.

In *Gl'Ingannati*, however, our minds are more fully engaged and our feelings are more drawn on. Like most of the other comedies this is in prose yet it achieves effects we normally think only within the power of plays in verse, elevation and beauty. It owes much of its success to the charm of the young girl setting out as so many will do in Shakespeare to be near her beloved. There is the most vivid sense of the wonder of her aspiration, of the charm of the combination of daring and timidity, and all this is given body and substance by the quality of the respect that is paid to virtue and to the thought that sustains it, and by the respect that is paid to passion. It is rarely that we find interests and attitudes that might be irreconcilable so complexly integrated, directness and decency being as complexly presented as the incongruities. And all is crowned with the sense of the beauty of the heroine.

But if the play presents to us the notion of a culture in which the complexities of morality are anything but passed over, in still another respect it offers us a view of quite another kind of society than such intrigues acquaint us with either in the Romans or in Shakespeare. It is still a man's world, but it is also a priest's and a church's. Always in the background waiting circumstances to bring them forward are the acknowledgements to be made to those who authorize sacraments, to those who oversee the distribution of property in dowries and inheritances, to courts and the administration of justice, and to custom and opinion in honouring truth and in exposing hypocrisy. On the whole, justice and law and the church are introduced less conspicuously than in Shakespeare's comedies but they set the context of the comedy more firmly. Here it is much as it is with Molière, humanity may be endlessly confused, social relationships are like Arachne's web and life after life can be stifled in them, but the claims of an aristocratic society will be met. And even though in this splendid play we are led in the usual manner to wish that love may overcome the rules of class, here the claims of society will be known to have the last word. In Shakespeare's first comedies the issue is not so sharply pointed although they go a long way towards developing an even more embracing complex of ideas in unfolding conceptions of nature and truth as the matrix of social as well as of the individual life.

Greek romances contributed richly to Italian comedy and not only indirectly through the uses Plautus and Terence had made of them.[3] For all that Boccaccio and Machiavelli represented, the appeal of romantic stories maintained itself and the material was of course well adapted to imbroglio and intrigue. It was not until Della Porta's comedies, some time after 1600, that the romantic character ever possessed the importance for Italian drama it possessed for Shakespeare, but it was vitally important to much of the drama and it was of immense value in enabling the playwrights to complicate their imbroglios by drawing upon the most far-fetched of causes and consequences of adventure and intrigue. The Italian comic writers were taking the lead from the ancients and carrying it to lengths not less elaborately than Shakespeare was to, though in less remarkable ways.

I think it not improper to speak of this as partly a humanist interest, at least to the extent that it represented a conscious imitation of the ancients, but it is also clear that the romantic plainly appealed to contemporary taste. These comedies in the vernacular will take every opportunity to bring current fashions and manners and issues forward, with Tuscan slang and humour and scandal and in England the colour of London and all that to a reasonably knowledgeable audience would persuade it to accept the imitation of an ancient mode as contemporary and up-to-the-minute, and with the romantic matter, as well, it would be contemporary sensibility that was being served.

In the *Suppositi* a young man who as an infant had been kidnapped by Turks is restored to his still grieving father. Through all the years he had survived as a servant he had maintained the nobility of character generally supposed to be the attribute of the well-born. When calamity came to his master this supposed servant acted not as a gentleman, however, but as a faithful retainer, with the tenderness and love of the Adam of *As You Like It*:

> Do not doubt that to save my young master's life
> I would undergo any suffering, I bear him so much
> love for the infinite favours he has done me. (V, iii)

An expression of friendship in *Il Negromante* goes beyond what the intrigue requires and is as tender as anything in Shakespeare:

> I have loved you as I love myself, nor would I ever have con-
> cealed from you, or been able to, whatever was in my thoughts,
> and now I don't think five or six years' separation will change
> my affection. (I, ii)

There is also the device Shakespeare was to use, a nurse whose coarseness by contrast illuminates the fineness in love.

But of all the plays in which the romantic quality mingles with the classic, so as to call Shakespeare to mind, Gianmaria Cecchi's *L'Ammalata* points most significantly to the major distinctions of Shakespeare's early comedies, their use of Christian sentiment and the complexity of the thought.

Professor R. W. Bond suggested this play as a source of *The Comedy of Errors*. He supposed that a company of Italian players performing at Windsor and Reading and elsewhere in England in 1574 might have included in their repertory plays of Cecchi as 'the most conspicuous and popular representative of the *commedia erudita* during the period 1560–1580'.[4] There has been no confirmation of Shakespeare's knowledge of this piece, but, even if one should not be interested in regarding it as a source, it is of great interest in its manifestation to a peculiar degree of the mingling of intrigue and romance.

Cecchi borrowed something from the *Menaechmi* for his comedy *La Moglie* but he owed to Terence for it too, and indeed both Roman writers were always his acknowledged models and sources. *L'Ammalata*, however, is the one of his plays that calls Shakespeare most to mind.

A young woman is in love with the moneyless foster-son of a man who will not help the young fellow to a position where marriage would become possible for him. As plans are being made to marry the girl to someone else she takes to her bed and lets it be given out that she will shortly die. Doctors, servants, nurses, soothsayers galore, to say nothing of widows, fathers, another suitor and another young lady figure in all the hub-hub this threatened disaster occasions. The preposterous, the buffoonery, the confusion are immensely entertaining but we are also being instructed from time to time about the difficulties of correlating appearance with reality.

There would never have been any resolution of the problems that were continually multiplying if there had not been discovered, quite unexpectedly, a magic ointment that made it possible to learn certain truths that otherwise would have remained hidden forever. The real state of the young lady's health was not one of these mysteries, although the ointment was of use in this matter as well, but the most astonishing revelation it led to included the discovery that the supposed foundling was brother to the hitherto favoured suitor. Years ago he and his mother had been sent off to be destroyed—*ammazzati*—for the father, unjustifiably it turns out, believed the mother an adulteress and the child not his. A man commissioned to kill them took pity on them and let them live. The boy, as we now know, had been adopted by his own father, and the mother was living nearby all the while as a nun. It is her skill with magic that is the means of discovering the true state of affairs.

The play ends in great happiness, in the reconciliation of husband and wife, father and mother,[5] in the restoration of a son and a brother and in the turn of events that enabled the sick young lady to gain the husband she wanted. A marriage is also arranged for the other brother.

Shakespeare's ending in all its complications would seem integral with the conception of the work from the beginning if one were to contrast it with the gratuitousness with which Cecchi winds up this *pot-pourri*. But in fact Shakespeare's ending does include elements for which there has been almost no preparation. Perhaps the very preposterousness of Cecchi's ending is a mark of superiority in this kind, where the least degree of coherence and the least suggestion of verisimilitude makes for more laughter. However this may be, the most significant point is that both playwrights resolve otherwise unfathomable confusion by the use of what passes as magic, and in the plays this is taken to testify to the work of a providential agency. Furthermore, this suggestion is not put crudely, for the language in both is grave and beautiful and care is taken to create a sense of wonder. The most significant likeness in the two endings is not in the inclusion of the reconciliation of parents in a story in which brothers once more come together, nor in the priestess-like function of a mother, nor in providing wives for both brothers, nor in all these together, but rather in the allusions to religious sanction growing out of the intensity of the romantic feeling.

There was something like this in the *Rudens* and the *Captivi*, but the religiousness was of course not Christian. In *L'Ammalata* the religiousness is only barely that, and this more in the suggestion of morality and contrition than of worship—the father is speaking: 'God be thanked that on this one day, at one and the same moment, I am made whole again, in mind and in body; and even more, what I never hoped for, that my most faithful consort is restored to me, and thou also, my dear son; and even more, and what counts for most of all, that I now know my ancient suspicion to be false. And so I render praise to God for His great gifts and I bless that moment in which the thought occurred to me that I should come to the place in which I have discovered all this happiness' (V, vii).

Neither the girl nor the mother comes on the stage in Cecchi's play. There is no opportunity for the wonder-working nun to make her pronouncements in person nor like Shakespeare's abbess can she come forward to invite all to a holy feast. We are left to infer that the happiness all are celebrating at the end is blessed and that holiness is being honoured. In this matter I think the difference between the two plays is more significant than even the likeness, but the likeness, putting aside the question of a source, is a witness to the fact that Shakespeare even in his limitless boldness is entering paths others were also discovering.

NOTES

[1] Nino Borsellino, *Commedie del Cinquecento*, Milan, 1962, I, xvi.

[2] '. . . en nostre temps, ceux qui se meslent de faire des comedies (ainsi que les Italiens, qui y sont assez heureux) employent trois ou quatre arguments [sujets] de celles de Terence ou de Plaute pour en faire une des leurs. Ils entassent en une seule Comedie cinq ou six contes de Boccace. Ce qui les faict ainsi se charger de matiere, c'est la deffiance qu'ils ont de se pouvoir soustenir de leurs propres graces: il faut qu'ils trouvent un corps où s'appuyer; et, n'ayant pas du leur assez dequoy nous arrester, ils veulent que le conte nous amuse'. (*Essais de Montaigne*, ed. A. Thibaudet, Livre II, chapitre x [Pléiade edition, p. 393]).

[3] Miss Sophie Trenker has constructed an ingenious theory with respect to the source of the *Menaechmi* as well as to Shakespeare's use of two sets of twins. She supposes an original folk-tale, and then a novella, in which identical twin brothers are accompanied on their adventures by identical twin servants. Plautus she thinks simplified his original but in its full form, or something like it, it was available to the pseudo-Clement and writers in the late Middle Ages, and in these versions a shipwreck and a story of separated parents also had parts. (*The Greek Novella in the Classical Period*, Cambridge, 1959, pp. 107–8). Some of this material may be found in Caxton's *Lives of the Saints* (*The Golden Legend* [Temple Classics], VI, 261).

I have not done justice to the complexity of Miss Trenker's argument but I have not found it useful in relating it to Shakespeare. The much more substantial and more rewarding treatment of Shakespeare's use of Greek romances is T. W. Baldwin's *Shakespeare's Five-Act Structure*, Urbana, 1947, as well as in his particular studies of *The Comedy of Errors*.

[4] *Early Plays from the Italian*, Oxford, 1911, p. cxi, and *Studia Otiosa*, London, 1938, pp. 43ff.

⁵ Lope de Rueda in imitating Plautus at least twice included the reconciliation of parents in the festivities of the happy ending—in the *Medora* and
in *Los Engañados*, the latter composed some time before 1565. This
incorporated features of *Gl'Ingannati*. The *Medora* is almost a translation
of an Italian adaptation of the *Menaechmi*. A shipwreck is the cause of one
of the separations. These plays do not ask so clearly to be brought forward
in a consideration of Shakespearean comedy but they do testify to the
interest in emphasizing the romantic features of Plautus-like plays. R. L.
Grismer discusses such matters in a valuable way in *The Influence of
Plautus in Spain before Lope de Vega*, New York, 1944.

There have lately appeared surveys of many of these matters in Douglas
Radcliff Umstead, *The Birth of Modern Comedy in Renaissance Italy*,
Chicago, 1969, and David Orr, *Italian Renaissance Drama in England
before 1625*, Chapel Hill, 1970.

Love's Labour's Lost

When Shakespeare commenced writing comedies on the model of Plautus he began with characters who had already embarked on searches. As the plot develops, the encounters and incidents lead ultimately to unions and re-unions, the restoration of families, engagements, marriages. Everyone at one time or another supposes he is moving towards a particular end when he is in fact moving towards a different one. Sooner or later the wanderings and errors lead to troths, and these often merely continue the errors. In the conclusion everyone, or almost everyone, gains the satisfaction of having his love requited, but the audience knows that the unions are inherently no more final than those that bound them before they were first separated. The coming into harbour we hopefully think to be a moment's peace in an eternally changing world.

The pattern of the action is so regular one must think of it as formalized, and by that fact alone we are disposed to accept the satisfaction of the conclusion also as formal, the pairings of couple after couple. Just how regular this is in *The Comedy of Errors* and what this signifies, is worth bringing out by a synopsis that must risk repetition as well as elaborating on the obvious.

Two sets of twins, unlike in character and circumstance but in appearance identical, so confuse all who come upon them that they themselves become confused. Dromio of Syracuse is commissioned to perform an errand that the other Dromio, who knows nothing about it, is being held to account for. The confusions continue. Following the command of one master, that

Dromio meets his master's twin and reminds him of the commission he had never made. The wrong Antipholus accepts the invitation of Luciana as she attempts to maintain her relationship with the other. Before anyone is able to square what he does with what he intended to do, he has set into action a chain of other confusions, and still other persons are involved, four different pairs altogether, masters, servants, parents, husband and wife and mistress and suitor. The mismatches multiply, and when all know enough to know they must find the right match they continue to confound each other—spiting a wife, favouring a mistress, putting money in a safe place, in precisely the way and at precisely the time that will thwart that very undertaking.

But the joy for the audience in all this confusion, which we understand because we have the clue to it, is in discovering the inadequacy of what everyone supposes to be adequacy—in discovering how the most obviously correct ideas and inferences turn out to be mistaken. And finally, when confusion appears to have exhausted itself, when every intention of ordering affairs is shown to be as ineffective as if it had been made at random, we are provided with what are apparently solutions to all the problems at once—several separated persons are re-united, others are brought together, Aegeon's wife is returned to him, Antipholus of Ephesus's marriage is restored, Antipholus of Syracuse obtains a wife, brothers and parents are all together again, and these marvellously happy unions, in part unsought for, were obtained through undirected as well as dedicated wanderings, through errors. The audience must therefore accept these happy unitings with their attendant happy promises as the results of no discernibly rational ordering on anyone's part, and whatever there is in them that accords to the heart's desire, whatever beauty and goodness and truth there was in the searching and the dedication, reached its ends through no other cause than the rules of the game, rules that were not known in a game that was not known to be a game. The rules of play provided the rewards, which we must suppose to be no better to be preserved than they were to be planned for. As with all play the happy ending itself is make-believe.

In *The Winter's Tale* Camillo tries to persuade the young lovers to take a course more promising than 'a wild dedication' of themselves to 'unpath'd waters, undream'd shores'. The figure of speech brings to mind great romantic adventures across the pathless seas, and the advice is that love, consulting only its own perfection, if it comes to shore at all, will do so only luckily. The same profoundly romantic assertion is also in Antipholus of Ephesus's plea not to be deflected from the course his 'soul's pure truth' has marked out for him. The idea is at the heart of all the early plays dealing with the tribulations of lovers—their motive is their guide, all else is random. The seekers, the lovers, of course make plans, and they are always hoping their plans will work out. Husbands, wives, suitors, out of their own needs, conjure up an order to events they suppose the universe will underwrite.

Berowne, as wise as he can be, points out the mistake in all this when men dedicate themselves to thought. The effort to defer all other claims life is making will defeat itself. Assured of his soul's pure truth though such a one may be, in the end he will find himself wandering blindly and he may get lost. No more than love is so sacrificing a service of thought enough to enable a man to square himself with the order in things. Thought can only be an index to its own inefficacy and to the intractableness and disorder of the world. The mind quite as much as the heart may be proposing for itself a satisfaction never to be attained.

Play after play will substantiate the lesson Berowne is offering but more often than not the playwright will make use of it to exploit the dilemmas of love. The early comedies especially will turn out to be representations of Love playing at cards for kisses and this will also mean that truth and reality are playing with men as trickily.

In *The Comedy of Errors* everyone is being matched against some spirit whose secret manoeuvrings confound him. In *Love's Labour's Lost* Nature is on the other side of the table playing its cards. Oddly enough, like the demon of *The Comedy of Errors*, Nature would like her opponents to win, or at least to draw, and they would be happy for such a result. How much she will let them in on, how much they must find out for themselves, is the question. Lords and ladies suppose there is a way to win, a system with which to beat the system. Nature and men and love they all suppose, if they only had the formula, would be known to behave as law directs, and if they knew this they themselves could help see to it that men and love and Nature should all keep in harmony.

Love's Labour's Lost adds to the fun by introducing ideas and philosophic speculation into the game, which now has debates as well as impulses to determine the moves. Arguments develop and the characters take sides although, as always with Shakespeare, as individuals they add the complications of idiosyncrasy, and so not only the improvisations of love but temperaments add their urgencies in proposing ways of coping with the events that always manage to be unforeseen. In *The Comedy of Errors* the patterns of the movement, after a single constant factor is allowed for, the disposition to loyalty and faithfulness, are determined by what seems to be a mysterious principle working through fortune. The disposition to faithfulness is in question in *Love's Labour's Lost* and the patterns of the movements of the action are referred to another source, a principle that if not wholly mysterious is not wholly intelligible. No wild dedication to another or to truth is enough to procure the benevolent protection of this power, but reverent and thoughtful service to what is definable as well as what is undefined in Nature, the thoughtful honouring of the disposition to loyalty, will at least sustain hope in obtaining Nature's concurrence with the aspirations of men and women. In this play 'the soul's pure truth' must be cognitive as well as oracular, and 'the glorious supposition' must be comprehensible. This is what those we wish well hope for, and if events permit—and at the end we are half promised they will—the play will bear them out. Which is to say, the playwright thinks their philosophizing finally not ill-directed, and yet not well enough, and he provides an epilogue to say so.

In *The Comedy of Errors* incident follows incident as one person mistakes the identity of another, in *Love's Labour's Lost* each incident follows as one person after another mistakes his own intentions and as they are all brought up short by the consequences that are indicated. The encounters and the results follow not as chance in itself would be accountable for, or as a controlling, immanent spirit, but, as the playwright determines the argument requires, in order that the action may reach its end in harmony with the appropriate conclusion to the argument that has been developed in discovering what the mistakes are that have been made. There are a couple of incidents that are as it were arbitrarily introduced from outside that are necessary for this manipulation—the first, the chance arrival of the ladies from France, the other, their untimely departure. But both these occurrences do no more than bring the arguments and the reasoning to a head, they do not redirect it, or introduce new factors, they merely make it possible for the playwright to lead the argument to the point of a determining crisis, and they allow him to suggest that the side that appears to have victory within its grasp may win an argument and still learn that life refuses to submit to thought. In short, the patterns of the debate and the patterns of the dances at the end coincide, all is similarly resolved, but the resolution is no conclusion, it is only a truce. Like the dancing, and like the meaning in the songs, we are persuaded that philosophy may indeed be treating with things as they are without knowing all there is to know. Reality is something other than Berowne's or anyone's reasoning will encompass. Much will remain unexplained. The future will still be wild. In Machiavelli's comedies the source of events accords perfectly with reasoned understanding, what is before us is the clear demonstration of the way things are. In *Love's Labour's Lost* it is not reason and criticism but philosophy we are attending to, thought whose beginning and end is in wonder rather than in clarification, and the play holds us by the felicity of the representation of its bemused gentlemen and ladies, not simply in observing their use in making a point.

The matters that concern the young men and women become moral as well as philosophical and the issues of morality lead into arguments in which the scenes and the drama itself move rather more pointedly although, again in contrast with the Boccaccesque manner, our interest in the morality is subordinated to the movement of the drama, to the charm of the representation. The example of Lyly is now before Shakespeare, and his achievements are being put to use in going on from Plautus. The obligation to Lyly is in part in his way of making use of sententiousness, and one of Shakespeare's greatest gifts was the power of presenting persons in debate so complexly created they never become mere mouthpieces. With no comparable power Lyly avoided much of the disadvantages that personifications bring with them by making use of mythological and legendary persons with their inherent resistance to simplification. Shakespeare was to end *Love's Labour's Lost* with a beautiful and also enigmatic use of mythological beings, and one may see in the ending, and in the manner the play follows in preparing for it, what Lyly has taught him and how he brings this in accord with the Plautine model.

In *Campaspe* Lyly commenced by ordering a succession of scenes with a different group of characters in each scene. A meeting is about to take place between Alexander, the conquering general, and several captives, among them Campaspe. In scenes between Alexander and Diogenes, we hear debates on the claims of power and philosophy for men's allegiance. In these as with the scenes with the captives the interest is in the matching of wits, and there is even a sense in which the issues developed in the meetings of Alexander with the captives are set off, somewhat satirically, against the issues in debate between the general and the philosophers. The whole is a polished and courtly work in which we see and hear actors playing glamorous or comic parts in interesting debates. There is nothing that can be called a plot, little to be called an action, we are simply offered interesting situations from a picturesque legend in which ideas are developed that have bearing upon the lives of these famous persons at a time of crisis. In the absence of anything like a plot, or, one is tempted to say, drama, there is offered us instead a somewhat tentative introduction into most reverberating ideas. The work may possibly possess the rudimentary unity inherent in an encounter and a parting, or in a series of slow mimes, but hardly more. Yet in its way, produced with taste, I should think the play capable of satisfying effects, with the charm that belongs to serious thought, gracefully expressed, expounded in a handsome setting.

In *Sapho and Phao* the scenes are more closely connected. Plot begins to take form although at the end it loses its chance for control, and in the confusion even the theme is all but submerged. But there is one constant element in the succession of scenes and within the scenes themselves that does establish a certain coherence and interest. This is the device of contrast—in the first scene the contrast of the life of Venus with the life of a ferryman; in the second, the contrast of the life of love and the life of the unloving; in the third, the contrast of the life of a page and the life of a scholar. This manner is of course the prime current of Lyly's prose as well, and here as in his other dramas the rhythm of the prose, formed upon the primary elements of parallels and oppositions, is the pattern not only of the debates but of the representation upon a stage of potentially dramatic tensions. The attraction of the dramatic representation is the same in nature and effect as the attraction of the language: 'Having received long life by Phœbus and rare beauty by nature, I thought all the year would have been May, that fresh colours would always continue, that time and fortune could not wear out, what gods and nature had wrought up: not one imagining that white and red should turn to black and yellow; that Juniper, the longer it grew the crookeder it waxed; or that in a face without blemish there should come wrinkles without number' (II, i, 60–6).

As time went on Lyly learned to develop contrasts into genuinely dramatic involvements, where the dialogue came to express conflicts of feeling, the confusions of defeat as well as the complacency of victory, so that we come to believe the characters are

68

genuinely involved in the consequences of their engagement with ideas. In one scene of *Sapho and Phao* each of the lovers is fearful of showing his feeling for the other, and in order to say what each wants to say, and yet to be interpreted in a different sense, each falls back upon puns. A conception of this sensitivity, in language expressing the poignancy of such a state, is of course what Shakespeare would know how to make the most of.

With *Endymion* Lyly moved into a more intricate manner of dramatic construction, for here the fundamental method of contrast is elaborated through allegory. Antitheses remain at the centre of the confrontations of argument and character—the love of the earthly opposed to the love of the universal, ordinary folk contrasted with royalty, mortals with gods, all this heightened with further richness through the Petrarchan exaggerations. These are all elements in *Love's Labour's Lost* too, where still more complexly, however, the discussions concerning the love of the temporal and the eternal are related to the interests of persons alive at the time. By contrast, on this as well as on other points, Lyly's success seems to be in but one dimension, a charming work but with a most limited set of overtones, and the Shakespearean work, however obvious its artifice, gives off resonance after resonance.

In *Campaspe* different aspects of a single theme were developed in a pattern of scenes in which different groups of characters pursued discussions concerned with their particular circumstances. In *Endymion and Gallathea* full-fledged themes were developed in part in representing changing circumstances. In these different methods there were the elements not only of a drama in which themes could be absorbed in the ordering of the action but in which a parallel action, or sub-plot, could serve to enhance not only the character of the primary action but the theme it developed as well. All this of course becomes Shakespeare's method in *Love's Labour's Lost*.

Shakespeare appears to have accepted all that Lyly offered him except his manner of representing persons as the simple projections of moral attitudes and doctrines. He seems never to have been able to confine himself to such forms except in the briefest interludes. For him the appeal of individuality was irresistible; any truth as truth or morality as morality that interested him in composing plays could only be expressed in imitating the processions of men and women across the stage, and however preconceived the pattern of the dramatic action, the drama and the beauty and the meaning must arise out of the apparent life of the persons being put before us.

Treating love matters, and being full of fun, these plays of Lyly like Shakespeare's are by definition playful, they exploit what seems to be spontaneous and random, and yet as they progress there seems to be method in them. As the scenes succeed each other a pattern fills out and we begin not only to hope but to expect that all we are attending to will somehow fit together. The plot, as that begins to shape up, may not be any more important than the spectacle—the view of persons moving about, their gesticulations in the throes of this or that, the harmonies and contrasts of form and colour, all these together with the words embodying as it were a single movement and life. As in games and dances there is a unifying spirit in the moving and in the coming to rest and in the starting forward again. In Lyly's plays and in *Love's Labour's Lost* the beauty of the persons, their dignity, their handsome dress, and in Shakespeare the special beauty of high spirits, are the show, and ideas, motifs, themes, plots are but elements in our wonder at their being and presence. I think we must credit fully Granville-Barker's judgment that *Love's Labour's Lost* was designed for production in a great house where 'a troupe of choristers' was maintained, that the play is never very far from the actualities of song and dance.[1]

No major source for *Love's Labour's Lost* is known, and although its obligations to Plautus and Lyly are plain, one sees in it so great a dependence on musical effects, so much interest in dancing and masking and stage play (the drama of the Seven Worthies and the dance of the masked Russians and the Epilogue are only the most obvious examples of this) that whether in intention or not the comedy seems to have absorbed another genre.

It is certainly a work designed to please aristocratic persons intent on all that was at the top of fashion. Further, it reveals a particular and apparently informed interest in certain currents of contemporary life in France, and this together with its special qualities makes it not unreasonable to wish to relate it to forms of drama that were coming into fashion in which music and dancing and spectacle were being developed lavishly. So far, I believe, there is nothing to relate Shakespeare's work directly to the famous and germinal *Balet Comique de la Royne* of 1581, which was to be a source for more than one production in England as well as in Italy, but there is a point to be made about it that applies to *Love's Labour's Lost* and to some of Shakespeare's later comic writing as well.

Beaujoyeulx in the preface to his work called attention to the use of the word 'comique', for he wanted it understood this was drama as well as dance. Moreover, 'Je me suis aduisé qu'il ne seroit point indecent de mesler l'vn et l'autre ensemblément [la musique et la poésie], et diuersifier la musique de poesie, et entrelacer la poesie de musique, et le plus souuent les confondre deux ensemble.'[2] It possessed also something of the character of the later masques in which at a certain point the spectators, royalty and nobility, were expected to become partners with the performers—in a spirit not unlike that of the dance with the masked Russians in Shakespeare's play. 'Les frontières entre la vie réele et la vie de théâtre s'estompaient même; le spectateur jouait un rôle presque aussi important dans la représentation que l'interpréteur qu'en pourrait considérer comme privilegié parce qu'il y participait d'une manière plus intense.'[3] Then too, the topicality of Shakespeare's play, as does the political allegory of so many other works in the genres of ballets and masques, exploits the sense of the participation of the audience in a work that is in so many respects a play about them.

In *The Comedy of Errors* it may be that school productions or Plautus himself had given Shakespeare support in making as much use as he did of something like dancing patterns, but in

Love's Labour's Lost there is that and much more—maskings, dancings, tableaux, and songs. How much also of what we would call accompaniment I cannot say, but partly from what we make of the style Lyly had set, partly of the success of *Le Balet Comique*, it is hard to think of a contemporary production of *Love's Labour's Lost* uninfluenced by the beautiful and spectacular styles of production one associates with ballets and masques. And certainly such richness is in the very nature of this play.

The structures of pattern as in dances—of advances and retreats—is here of course almost inevitable when the play was to proceed so much according to the turns of an argument. In this connection one must always think of what is said of the origins of philosophy in rhythmic movements, even in song, according to the legend of Orpheus. Furthermore, the particular philosophy that exercises the persons in the play is itself always exploiting contrasts and opposites—the Platonic oppositions of light and dark and spirit and flesh on the one hand, the conflict between the life of the mind and the life of nature on the other. Moreover, since so much has to do with love between the sexes, almost everything is presented in terms of the Petrarchan antitheses, of fire and ice, bliss and torment, of all or nothing at all. That is to say, a comedy of imbroglio or satire, or of character and manners, might proceed according to patterns of causality and chronology in which there would be little need to arrange matters according to contrasting systems. Here where almost everyone is conscious of such contrasts, it is of the greatest use to the progress of the play for the contrasts to be represented, even, one might say, enacted.

The antitheses of argument as philosophy presents them are matched against the oppositions nature opposes to abstraction, and the resolutions are at once resolutions in the modification of the argument and the accommodations the persons make in coming to terms with experience. The Plautine form, in short, now follows not merely the principles of music, thought itself runs parallel to the movements of music as the dramatic action runs parallel to the movements of dances.

A theme embodying an argument allows for the oppositions of thought to be developed in the representation of contrasting persons, ranks, scenes, and actions, so that now we see pairs of persons—not kindred this time—moving towards unions in companionship or marriage, separating, forming ranks again, encountering each other, or semblances of each other, again and again, dispersing again. Sometimes in their encounters and separations they are moved according to the necessities of actions they have already undertaken; sometimes according to the obvious manipulations of the playwright contriving a plot. There are ironic parallels in the affairs of the serious and the pedantic, the high and the low. Sometimes the plot indeed is thought to be the contrivance of something else—destiny, or chance mistaken for destiny. Sometimes the intrigues of the persons are plots of their own, sometimes it may seem that some such pervasive spirit, this time a mocking spirit, is the soul of the little universe of their devising. But most plainly the steps and resolutions of an all-embracing argument are determining the juxtapositions to come next, what contrast, what consequence—in action, in the emotional involvements of the persons, in outcomes. The idea of a happy life, the idea, for example, that must prevail if neither the claims of philosophy nor of mere appetite are to attain an unworthy victory, will be shown to be harmoniously correspondent to the very natures of men—particularly of good men—so that the audience may even come to believe that the ideas themselves, the arguments, and resolutions, are the life blood of the King of Navarre, of Berowne, of Catherine, and many another. That is, as if indeed life in drama might be taken to be the embodiment of thought, as if what distinguished men from puppets were their inability to act without thought. Which is both a serious and an ironic idea, and the play is ultimately ironic from the very fact that there is so much to be said against the notion that life is in any sense indebted to thought as men come to their end.

Act IV, scene iii, illustrates the manner to perfection. The scene opens in the park with Berowne in soliloquy revealing he has written a sonnet to his love and sent it to her. He moves aside as the King comes on reading a sonnet he has written to *his* love, which he means to leave for her, and he in turn steps aside as Longaville enters, reading his sonnet. Dumaine then comes on, composing a poem, and Berowne, in the wings, comments on this line by line as Dumaine puts his poem together. After Dumaine reads his lovely song entire—'On a day—alack the day!'—one by one the others come forward to rebuke and tease him for betraying them all, but Berowne will not permit this and exposes the general defection. All ends in the agreement of the men to admit their subjugation by love. The mockery and the compact conclude with Berowne's great speech on love and wisdom and charity, and the scene ends with all going forward as troops marching to battle under Love's banner in splendid, mocking show.

The three poems that are recited develop different ideas about love and perfection and divinity. The theme of the King's is that the lady he loves is more beautiful than all else in nature. Longaville praises his love as a very goddess and in service to her he is freed from all oaths that would bind him anywhere else. Dumaine's theme is that his love, a mortal, surpasses any goddess, and to be forsworn for her sake is no sin. They are all playing about not only with justifications for unfaithfulness but with confused ideas about the love they feel powerless before. So when Berowne provides the capstone, we may doubt how far he can free himself from casuistry, not only because he himself has been forced to reverse himself but because anyone is hard put to reconcile the claims of love and philosophy and religion when they are most absolute. Accordingly—and partly, too, because he is such a scoffer—we may not take wholly seriously the reasons he now offers that wisdom may be found in the holy of holies, a lady's eyes, but as more than one commentator has explained, his reasoning is as deep as it is complex, and the reconciliation of conflicting claims is made not only brilliantly but seriously.

Not every scene in *Love's Labour's Lost* matches this in its obvious formality, in the development of an argument in stages as formally distinguished as the entrances and withdrawings, with a great fanfare of a speech in conclusion preparatory to a march into battle. But this is unique only in itself, other scenes are comparably formed, and all are in harmony with the spirit informing the rhythmic movement of the play as a whole.

Love's Labour's Lost depends upon what *The Comedy of Errors* hardly knows, mockery. In that play there is ridicule and occasionally even satire but the thought is predominantly developed within the perspectives of humour and of the picturesque. There is very little of the criticism of the particulars of behaviour and of attitudes of mind that plain mockery feasts on. In *The Comedy of Errors* at times we recognize a certain melancholy in those who seek what they fear is unattainable, yet in the comic action very little point is made in contrasting the merely human with the pretensions that outgo the reach of humanity. As it was in Plautus, pretension, boasting, vainglory has only to be brought into view to be laughed out of court, and the fun, in the events and the discomfitures, springs from very different emphases. It might almost be said that *Love's Labour's Lost* on the other hand exists in order to mock pretensions, and particularly those of the young in the higher ranks of society. Being who they are, they are head over heels in self-confidence, at one time aspiring after truth with as much purity and zeal as if they were philosophers (or so it seems to them), at another they think they can be as dedicated to the heart's fancy as to truth. In mocking them the play goes on to prick at the claims of philosophy itself, and then at the claims of love—not only at the aspiring of the young but at the very things they aspire to. The mockery in short entertains increasingly comprehensive ideas, as ideas and as guides to living.

Dramatically the play begins with the delivery of an edict—the decision to leave the Court has been made—but the King's authority is supported by an argument. Philosophic study is of such absolute value that its claims now must supplant all others. Through this at once fanciful and serious matter the audience is inducted both into the dramatic action and the world of ideas.

75

Our interest is immediately increased by circumstances which heighten the potential conflicts and emphasize the issues. There are the particularly provocative suggestions that we may have in prospect adventures of the kind we are accustomed to in stories of chivalric adventure.

The courtiers plight their faiths as if they were departing on a quest from the Round Table itself, and the terms set in keeping their oaths turn upon deprivations ordinarily appropriate to the monk-like sacrifices of knights on holy missions. As a consequence the mockery that begins to play on all, as Berowne makes his objections to what he thinks is nonsense, is partly criticism of the philosophy of the King, but it is also mockery of the idea that courtiers might practise asceticism in any cause. Berowne can conceive of dedicating himself to a cause, but asceticism as extreme as this is something else—

> So much, dear liege, I have already sworn,
> That is, to live and study here three years.
> But there are other strict observances . . .
> Which I hope well is not enrollèd there. (I, i, 34–6, 37)

He says that the purpose of study is to learn how to live in the world—

> to study where I well may dine
> When I to feast expressly am forbid;
> Or study where to meet some mistress fine
> When mistresses from common sense are hid;
> Or having sworn too hard-a-keeping oath,
> Study to break it and not break my troth. (61–6)

To which the King replies that such study and such a life refuses 'study's god-like recompense' (58). Although the King does not say enough to require us to interpret his purpose as the study of the Divine Ideas, or of God, we see that the tenor of his argument goes that way—as Berowne protested,

76

I have for barbarism spoke more
Than for that angel knowledge you can say . . .[4]

(I, i, 112–13)

The conventions of the Academy are to be picturesque, and in addition to the oaths, the monastic character of the fasting, and the limiting of the time of sleep, they include some of the more outlandish features of the old romances, as, for example, the rule that no woman shall come within a mile of the court 'on pain of losing her tongue' (123–4). Thus what was initially proposed as a plan to free the philosophers from distraction came to seem somehow a life of hideous deprivation and the initiates felt compelled to punish almost vengefully those who would threaten their withdrawal.

The extremity to which the aspiration for single-mindedness goes is mocked, oddly enough, not so much as a Puritanical or morbid disposition, but as intemperance, and this is plainly seen in the initial compromise, for it is in observing decency and propriety that the King agrees to the visit of the daughter of the King of France. Navarre sees no humour in this, but Berowne sees it as the foundation of more and more ridiculous things to come—

Necessity will make us all forsworn (148).

Necessity, in the nature of things, mocks extremity, mocks pretension, mocks idealism, mocks philosophers, mocks the noble generally, who will—also of necessity—continue on their ways. Men are necessarily committed to commitments, or at least men of the court are, men of mind and aspiration who set as high a value upon truth, say, as upon loyal service generally, and upon the charm and independence of women. So it is not the romantic or the grotesque or the superstitious that the play mocks, so much as the nature of intemperance even within the very need that the play does not mock, the need to maintain 'troth'. The mocker himself, with the playwright's sympathy, is committed to the idea of commitment:

No, my good lord, I have sworn to stay with you;
And though I have for barbarism spoke more
Than for that angel knowledge you can say,
Yet confident I'll keep what I have swore,
And bide the penance of each three years' day.
Give me the paper, let me read the same,
And to the strictest decrees I'll write my name.

(I, i, 111–17)

In *The Comedy of Errors* ideas are seldom discussed, none comes anywhere near governing the action of the play, and none as an idea comprehends the rich suggestions of meaningfulness arising out of this or that encounter or dilemma. Circumstances control the play's movement, and the characteristic lavishness with which Shakespeare must always lay out his poetry and drama is limited there by the plot alone. In *Love's Labour's Lost* governing ideas do not so much limit as they adorn the lavishness—the variety and beauty in the characterizations, in the mockery, in the music and songs and dancing and horse-play have almost free rein, but not so free that they escape the playwright's intelligence asserting its continuous judgments, laughing at the foolishness and fancifulness of these young people taken up with notions of their own power and importance, explaining the ridiculous as the luxuriance proper to thought as to life.

The initial circumstances of the play bring out the fundamental absurdity. The King and his friends suppose it will be quite easy to turn to a life of study and denial. The folly is further defined by the character and class of these deluded ones, young, wealthy, untried—in short, sheltered not merely from the trials of society but from the knowledge of nature. They take their excellence and self-sufficiency for granted and know of no circumstances that might confound them. They are as ignorant of any magical spirit at work in the universe to guide or vex as they are of any destiny than of their own contriving. They appear not to know of a moral or religious law which mortals—they

78

hardly think of themselves as mortals—must obey. Untroubled, in their very peacefulness they reject the possibility of unknown powers in nature and in their own natures to call any other tune than they themselves make up. As the play turns out they will learn that they have been mistaken, that in their ignorance they have been defying powers beyond their knowledge, and in their labours as in their playing they will come to know that they have been fortune's fools beyond anything the spirit at work in the world of *The Comedy of Errors* would ever have made of the inhabitants of Syracuse and Ephesus. They have asked for life to mock them and it turns out that perjury, perfidy, abnegation and purification are required to bring them to their senses. The point is clear, the mockery now is mercifully light, for all this is in the nature of the young and civilized, but the stakes all the same are the only stakes there are, truth and troth.

The Comedy of Errors seems to carry over something of the religious awe of Plautus. The continuous references to sorcery and witchcraft lead the audience to half-believe that there may indeed be something mysterious at the root of all these contretemps and confusions. There is a charm here that harmonizes with the note of the romantic yearning that moves young and old alike from the beginning to the end of the play and that finds expression in many beautiful verses. It is the poetry of 'the soul's pure truth' and of witchcraft that holds the play together, and the author never allows criticism to point up the foolishness in all this. Ideas as ideas have almost no part in governing the progress of the play, they are hardly brought into it, they are almost never taken up in significant ways, and they are not involved in effecting recognitions and reconciliations any more than in the initial confusions. It is precisely because ideas are not inherent in the work that the world of the play can seem a seamless world in which commonplace quarrels, ordinary intrigues, and the most obvious mistakes can appear to be the work of magicians and sorcerers or of the spirit such beings live by. And in the reverse, it is the very exploitation of a single spirit informing all things, effecting finally—there can be no other explanation—the

79

return of his wife to Aegeon, the restoration of sons and brothers —that requires the exclusion of anything that would quicken the critical judgment of the audience. Above all else the audience must be prevented from looking at all this preposterousness in anything like the perspective the exploitation of ideas would immediately call forth.

Love's Labour's Lost begins with ideas, and simultaneously with the mockery of them. By that very act it can never give any hint that it is a play about a world itself dreaming of things to come, by that fact it presents us at once and immediately with two worlds—the contrived world of the play before us and the world of the mocking audience. The mockery attests to the presence of another mentality. Even as we are being charmed into sympathy now with the King, now with Berowne, now with the ladies, we are being drawn to consider something quite different, we are being led to ask what all this nonsense has to do with the serious business of our own lives.

The King is meeting with his Court. He proposes that they form an Academy. The proposal is accepted over some objections. This is too great a change, Berowne says, not merely in so swiftly transforming the ways of courtiers but in disregarding the nature of men. By his objections Berowne helps establish a different point of view in the audience than was being formed as the King made his proposal. It is being led to put the whole matter into a critical perspective. Berowne is saying in part that men do not change easily and that nature is recalcitrant to schematic impositions, not least in dedication, and without the most careful and sustained preparation. He is not able to win his point with the King but he does make it with the audience. We agree that this new undertaking must be prepared to cope with stubborn and deep-rooted ways, that the King may be proposing a programme that may not succeed, and while the whole scene is set up to cause us to wish the undertaking well Berowne's criticisms have put the matter into the perspective of sound judgment.

Ironically, both the King and Berowne, now and later, are

appealing to unchanging truths. The King is appealing to the idea of eternal truths to be discovered beneath the flux of things, and in this discovery he supposes the Academy will find the richest kind of life, even immortality. Berowne is asserting the fixity of nature's laws, in which he maintains that the devotion to thought cannot be pursued without due regard for men's other needs. He will carry his point too far, of course, for he wishes to make all the claims he can for love and for pleasure, and he will later say that the very philosopher's stone the King is seeking can better be sought by looking into a lady's eyes, as if in those quick motions of light and dark and passion itself the shining truth of reality is there for all to possess. As the play turns out we shall come to see that Berowne is about as simple-minded as the King, and we shall be left in no doubt at all that there is as little constancy in the hearts of lovers as in the minds of philosophers. The play, however, will not rest with this point but will go on to another, for it will treat both arguments kindly, or at least it will treat the arguers kindly by presenting another hopefully-reconciling doctrine that there is indeed a constancy men may rely on and take comfort from, constancy in change. It is this truth men must learn to live by, must search into, and must make peace with. The idea is presented as a paradox that saves the sweet with the bitter, and it is the more thoughtfully presented in that it mocks the very point of view from which the mockery of the play has been worked out from the beginning, letting us understand that the very standards we have been employing in our mocking judgments are themselves subject to change.

The play, presenting arguments in which the action is in part an illustration of the issues at debate, proceeds as the arguments require. In *The Comedy of Errors*, Antipholus of Syracuse lands at Ephesus at a time set either by fate or chance, his arrival has not been arranged at that particular time in order to illustrate an idea or to propose an issue in an argument. By contrast with this, in *Love's Labour's Lost* when news is brought to the King of Navarre that certain ladies from France are about to pay his

Court a visit, the meeting at that point is called for in order to test the reasoning of the King for going into retirement.

Because this is a play, a confronting of persons as well as ideas, and because as persons poetically and dramatically conceived they are something more than counters in a game, the play proceeds in holding our attention to its movement, its colour, its humour and vivacity, the sensibility and even passion of the players. Yet although this dramatic imagining takes the production away from the simplifications of allegory, the argument as argument controls what the persons address themselves to in their talk and it provides the guide-lines for the ordering of the incidents.

There is to be a visit of ladies from the Court of France and as a first consequence the debate between the King and Berowne is postponed. Hospitality and certain political negotiations require the lords' attention, but the main matter turns out to be something else. In the course of the meeting the gentlemen and ladies become attracted to each other. What commenced as a temporary delay in the flight to Academe leads to the raising of doubts about the whole undertaking. The oaths the courtiers had taken are apparently to be broken and the noble lords find themselves at odds with each other and even with themselves. They will give up the idea of retreating from the world if only the ladies will marry them. Affairs are not to go so simply, a death causes the ladies to return to France, and in any event they decide they will not respond to the men's beseechings until the suitors show themselves capable of keeping oaths. The play ends with this matter not resolved and, curiously for the men, in a strange return to something like their initial proposal. Instead of retiring from the world to study philosophy they now engage to retire from the Court to a life of sacrifice, charity, and harsh asceticism, in order to establish their character, to establish their right to be believed in. At the end of a certain time it will be for the ladies to determine if the men have redeemed themselves. The play ends in the hope they will and in the hope that marriages will crown their rehabilitation with happiness.

This has been a steep fall for those who once aspired to immortality through the study of philosophy, and even for Berowne who had argued that divinity might be attained by gazing into a lady's eyes. The philosophers will now be happy enough if they are granted what fortune keeps in store for ordinary mortals. The point is made in a number of ways, most brilliantly and ironically by the Princess in refusing the King's request for an immediate betrothal. Her words are as beautiful in their feeling as they are witty in their rebuke—this has been, she says,

> A time . . . too short
> To make a world-without-end bargain in.
> (V, ii, 789-90)

It is a point the audience would have thought of many times in the midst of the extravagant language one after another of the characters had let himself use, and even though Berowne had some sense of what the world is really like he may not have understood the full import of his words early in the play—

> At Christmas I no more desire a rose
> Than wish a snow in May's new-fangled shows,
> But like of each thing that in season grows.
> (I, i, 105-7)

But it is in the concluding songs that the gist of it all is most stunningly presented. There we are told of Spring and Winter and of the terms on which men live with time. We are told of faithfulness and the threat of unfaithfulness and a great deal about stability in the midst of change. The songs are exquisitely beautiful although the subject is homely. Where the play had commenced with the mockery of extravagance and of the pretensions to something like divinity, it ends with a celebration of the beauty of the commonplace. Where it had commenced with most unreal aspirations for unbending constancy, it ended with the praise of a world of change. All this to conclude a play about lovers for whom the future is still uncertain.

The mockery that has been central to the conception of the entire play has been transformed. It depended originally upon standards of consistency, of reason and logic, and now these songs mocking human affairs in their most trivial uncertainties —winter colds, boring sermons, cuckolded husbands—turn into the praise of all that has been mocked, change itself, mortal life, and the ways of time. For the final irony the point is made that there is an abiding and salutary truth discoverable in the very stuff of mutability.

Miss Frances Yates has shown how *Love's Labour's Lost*, in all the interplay of ideas between the claims of philosophy and love, is treating concerns that Bruno, Sidney, Raleigh, Florio, and a whole lively set were taken up with.[5] Much of the mockery of the play is a mockery of contemporary fashion, and Bruno is at the centre of it. The ideas, however, are serious, and in making use of them it appears that Shakespeare is coming to grips with issues central to Bruno's thought, the efforts he was making to resolve conflicts between Platonism and naturalism.

Miss Yates observed that many persons in the play were expressing contradictory aspirations as they made references to lady's eyes and stars, to light and darkness and the light of the mind. Her point was that the conflicts between the claims of philosophy and of love as they were manifested in these expressions were those that engaged Raleigh's circle where so much was being made of the study of astronomy and the bearing of that science upon philosophy. These interests also bore upon the cult of love supporting the ideas Sidney was developing in the sonnets to 'Stella'. The part of Bruno in all this was to encourage his friends to give up earthly love for heavenly love, particular earthly love for particular heavenly study, and of course to do so in accordance with a particular philosophy.

I am convinced that Miss Yates has illuminated a matter of considerable importance, and that *Love's Labour's Lost* treats philosophic issues in substance as well as indirectly. Poetically, the references to eyes and sight are initially significant for their indication of the mannered style of conceit in these courtly persons, in Berowne particularly as he all but harps upon the figure—

> Thy eye Jove's lightning bears. . . . (IV, ii, 117)

> O but her eye! By this light, but for her eye, I would
> not love her—yes, for her two eyes. . . . (IV, iii, 9–11)

> My eyes are then no eyes, nor I Berowne. . . .
> (IV, iii, 231)

The eyes, themselves continually moving everywhere, changing from what they light upon, turning here and there, become the symbol of the mind and perhaps of love itself, by nature restless, changing back and forth from true and false, sight and mind and love all true sometimes, and they are also deceiving. Love changes, the object of love changes, and yet when the great speech is done with we have been told that men in their most restless life are ever seeking to take hold upon permanence, that the true Promethean fire does exist, and that through love it lights men truly. In another aspect, as suggestive, the words lead us into thoughts about a world in which truth and being are one, the light of the mind at one with truth.

> But love, first learnèd in a lady's eyes,
> Lives not alone immurèd in the brain,
> But with the motion of all elements,
> Courses as swift as thought in every power,
> And gives to every power a double power
> Above their functions and their offices.
> (IV, iii, 326–31)

Berowne is refuting what he had first argued—

> Light seeking light doth light of light beguile—
> (I, i, 77)

85

but he has known, as they all have, the language of philosophy and even his pleas in behalf of common sense have never freed him of the vistas of heavenly contemplation in that first enterprise. His effort is to keep the balance.

Shakespeare does not, of course, permit his characters to pursue their philosophical interests to the point that the drama suffers, but the issues he focuses on in this play were to be of lasting concern to him and he is to explore their depths in the years ahead in many forms. His method is not in any strict sense ever dialectical, although here, as in Berowne's speech, he will lay forth the essentials of an argument in some fullness. I think there is indeed in *Love's Labour's Lost* more of the sense and spirit of the *Eroici Furori* than even Miss Yates has shown.

For one thing, in the ending of both works there is a kind of stand-off, a truce between opposing views, in which we see not only a similar understanding of the complexity of the problem but a remarkable concurrence in at least one conclusion, time and nature have it within their power to bring to fruition what humans in themselves cannot. In reaching the conclusion the two treat similarly with certain attitudes towards absolute truth and divinity even though with important divergences.

The ending section of the *Eroici Furori* is largely the recounting of a story of nine blind young men. We learn that they are nine by analogy with the nine spheres and the intelligences that govern them. They are in despair of attaining the creature they have all learned to adore, a divine lady who bears some resemblance to Dante's Beatrice. They depart from their happy homeland swearing to find if not a more divine creature at least one her equal except that she would also possess the virtues of mercy and pity. They come to the home of Circe, daughter of the Sun, who is the generative power in all the things and forms of nature, bearing within herself every seed of generation and corruption, of all metamorphoses. The nine young men are dazzled at first with the splendour of the variety of things in Circe's power but they end by being blinded by it. Their

86

journey, far from bringing them to their goal has led to their undoing. Seeking divine beauty they have become lost in the mazes
of the world itself. Yet this defeat—as Bruno sees it—paradoxically is to be the means of their arriving ultimately at their
original goal. Dismissing them as ones who have directed their
gaze too high, Circe tells them that nevertheless through their
very immersion in the world under her sovereignty they now
may know that they too bear within themselves the seeds of
every change. This means that they also know that they bear
within themselves the potentiality of all that they were seeking.
They had thought initially that they would come upon their
divine lady through some such ascent as the Platonists describe
as the way to attain truth and goodness, but now they may
expect to attain it in a quite different manner. They will attain it
in passing through if not all at least a very great number of the
forms that are contained within the wheel of the species of
nature. Thus dismissed, they undertake a final journey. It is a
long one. They come ultimately to a place where they find the
nymphs of Ocean with their leader, and here Circe's promise is
fulfilled. They now behold at one and the same instant 'the most
brilliant and the most obscure, the beginning and the end, the
greatest light and the most profound darkness, infinite potency
and infinite act coincide.' They burst into song, joining with the
songs of the spheres, 'so that the heaven, the movement of
worlds, the works of nature, the discourse of intellects, the contemplation of the mind, the decree of divine Providence celebrate
in complete accord that lofty vicissitude which raises the inferior
to the superior waters, changes night into day, and day into
night, so that the divinity may be in all, according to the mode in
which the infinite goodness is infinitely communicated according
to the entire capacity of each thing.'[6]

After each of the nine had played his instrument and sung his
song, they danced together in a circle, and joined in a final song,
the 'Song of the Illuminated'. This takes the form of a dialogue
between Neptune and Jove. Neptune claims that his realm, the
world of infinite change, is more divine than the world of the

eternal heavens of Jove. But Jove answers that no realm may be more excellent than his, rather—

> 'O, god of the tossing seas, that any one be found
> more blessed than I is not permitted by fate, but my
> treasures and yours run their course together.
> 'The sun prevails among your nymphs through this
> one, and by the force of eternal laws and of the
> alternate abodes, she is valued as the sun among my stars.'[7]

At first glance one may discover certain resemblances between ideas and even conceits in this story and in *Love's Labour's Lost*, although the writing is proceeding very differently. Yet if we follow attentively the procedure in each we may discover not only the points at which the thinking coincides but also, in the form Shakespeare's work is taking, how he is diverging from the position Bruno holds and from certain of his conclusions also.

There has been dancing and play-acting in the last scene of *Love's Labour's Lost* and at the very end a song in dialogue—'the dialogue that the two learned men have completed in praise of the owl and the cuckoo.' In the performance one might say that the song is offered emblematically. Spring and Winter, half bird-like creatures, half deities, conjure up picturesque incidents in the life of the countryside characteristic of the seasons for which they stand. By implication the pictures created in each stanza answer arguments developed in the play. As images of static scenes, almost still-lifes, they further contrast with the play as a representation of actions. So, by their burden, which they express indirectly, and by their nature, which is undramatic, they stand out in the first place as distinct from the nature of the composition to which they are appended, and in that distinctness they further emphasize the difference of their substance from that of the play.

As songs, apparently separate from the play, they are nevertheless formally staged as tableaux with the single obvious connection to the play in the master of ceremonies who introduces them, Armado the grandiloquent youth of the play proper. He is in character in offering the songs as if they were some learned production—introducing the singers not only by their names but by their Latin names as well, and he is wholly out of character with the style of the songs themselves which are plain in the extreme. This contrast in itself mocks pretensions of grandeur and god-likeness. It does this in treating of ordinary matters in plain language. It does it also in confining the image of human life within the idea of the seasons of the year. We are being led to infer that the quality of life is not other than this, just as the seasons are always just these, and further, we are being led to celebrate this very state of things, the health, the discomforts, the changes time brings. We are being left with the last inference that all men have access to all that life offers without the sanction of philosophy. And yet, these songs in praise of a simple life, sung by fantastic beings, are also continuing a dialogue with the play that has preceded, and their burden is matching what was wise and lovely in the thoughts of contemplation and the love of women.

The figure of Spring, *Ver*, in the form of a cuckoo sings his song first. It is pleasant to think of him as wearing a Lurçat kind of costume, a partly feathered god. Opposite on the stage is another strange creature, half owl, called Winter and *Hiems*. The Latin names accompanying the English suggest mysterious personages, and whatever form they take they are certainly grotesque enough, for birds or not they sing with human language and so wisely and beautifully that at the end they are compared to Mercury and Apollo.

> When daisies pied and violets blue. . . .
> When shepherds pipe on oaten straws. . . .
> When icicles hang by the wall. . . .
> When all aloud the wind doth blow. . . .

Whenever—when the seasons change, when the course of nature halts, when men and wives fall out, when men come indoors to warm themselves, in the revolutions of time and the seasons—human life finds its measurement and end. The emblems seem to say that in such particulars we are looking at the vortices that are at the heart of reality. It certainly takes very little imagining to see in their succession an image of the life of man.

The pictures are put before us as if we were able to see them all in a single instant and yet as if they existed in the perspective of all time, just as visually the few particulars in the descriptions seem to embody all the generalizations we could ask for to explain the course of ordinary life. The images are brilliant in the economy of the particular details but somehow they sustain the generalizations fully. And although everything has to do with changes, there is very little movement, the pictures are fixed in stillness, I think in order to sustain the idea of timelessness— that the seasons are always like this, that life is always like this. There are the endless repetitions, the eternal likenesses. It will always be the same owl, the same song, the same sermon, the same cough—misery, delight, boredom, comfort, love and unfaithfulness, endlessly repeated, endlessly cherished. A feature here and there is sharply focused—'Dick the shepherd blows his nail'—but the audience is left to its own liberty to picture him, young, no doubt, hearty, taking his work as it comes; greasy Joan, vigorous, spirited, not much of a scold probably, generally content. And so it goes, vivid because at once pointed and typical and bursting with life. Because it is all these things and because the seasons in their passing typically give the idea of all seasons and all times, an endless repetition, as if too the circumstances of life in the country are equally the same forever, equally spirited and vigorous and enjoyable—the miseries are endurable, the boredom too, and the cold and the warmth and the hot drinks and bright days and the flowers and marriages and fallings-off are all part of the quality of life when the love of it endows it with everything love can.

The character of what is represented in these songs is consequently the character of serenity. By this way of putting the

scenes together we are being granted a view of the common condition, of the general vista, as at once still and lively. What was
everywhere in the rest of the play regarded fancifully and mock-
ingly is here more complexly represented—fanciful enough and
even gorgeous in the setting, mocking rather more obviously
with mentions of Marian's nose and the parson's saw, but most
strikingly mockery now through the emphasis on the plain and
homely rather than on the pretentious and refined. The result is
to concentrate the drift of everything that has gone before, the
poetry and the criticism, into a still and witty acceptance of
mortality. The mockery of aspiration, of pretension, of ignorance
and mistakenness, is all dissolved, not into laughter—although
there are many things in these songs to make us smile—but into
serenity and enjoyment. The deities of ballet and masque, singing 'one of the best songs in the world' about Dick and Tom and
Joan and fearful married men, leave us happily in possession of
all that is enjoyable and tolerable in the way the world will
always go.

If one were to attempt to grasp the degree of cultivation, the
depth and authority of culture in the conception of this mytholo-
gized epilogue, of the complexity of mind in the poise and
balancing of the features of English country life, of the intellectuality that makes the poise and the detachment even conceiv-
able—able to estimate that, and then by some power be able to
value the art of it all as art, one could only end with an appreciation of art at its superlative. To end in this way—the summary,
the expansion of meaning and feeling, the introduction of an
unexpected and even miraculous charm—this is the touch of a
mind at work at its fullest power, Athena-like, Jove-like, the
apparently effortless bounty of an imagination which never
bothers to calculate effects and thus outgoes calculation. Shakespeare's mind in thus bringing the whole to perfection is in effect
already beginning still another work.

One must believe that the force of Bruno's imaginings and
the force of his thought gave Shakespeare something to go on
here.[8] The technique, too, is comparable. But while Bruno may

end in the assertion of a reconciliation of opposites, a resolution of conflicts, it is not at all clear that there is in this the assurance of tone, the serenity of Shakespeare's ending. With Shakespeare these speaking emblems, representing the contrasts of poetry and wisdom, uttering the contrasts life and humanity inevitably treat with, set up patterns in which extremes are set against extremes—the gorgeous, the homely, the trivial, the eternal. The stanzas themselves might be words glossing *Les Images* of the Duc de Berry at Chantilly. But in spite of all that brings this comparison to mind, a more appropriate likeness would be to paintings of the High Renaissance or the back-drops to *intermezzi* constructed by Brunelleschi and Leonardo, the grandly mythological combining with the miniature and the homely, the fanciful and the real regarded with equal wonder. Half-emblem, half-choral movement, picturesque, simply worded, the effect is almost miraculous, the details of ordinary life as ravishing as the forms taken by gods, the crude imitation of birdsong in words whose own music is exquisite. All this more than crowns the meaning the play has been preparing for, the celebration of the potentialities in change, in picturing and in sound to give body to the contentment possessing the mind that honours this truth. The wit, the playfulness, the display of art in this formal close is as enchanting with thought as it is with beauty.

Bruno's universe was ordered and harmonious, and his terms were the traditional ones of philosophy, 'the harmony and consonance of all the spheres, intelligences, muses and instruments', and this harmony pervaded the heavens, the motions of the planets, the works of nature, and human discourse: 'all together join in celebrating the lofty and magnificent changes that raise the waters beneath to the firmament above, the changes of night into day and day into night in order that divinity may be in all things in such a way that everything holds within itself the potentiality of all else, and the infinite bounty diffusing itself infinitely everywhere that all things may partake of it.' All is change, divine change, but it is harmony too, following laws. Men must live in harmony with the universe, obeying the laws that govern it, and bring their own lives—their life in the body, their life in the intelligence—into composure and thereby into tune with the rest. Bruno puts this in terms that, I think, correspond to the issues raised in *Love's Labour's Lost* and they point as well to the conclusion the play leads to in the songs that end it, a conclusion that in eschewing abstractions appears to reject Bruno's way of linking nature with divinity as strained and laboured.

The songs of *Hiems* and *Ver* in their tone of serenity are affirming concord in the order of things. The changes of weather, the warmth of fire, the taste of cider are excellent themselves, although some things like cuckoldry and bitter cold are not, but in their sum and in the processes of time there are grounds given us, we are being told, for joy and contentment. In all such matters Bruno would be proclaiming a divine being to be immanent and to be known through them. In Shakespeare's songs all these particulars speak of the love of life and of the certainty of change and so we take satisfaction in whatever truths we may draw from such a focus. We may even think that in the pleasure we are getting from such perceptions we are honouring and praising the very principle of change and every form and shape change takes. The songs one might almost think designed to exclude any notion of immanence, yet their very loveliness recalls a metaphysical suggestion the King had only just made—

> The extreme parts of time extremely forms
> All causes to the purpose of his speed,
> And often at his very loose decides
> That which long process could not arbitrate.
> (V, ii, 741-4)

The *Eroici Furori* ends in a poem in which the main speakers are also gods—Jove and Neptune, and in which there is a contrast in what they speak of, Jupiter telling of supernatural truth, Neptune representing nature. There is a kind of truce in their debate too—if it is quite that—for Jove concluded by saying that what each represents must live in concord with the other—

> 'Ma miei thesori et tuoi corrano al pari'—
> 'My loved ones and yours run an equal race.'

The details in Bruno's poem and the language are not so plain and homely as in Shakespeare's, but then they have not had the mocking frame of the flowery Armado as master of ceremonies nor are Bruno's words directed to an audience that from the beginning has expected mockery. There is, however, much that is identical in the meaning—in one the gods, in the other mortals, know the world for what it is, take it for what it is, take pleasure in accepting it. But the difference in manner accounts for vast differences in meaning.[9] In Shakespeare there is the joy of celebration, there is the limitless delight in the sense of all that remains untold, there is rejection of the claim of reasoning to have the last word. The songs mock all that Berowne has stood for, and in expressing so much in mere particulars that Bruno has argued for in abstractions, they mock his methods as well.

If the poetic qualities of the play are of this order, one must still also take account of the character of the thought informing such beauty, a certain rationality and a certain theological drift that supports the rejection of philosophy. For although one must interpret this Epilogue as far as may be independently, as if only the most limited reference to the context of the play were desirable, yet one must also interpret it as cohering with the fullest burden of the play's meaning. Although I think it right to take the Epilogue as an indication of Shakespeare's rejection of the idea of immanence as we know that in Bruno, yet throughout the play we have been presented with ideas of perfection, of satisfactions spoken of as heavenly, of faults of a damnable kind, of disciplines looking towards the purgation not only of impurity but of sin, and of forgiveness. The very texture of thought in the play, making so much of the love of wisdom and of love and marriage, testifies to a set of values of a generally Platonic character and not alienated from Christian belief. I think one must regard this as a matter of texture rather than as an articulated scheme of thought such as appears to underly *The Two Gentlemen of Verona*, but one ought to take note of its character for whatever help it may give us in interpreting the Epilogue, and also because it may help us in recognizing the basis of the appeal of Bruno for Shakespeare, as well as what he could not accept.

The idea of oaths is at the centre of the concerns of both the gentlemen and ladies in the play. Initially the lords committed themselves to the most serious study of truth and later offered themselves to the ladies. Both commitments are sworn to, and while much is made of perjury and inconstancy as if the perjurers were wholly responsible for their acts, it is not only in self-deceit that the plea is made that inconstancy has been forced upon them. The suggestion is that there is more here than the lords and ladies or than anyone comprehends, the claims of truth and faith are not wholly understood, and love whether of truth or of persons hardly knows itself and certainly does not know what it loves. The uncertainty is expressed as a conceit and a paradox and a contradiction—the path of truth is the path of error:

> Therefore, ladies,
> Our love being yours, the error that love makes
> Is likewise yours. We to ourselves prove false,
> By being once false forever to be true
> To those that make us both—fair ladies, you.
> And even that falsehood, in itself a sin,
> Thus purifies itself and turns to grace.
>   (V, ii, 771–7)

It is the dilemma of Proteus in *The Two Gentlemen of Verona*, but in this play the final appeal is to grace, sin is to be purified.

The love that takes hold of these courtiers is close to adoration—

> All ignorant that soul that sees thee without wonder.
> (IV, ii, 115)

At one time there will be the usual hyperbole,

> Thou being a goddess, (IV, iii, 64)

almost immediately to be characterized as

> Pure, pure idolatry. (IV, iii, 74)

It is hyperbole also that all might take to with Dumaine in praising each mistress, that Jove would willingly consider

> Turning mortal for [her] love. (IV, iii, 119)

Yet it is certain that the courtiers are seeking in love a blessedness greater than even study would have conferred, assured that within it is a power that will lead to their redemption. They have behaved grievously, and only grace can redeem their perfidy.[10] The means of grace are evidently to be made available through their mistresses, and through the new service which their perfidy makes possible:

> Let us once lose our oaths to find ourselves. (IV, iii, 360)

The reasoning here is intricate. These are not the paradoxes that engage Bruno's nine young men who are bowing before Nature, yet there is an inherent serenity in the wonder of these souls even as they discover that their limitations as mortals, requiring the inevitable perfidy, are the very means of their redemption. I think we are obliged to accept Berowne's argument as one the others would also offer: 'Since our love for you

ladies puts us wholly in your power, the mistakes are yours as
well as ours. We are false to ourselves in swearing to be true to
you for all time, and it is you who are therefore the cause both of
our falseness and our truth. And yet that very falseness, a sin in
itself, being the means of our swearing to be true to you, is by
that fact purified. Causing us to err you provide the means by
which grace saves us, making us constant now by making us
perfect' (IV, iii, 356–64).

The period of trial will last forever, not merely that one year
of the engagement. The conviction of the prodigality of grace
will nevertheless abide, year in, year out.

There is a remarkable similarity and a remarkable difference in
the ordering of *The Comedy of Errors* and *Love's Labour's Lost*.
The similarity is in the elusiveness of the principle the characters
in both plays suppose to be at the heart of things. In *The Comedy
of Errors* one after another takes refuge in the thought of potions
or dreams or madness. In *Love's Labour's Lost* first the King,
then Berowne, and even Armado appeal to some power or other
that will stand by them as they commit themselves to extraordinary goals. Most of these self-confident young people fall
into confusion, of the world's making and their own, and according to which it is, or which we determine it to be, the play may
conclude as a comedy of circumstance or a comedy of ideas.

The most significant difference is that the spirit at work in
The Comedy of Errors is a spirit known to intuition or to dreaming, and the soul's pure truth and the glorious supposition with
all their great authority are related to the scheme of things in no
rationally intelligible way if they are to be related to it at all. But
in *Love's Labour's Lost*, just as there is coherence in the mockery,
there is coherence in the ideas that relate what is true or useful
in the King's conception of the study of divine truth and
Berowne's and others' arguments that count on a transcendent
tutelary force. I believe that, as in *The Two Gentlemen of Verona*,
the texture of ideas is closer to traditional Neo-Platonism than to
Bruno's, and it is agreeable to Christian spirituality. But putting

aside for the moment the character of the philosophy that is being called on, we know we are observing in this play a more complex use of ideas for comic purpose than in any preceding English work or in any of the ancient comedies. Of works prior to this it seems to me that only Bruno's *Il Candelaio* (1582) matches or surpasses it in this respect. I do not know if Bruno's example in this play was of use to Shakespeare, but I believe a certain comment to be made about it in the light of the use of ideas in the Italian comedy of the century will help in pointing out the special originality of Shakespeare's play as well as a meaningful similarity.

In general the world in which the characters of Italian comedy find themselves is simply society, aristocratic, churchly society. Men are held together by good sense, by force, and by fear. There is very little to indicate any cosmogonic principle, any over-ruling Fate or Providence, any power for retribution or reward working within a system of ethics, little or no sense of natural law. Machiavelli's characterization of the province of comedy in the prologue to *Clizia* says almost all: 'Comedies are meant to profit and delight the spectators. They are valuable enough if they acquaint people, and particularly the young, with the avarice of an old man, the frenzy of a lover, the wretchedness of a poor man, the gluttony of a parasite, the flattery of a harlot, the little faith in all men. Comedies are full of such examples, and they are allowed to represent them with the greatest honesty.' In this sense comedies offer us representations very like those of the ancients who were pleased enough with pictures of a world in which almost everything depended on men's wits. In almost all this comedy except Ariosto's there is even little sense of the profundity in the affections and he, of course, would appear to hold love in honour at no matter what cost.

But if ideas and wit never supply other than a moral system to sustain the satire and humour, intellectuality as such, wit as such, is developed to the fullest in creating, as it does in Machiavelli, a truly comprehensive criticism. Amplification rather than luxuriance is the Italian mode, elaboration for the sake of caricature and the grotesque, for humour in making finer and finer and finally more absurd discriminations, even in developing a single, supposedly all-embracing point about selfishness or avarice or lust. Machiavelli needed to represent a certain matter in the most elaborate of ways if he was to present it in a manner worthy of his intelligence. And so the complicated absurdities about dowries, pedantry, astrology, parental authority, lovers' whims, are held together before a single court of judgment. Nothing is more informative in this respect than Bruno's remark in commenting on his own play. In the Argument Bruno speaks of the three main matters of the work, love, alchemy, and pedantry, as these are embodied in the three chief figures. The lover is insipid, the alchemist sordid and avaricious, the pedant stupid. Bruno goes on to say that the unity of the work is in part manifest in the fact that the insipid character has his share of stupidity and sordidness, the sordid one is flat and stupid, and the stupid one is as sordid and insipid as he is dumb. The vices, it appears, are indivisible, all is one comprehensive interlacing of depravity.

In Machiavelli the elaborations establish the authenticity of a point of view. In Bruno they establish a theory. It is not until Della Porta's later works, after 1600, that Italian comedy will undertake to use its habitual intellectuality to establish the kind of philosophic context Shakespeare seems to have introduced into his conceptions from the beginning.

In the middle period and in the last plays we are accustomed to the idea that Shakespeare is always relating the dramatic action, and the pageantry, to use Prospero's word, to an idea of the universe itself, and this indeed provides part of the interest of the plays. Not even Bruno wrote with anything like such a conception of drama, all the same he is the one writer before Shakespeare among the followers of ancient models whose comedy depends on a schematization of ideas. Although *Love's Labour's Lost*, and perhaps *The Two Gentlemen of Verona*, are not so mindful of providing all the details in an articulated scheme of thought as *Il Candelaio*, their success in the end depends upon the coherence of the philosophic affirmations the chief persons draw on as they discover the consequences of their commitments.

NOTES

1 *Prefaces to Shakespeare*, Vol. II, Princeton, 1947, pp. 422–35.

2 Baltasar de Beauioyeulx, *Balet Comique de la Royne, 1582*, ed. G. A. Caula, Turin, 1965, sig. Ciii^v.

3 M. M. McGowan, *L'Art du Ballet de Cour en France, 1581–1643*, Paris, 1963, p. 247.

4 By the phrase 'angel knowledge' Berowne may be signifying more than the philosophizing of the academies. The phrase may take in what is meant in *The Two Gentlemen of Verona* when there is mention of Silvia's angel-like perfection and the state of knowing it. The significance of this is discussed on pp. 142–9.

5 *A Study of Love's Labour's Lost*, Cambridge, 1936.

6 P. E. Memmo, Jr., *Giordano Bruno's The Heroic Frenzies, A Translation with Introduction and Notes*, Chapel Hill: University of North Carolina Press, 1964, p. 77 (*Argument of the Nolan*).

7 *Ibid., Fifth Dialogue*, p. 266.

8 Miss Yates recently reaffirmed her conviction that *Love's Labour's Lost* has profound and intimate obligations to Bruno: 'It now seems to me absolutely clear that Berowne's great speech on love is an echo of the *Spaccio della bestia trionfante*, in which all the gods speak in praise of love in one of the constellations. . . . The foils of the poets and lovers in the play are the two pedants, one a Spanish soldier (Don Armado), the other a "grammarian" (Holofernes). Once again the *Spaccio* with its two types of pedantry . . . provides the answer to this' (*Giordano Bruno and the Hermetic Tradition*, London, 1964, pp. 356–7). Miss Yates has not so far supported these assertions with full detail, but I believe other indications of such an influence may be brought forward to support the general claim. Berowne's argument that what we love in women is the divine immanence itself is very like Bruno's 'Divinity reveals herself in all things, although by virtue of a universal and most excellent end, in great

things and general principles, and by proximate ends, convenient and necessary to diverse acts of human life, she is found and is seen in things said to be most abject, although everything, from what is said, has Divinity latent within itself. For she enfolds and imparts even unto the smallest beings, and from the smallest beings, according to their capacity. Without her presence nothing would have being, because she is the essence of the existence of the first unto the last being' (*The Expulsion of the Triumphant Beast*, translated by A. D. Imerti, New Brunswick, 1964, p. 242). This would be Berowne's 'true Promethean fire' that one finds in ladies' eyes: 'to the extent that one communicates with Nature, so one ascends to Divinity through Nature, just as by means of a life resplendent in natural things one rises to the life that presides over them' (p. 236).

The attack upon pedants is everywhere in the *Spaccio* (as of course in *Il Candelaio*) and this is the term for all those who betray the spirit: 'good-for-nothings who are hostile to the state of republics and who, with prejudice to customs and human life, offer us words and dreams' (p. 149).

Miss Yates' assertion can be re-inforced at innumerable places and I should care here only to point to a couple of matters which may be relevant to the composition of the ending songs of *Love's Labour's Lost* as well as to their imagery. There is for example Bruno's adaptation of some verses of Tansillo:

> They rejoice who are not displeasing to Heaven,
> And who were not cold to, and disrespectful of high enterprises.
> They then, when snow and frost fall
> Upon the hills, barren of grass and flowers,
> Have no reason for which to mourn their happy seasons,
> If they, changing in hair and countenance,
> Will change life and pursuits.
> The farmer has no reason to grieve,
> If, at the proper time, he gathers his fruit.

(P. 194. The Tansillo poem is *Il vendemmiatore*, stanza 5.)

The idea of constancy underlying mutability, as illustrated in the very particulars of existence, is expressed in images which in Bruno's sense are true emblems, and the homeliness of the detail is worth pointing out also in view of the images in Shakespeare's songs: 'Jove sometimes, as if he were bored with Jove, takes certain vacations, now as a farmer, now as a hunter, now as a soldier; now he is with the gods, now with men, now with beasts. Those who are in villas take their holidays and recreation in cities; those who are in the cities take their relaxation, holidays, and vacations in the country. Walking pleases and benefits him who has been sitting or lying down; and he who has run about on his feet finds relief in sitting.

He finds pleasure in the country who has for too long dwelt under his roof; he yearns for his room who is satiated with the country. Association with one food, however pleasing, is finally the cause of nausea. So mutations from one extreme to the other through its participants, and motion from one contrary to the other through its intermediate points, come to satisfy [us]; and finally, we see such familiarity between one contrary and the other that the one agrees more with the other than like with like' (p. 90).

9 The *Eroici Furori* presents reasoning by which the soul may be understood to be capable of rising to the realms of divinity. Following a long argument is a series of 'dialogues' in prose interspersed by sonnets and other verse forms. It is a form partly deriving from the Platonic and Lucianic dialogues and partly from the medieval conventions of prose explications and commentaries on poems. Emblems with Latin mottoes precede twenty-eight of the sonnets. The philosophizing, the commentary, and the language are at innumerable points dominated by the exploitation of contraries in the Petrarchan manner. Many of the emblems used had been invented by others, some were used in alchemical illustration, and some were apparently of Bruno's own devising. Bruno's emblems generally illustrated the efforts of the lover of divinity to attain the goal that continually eluded him. (See Memmo, *Giordano Bruno's The Heroic Frenzies*, pp. 54–5.) In a significant respect they are of the same character as the figures in the Shakespeare ending—they are to be accepted at face value and they do not require the searching out of meaning that allegory does, this is Bruno's own distinction (Yates, 'The Emblematic Conceit in Giordano Bruno's *De gli eroici furori* and in the Elizabethan sonnet sequences', *Journal of the Courtauld and Warburg Institutes*, VI [1943], 104). One was to imagine the verses sung and accompanied by dancing. Bruno's writing often took on a quasi-dramatic character, and this was one of the reasons his *Spaccio della bestia trionfante* was of use to William Carew in his mask, *Cœlum Brittanicum*. However revolutionary his meanings Bruno continually conceived of his work as courtly entertainment, and the emblems and the dramatizing were designed with such an audience in mind. This aspect of his work would also seem to have interested Shakespeare in the composition of *Love's Labour's Lost*. The use of the word *dialogue* is a case in point—the end to the play was in fact Armado's undertaking to entertain the King—'Will you hear the dialogue that the two learned men have compiled, in praise of the owl and the cuckooo?' As the editors point out, this use of the term by Armado is analogous to Bruno's, and I should add, also, that the particular dialogue has elements of form as well as of substance in common with the verse dialogue that concludes the *Eroici Furori*.

[10] Both in this play and in *The Two Gentlemen of Verona* the 'villains' do penance for breaking oaths. It is indicated that they will become purified through practices identified by the language as practices Christianity proposes. However lightly spoken in these plays, the conditions set for removing blame and for re-institution of the conditions of confidence are precisely those that are called for when perfidy and perjury partake of the character of sin. Accordingly we are obliged to view the oaths themselves in the traditional character of commitments made in the sight of God; having that character, broken oaths are to be forgiven and amended only in concurrence with what is understood to be God's arrangements for such forgiveness—repentance, contrition, sacrifice, in the terms in these plays laid down by the Princess and Valentine. What lacks is only the reference to a church and sacraments. Otherwise, we are asked to consent in sympathy with procedures we cannot detach from churchly practices and which in any event we understand in the terms traditional in Christendom. I myself find that a modern Catholic theologian writing philosophically characterizes the nature of oaths in precisely the sense that Shakespeare is using, and his language in another era is, I think, a testimony to the traditional character of Shakespeare's ideas: 'Le propre du vœu, c'est d'affecter la chose vouée d'un caractère sacré, de la faire passer dans la sphère du divin. Et avec elle, c'est la liberté qui se trouve engagée et consacrée. En disposer autrement ne serait pas simplement inconstance ou infidélité commune, mais, au sens littéral, profanation, c'est-à-dire usage profane, non rapporté à Dieu, de ce qui est sacré. . . . il faut que l'Absolu auquel le vœu s'adresse, non seulement existe, mais intéresse notre existence et s'y intéresse, en sorte qu'il puisse connaître, agréer et ratifier notre engagement envers lui' (J. de Finance, *Essai sur l'Agir Humain*, Rome, 1962 [*Analecta Gregoriana*, CXXVI], pp. 334-5).

The Two Gentlemen of Verona

'Who is Silvia?'—the sound of the words answers the question. In this play so full of courtiers' exaggerations, fearsome betrayals, and romantic adventures, we are asked to value her beyond praise, the greatest wonder of all. When there is to be the offering—

> To her let us garlands bring—

we are led to think of May Day, or of some more ancient practice such as those honouring a goddess. Even in her presence she is spoken of as someone apart although she is loving and loved.

At the end of the play there is no need to repeat the question, we know her quality and what it attests to. What she is, the state she has attained, provides the light by which the confusion and evil and pain in the play are known for what they are, and what is to sustain men in such a world is known for what it is. She is the beacon.

The play turns upon constancy and inconstancy in lovers, and the action follows upon the change of affection in one young courtier. This does not lead to the confoundings and the imbroglio of the kind Shakespeare might have contrived if he were keeping to some such happy end in view as that of *The Comedy of Errors*. Nor, in fact, is the action articulated in any such economy and perfectness. All does work out after a fashion but it appears that the burden of the involvements and the resolution counts for at least as much as the adventures.

In the first part of the play there is a succession of scenes in which we see the chief persons in their happiness, happy at least in their prospects, and then we soon see them in distress. They become separated from each other and at odds. One after another is driven to flight, one or another becomes a pursuer. Because the scenes present us with these manifold effects of one young man's transferral of his affections and because so much attention is given to representing states of feeling, our interest in the events is for some time relatively subdued. The drama thus comes to centre on the pain and disruption in the betrayed and the betrayer in their immediacy.

Love's Labour's Lost also tells about perjuries, lightly of course but seriously enough, too, to require seriousness in the winding-up that will put an end to the separations. *The Two Gentlemen of Verona* tells of wrongs that follow upon inconstancy and a breach of faith not in so high-spirited a way, although there is enough of the fanciful and enough humour to lighten its more troubled seriousness. The audience will not be led to respond with the fullest sympathy to the depth of pain these wrongs point to, partly because there is so much that is fanciful but partly, too, because so much of the expression of feeling is instantly translated into analysis and into philosophizing. So many of the scenes in the first acts are given to acquaint us with what it is that Julia feels for Proteus, that Silvia feels for Valentine, and also what the significances of these feelings are— Valentine uses quite philosophical language in speaking of Silvia, and Julia expresses her devotion for Proteus half religiously. Even Launce takes to speculation in speaking with his dog. Quite differently than in *All's Well that Ends Well*, say, the depths of pain at the centre of the action are sounded more in the development of thought than in the representation of anguish.

The character of the wrongs and the pain is defined by the largeness of the hopes for happiness. When Antonio, unmasking Valentine, speaks scornfully of one who aspires to love Silvia, he likens his ambition to a god's—

Why, Phaethon—for thou art Merops' son—
Wilt thou aspire to guide the heavenly car,
And with thy daring folly burn the world?
Wilt thou reach stars, because they shine on thee?
                              (III, i, 153–6)

When Julia speaks of Proteus she hopes as greatly—

A true-devoted pilgrim is not weary
To measure kingdoms with his feeble steps;
Much less shall she that hath Love's wings to fly—
And when the flight is made to one so dear,
Of such divine perfection, as Sir Proteus.
                              (II, vii, 9–13)

All aspire equally ambitiously, and when it seems they will be disappointed they take to desperate, however conventional, devices—Julia masking as a page, Valentine joining outlaws, Silvia in flight to the country, Proteus to outrage. All is sufficiently preposterous and sometimes picturesque and amusing enough to conceal the force of the distress that has brought about the flights and the threats, but the terms which all of them use in thinking of their joys and troubles are the terms of absolute good and evil, of life and death, of constancy and falseness—

                         All I can is nothing
To her, whose worth makes other worthies nothing.
                              (II, iv, 165–6)

I fly not death, to fly his deadly doom:
Tarry I here, I but attend on death;
But, fly I hence, I fly away from life. (III, i, 185–7)

                         better have none
Than plural faith, which is too much by one.
                              (V, iv, 51–2)

But just as the romantic exaggerations allay the intensity of feeling inherent in the separations and the wrongs, a certain attention to the details of common life tempers the exposition of philosophy that is required to explain the reconciliations at the end. Ultimately it is made clear that the issues in the play are conceived of in the most far-reaching of meanings, but the solutions that are provided, humans must settle for as humans. The particular problems before us have to do with engagements, marriage contracts, preparations for life in the world of affairs. The lovers are the wards of parents, fathers send their sons to court to enlarge experience, and so we see these young romantic lovers in circumstances that we all recognize as belonging to social life and maturing. At the end Valentine, educated as his father had intended, acts as a true prince and not as the fanciful ruler of good-hearted brigands in an idyll, but in the society they have all inherited, governing, dispensing justice, even pardoning. The wayward Proteus is brought to his senses and forgiven, the lovers and friends are united as they should be, and Valentine in his new authority points to a happy prospect for them all. Even in this there is the obvious recognition of the nature of the world as it is—where there is the necessity for compromise, and where reconciliation must go forward even when all the issues in the quarrel have not been settled. In this ending that looks towards the restoration of ideal loves the compacts are those all men must make.

This counter-balancing of the philosophic and the circumstantial, the ideal and the real, poetry and prose, is of course characteristic of Shakespeare, and he is able in quite different works to mingle these emphases to a variety of effects. In this play the romantic exaggerations and a series of scenes in which there is little dramatic development permit him to play down the depth of passion and anguish inherent in the betrayals and disappointments and to give fuller play to commentary. At other times, in *A Midsummer Night's Dream* and *As You Like It*, the fantasy and the poetry open up into the loveliest of visions. Here they lead more into the vistas of philosophy and religion.

And in the reverse, the real and the circumstantial, even with Launce and Speed, tempering the lyric and the fantastic, set significant limits upon the philosophic, above all in establishing the humanity of these young persons who call to mind ideas of the immanent and transcendent. As Valentine sees it, grace is a function of the sovereign. When he is merciful to the penitent they escape the eternal wrath (V, iv, 81). As it was in *Love's Labour's Lost*, the guilty follow the precise, traditional procedures that ensure forgiveness.

It is even the earthly and the spiritual that balance each other, although in the conclusion there is doubt for once that Shakespeare has brought this off. The lovers and friends who have been separated are rejoined and reconciled and they are to live together now in untroubled happiness. This should be a conclusion the audience would be happy to accept, as it is in fairy tales or when a *deus ex machina* intervenes as our sympathies require. Such a satisfaction is evidently aimed at here, but in this play it is not only the requirements of probability that must be met or else disposed of, the resolution of the issues must be in accord with the reasoning that has been so complexly presented hitherto. Valentine pardons as a governor, but he also blesses. It is almost as a priest absolving Proteus that he attests to the allaying of the eternal wrath, and Proteus is expected to follow just such directions as a priest would set. And finally, in the language of the reconciliations there opens up the prospect of the harmony for which the prior philosophizing was an introduction.

With such ends in view the play is accordingly managed in complex ways. At the beginning there is a certain obviousness inherent in the oppositions that are laid before us, of wholehearted love and none at all, of undying friendship and betrayal. The themes, too, are explicit but as always with Shakespeare the issues inherent in the oppositions are being presented indirectly, for the initial confusions and deceptions are but preparations for more far-reaching ones whose consequences are all but unimaginable. What is peculiar to this play, in contrast with *The Comedy of Errors* and *Love's Labour's Lost*, is the fullness with which the states of mind and being of the characters are being laid forth prior to the commencement of the action. Several of the first scenes are more vignette than episode, and they are as they are in order to acquaint us with the quality of feeling and mind of these young persons.

At first glance it might also seem curious that the sense of the moment, concentration upon the immediate state of being, should be so stressed in a work in which ideas of the eternal are to be so seriously invoked, when *Love's Labour's Lost*, which has so much to do with the processes of time, should follow another course. I think, however, this is in harmony with the ending celebration of the play, with the words—

One feast, one house, one mutual happiness,

which not only signify the conclusion to strife, they speak of a state of happiness and peace. The reasoning in the play as well as the turn of events have prepared for this, but it is the attention given from the very beginning to the representation of states of feeling that prepares us for the sense these words give of a life of ever-continuing love.

The success of the ending—and it is far from being what we need—must be founded in all that has been presented in showing the forms life takes in suffering certain wrongs, founded in the representation of the growth of understanding in these friends and lovers of what suffering as well as reason teaches about friendship and love.

There are features of *The Two Gentlemen of Verona* that remind us of the Plautine comedies. The characters come, so to speak, in pairs—the two friends, the two young women, the two elders, the two servants. There are separations and re-unitings, even of the servants, and there are alienations that need to be healed. There is one considerable set of circumstances in which an identity is mistaken, through Julia's disguise as a page, and there are other lesser confusions caused by Valentine's change into a king of brigands and by Silvia's flight into the wild. There are confusions of another kind as well, like some of those in *The Comedy of Errors*, and still more like those in *Love's Labour's Lost*, when lovers break faith and make new vows, although the breaking of the oaths to the masked ladies cannot be taken as seriously as Proteus' disloyalty to Julia. Also, as it is characteristically in the Plautine plays, the mix-ups are sorted out in the conclusion, the pairs are joined as they should be—that is to say, as we and they, in goodness of heart and soundness of thought, would wish them to be.

But much differently than in *The Comedy of Errors* mere circumstance is not at the root of the confusion. It is more as it is in *Love's Labour's Lost* where a certain force—in this instance, love—is moving first one person and then another to a course of action that causes other persons, also moved by love, to respond through other actions. Passion, not calculation, is the spring of all that occurs. In *Love's Labour's Lost* sometimes the love of wisdom, sometimes love itself, is setting events in motion and it is often difficult to tell which it is.

Then, in *The Comedy of Errors*, after the first entrances almost everything follows partly in coping with confusing happenings and partly in attempting to outwit those who appear to be causing the confusion. The imbroglio is extended through intrigue. Here, however, intrigue, except when Antonio unmasks Valentine, although present in Julia's service as a page and in the complicated incidents in the forest, is of little importance in forwarding the action. Intrigue plays a more significantly dramatic part in the devices of self-deception, or self-enlightenment—whichever one wishes to call it—when Silvia in the letter she has Valentine write at once conceals and reveals her love for him; and when Julia pretends to Lucetta that Proteus means nothing to her. The emphasis is turning inward.

And although passion rather than calculation is determining the events of the drama, and even though so many of the elements are those of Roman comedy, something other than debate in the Lyly fashion is the means of ordering the sequences through which the confusion comes to a climax. A major theme is indeed being unfolded, and in a more complex form than in Lyly, or in *Love's Labour's Lost*. The example of *Il Candelaio* again comes to mind, of which it was true to say that each main figure, the standard-bearer of a particular vice, was no stranger to the vices of the others, and in the interweavings of their intrigues a whole complex of vice revealed itself in its fullness. There is in *The Two Gentlemen of Verona* much less of the comedy of intrigue than in *Il Candelaio*, but the weaving of ideas is possibly as extensive and as comprehensive.

As I see it, the governing movement of the play arises from the exploitation of opposites, in which opposition in the nature of the dynamism of life gives rise to a disposition or an act which in coming into being meets with its own opposition. The Petrarchan conventions and psychology offer much in enabling the playwright to develop such a movement and rhythm, but still other antitheses than these provide are also at work.

In the beginning scene the two friends play about with ideas of what life may be like for them in the days ahead—at home or abroad; days spent in love and idleness or given to ambition and adventure. If it is love they shall be following, it will be love followed with the ardour of Leander; love leading to felicity; love all scorn and grievousness and folly; love the companion of wisdom; love the ruination of good hopes. Or they may reject love and seek honour. After mentioning all the possibilities the friends find themselves in agreement upon one thing, that he who seeks honour forgoes love, and he who forgoes the search for honour is free to love. As Proteus summarizes—

> He after honour hunts, I after love.
> He leaves his friends to dignify them more.
> I leave myself, my friends, and all, for love,
> . . . neglect my studies, lose my time,
> War with good counsel, set the world at nought.
>
> (I, i, 63–8)

A quite different oppostion becomes a theme in the second part of this scene. Proteus and his servant Speed engage in a wit combat. There is a lot of twisting and turning about—just who is who, who master who servant, who shepherd who the sheep— and the playful paradoxes conclude with the nonsense that something is nothing. There are certain points in this banter that bear upon the action and even the issues that Proteus and Valentine have raised, but the manner itself is a continuing manifestation of the drift of meaning that got under way in the first part of the scene as oppositions and contradictions were developed, the suggestion taking form that there are no resolutions to the conflict, or, more pointedly, that what are offered as resolutions in fact resolve nothing. Speed finally obeys Proteus' order to leave, and there is nothing else to do. Earlier there was not only the point that love immobilizes honour, there was the other one, that love does not always meet with the return of love.

In the second scene Julia goes through the motions of saving her dignity by refusing to accept the letter she so eagerly desires. Love and shamefastness are opposed and love and the impossibility of loving. The major and wonderful effect of the scene is to make vivid and sympathetic the character of a young woman as honest as she is deep, blessed with the spirit of truthfulness, and witty to boot, but in the developing of the paradoxes the rhythm of the preceding scenes is maintained, partly through the help of the same style of language but chiefly in adding to the sense of life as a continuous ebb and flow. We are conscious of this, for example, when Julia gathers up the pieces of the letter she has torn up:

> Be calm, good wind, blow not a word away
> Till I have found each letter in the letter,
> Except mine own name: that some whirlwind bear
> Unto a ragged, fearful-hanging rock,
> And throw it thence into the raging sea! (I, ii, 118–22)

It is she who is one moment calm, the next uncertain, but it is

Proteus at the end of the next scene who speaks the words that best tell how all is to come to pass:

> O, how this spring of love resembleth
> The uncertain glory of an April day,
> Which now shows all the beauty of the sun,
> And by and by a cloud takes all away! (I, iii, 84–7)

The oppositions are in nature originally, and this time more intrusively urgent than in the succession of the seasons.

In the course of events one after another of the four chief persons in the play moves from one state to its opposite— Proteus from complacency to furious pursuit; Julia from tremulous happiness to fear and another kind of pursuit; Valentine from a hopeful life of study, first, to love, and then to exile; Silvia from love and security into great danger. These reversals affect us less as misfortunes leading into disaster than for what they signify as the corruption of peace and joy. It is certain that no mere quasi-divine revelation, as in *The Comedy of Errors* and *L'Ammalata*, can set things right, more is involved than bringing people together and removing misunderstandings. Change of circumstance in itself cannot allay the trouble, restore trust, and allow love once more to prosper. Proteus must cease to love Silvia and return to loving Julia. He must make peace with Valentine, and Valentine must know how to forgive him. Silvia and Julia are also called upon to forgive. With them all there must be complex and profound changes, although these are not to be shown to us in a brief final scene, but merely indicated. Yet even here the same pattern remains clear—forgiveness is the means proposed of reconciling the oppositions of love and rivalry, and of love and honour, and of nature itself, where love does not inevitably obtain the return it hopes for.

At the end of *Love's Labour's Lost* everyone is asked to wait to see if a year spent in holy discipline can make the men better disposed to be true. In *The Two Gentlemen of Verona* forgiveness is offered as if more profound betrayals could be absolved and deeper disturbances erased in no time—through an instant's remorse on Proteus' part and through a simple blessing from Valentine. In the one play nature is given its due, and the processes of reformation and absolution are known to require time. In the other, miracle-working means, if not sacramental power, effect the changes, and so abrupt is the appeal to these that the sense remains of conflicts continuing in the very nature of things.

Dramatically and poetically it may appear that the reconciliation has not come off, but putting that matter aside for the moment, one may observe this, that we have here at the end the continuance and indeed the climax of the oppositions set up in the chaffing with which the play began, in the Petrarchan antitheses, in the dilemmas of those for whom love is not requited, in the dialectics of love worked out in philosophy, and in the disharmonies of nature itself. And as the pattern of opposition became more and more comprehensive, taking in more and more of the issues of existence, there was concurrently developed a more and more comprehensive formulation of what could contain change, what could guide lovers who were only human, what could hold friends together. The question became increasingly how could even the best of men, and all who aimed for the best of ends, perfection, justify trust. The answer was, hopefully, through knowing truth.

Constancy, evidently, that composition of the affections that allows for unwavering behaviour, is impossible under the conditions in which mortals find themselves. Proteus is only the extreme example of the state of men in nature, at once entertaining hope and fear, knowing calm only as a respite from storms, in peace prepared for danger, love itself being fire and ice, or master and slave—in one of its worst tyrannies, making its postulants servile:

> Yet, spaniel-like, the more she spurns my love,
> The more it grows, and fawneth on her still.
>
> (IV, ii, 14–15)

This is a lesson very unlike that Berowne was able to draw, the prospect he held to of each thing prospering in its fit season, as if nature in its wisdom kept an eye on men and what was good for them. For almost everyone in the world of *The Two Gentlemen of Verona* it will always be as it is to be for Helena in *All's Well that Ends Well*, love always reaching beyond itself. So Julia will in effect say, Proteus concurs, and if the vicissitudes of the others tell us anything, it can hardly be different for Valentine and Silvia except that Silvia knows peace more consistently.

But although mortals are inconstant, the idea of constancy persists. From within every mortal, and most splendidly in the 'angel-like' (II, iv, 65), there shines all-ruling truth, the authority for the marriage of minds, invincibly redeeming. Petrarch who celebrated as much as any the loveliness of the beauty of mortality, and who did so much to discover the language for all the oppositions men sound in their loving, expressed as exquisitely the serenity and authority of the source of constancy:

> Stiamo, Amor, a veder la gloria nostra,
> > Cose supra natura, altere e nove:
> > Vedi ben quanta in lei dolcezze piove;
> > Vedi lume che 'l Cielo in terra mostra.
> Vedi quant'arte dora e 'mperla e inostra
> > L'abito eletto e mai non visto altrove;
> > Che dolcemente i piedi e gli occhi move
> > Per quanta di bei colli ombrosa chiostra.
> L'erbetta verde e i fior di color mille,
> > Sparsi sotto quell' elce antiqua e negra,
> > Pregan pur ch' l bel piè li prema o tocchi.
> E 'l ciel di vaghe e lucide faville
> > S'accende intorne, e 'n vista si rallegra
> > D'esser fatto seren da sì belli occhi. (CXCII)

> Here tarry, Love, our glory to behold;
> > Nought in creation so sublime we trace;
> > Ah, see what sweetness show'rs upon that face,

What brightness to this earth the heav'ns unfold!
See, with what cunning, crimson, pearls and gold,
  Her chosen vest, ne'er yet seen elsewhere, grace:
  Mid the hills' arching shades observe her pace,
  Her glance replete with elegance untold!
The variegated flow'rs, the verdant blade,
  That grow beneath yon aged holm-oak's gloom,
  Court her fair feet to press them, and to tread;
The golden stars that stud yon beauteous sky,
  Cheer'd by her smiles, assume
  Superior lustre, and serenity. (Nott)

Through the changes all the persons in the play come to know
there persists the idea of attachments that are not the playthings
of time, of resolutions that are not mere truces. In Valentine's
praise of Silvia, in Julia's praise of Proteus, in the doctrine of
forgiveness at the end, there are allusions to a transcendent
world of truth. There are many suggestions of some other
sovereignty than that of the passions or of nature, and while the
elaborations of argument are indispensable in the presentation
of the idea of truths that do not mislead, the power of the play
will ultimately depend on the degree to which the characters in
their life-likeness will substantiate the doctrines. So much has to
do with the condition of mortals, rooted in change, and yet we
are to discover in the beauty and charm and strength of Valentine and Silvia and Julia and even of Proteus the qualities that
are to justify reason and faith both. The benediction with which
the play ends is to provide more than the culmination of an argument, it is to represent the condition nature in humans aspires to
and on occasion attains.

The patterns of parallel and opposition are the initially for-
mative elements of the first scenes, but they are soon assimilated
within other developments as the relations between the various
persons take form in the expression of more complex feelings.
In the juxtaposition of scenes in which the interests of the

different ones are seen to bear upon each other there begins to form the sense of a single power at work in bringing these lives together and in complicating them, and a theme as well, or several themes, arise out of ideas and words and out of conflicts in which there seem to be clear issues. There are times when the assimilation of the various interests is less than perfect, in which one or another comes forth in such a way as to unbalance the movement of the work, but generally all is managed with success and the parts lose their identity in the life of the whole.

Shakespeare's primary source for *The Two Gentlemen of Verona* is a narrative, Montemayor's *Diana*. This story is very unlike the comedy of imbroglio that underlies *The Comedy of Errors* and, although in *The Two Gentlemen of Verona* Shakespeare is continuing to make use of the resources of the Roman type, Montemayor's narrative manner is influencing him greatly, particularly in the first three acts.

On the face of it the play commences with a situation that could very well be—and we even expect it to be—an introduction to an action. Two friends are about to embark upon different courses which they hope will not separate them forever. It soon turns out that they will be coming together again sooner than they anticipated, and also it becomes evident that the cause of their separation—ambitions of very different kinds—no longer holds, for both now were being ruled by love. But even as they find themselves of a mind in this respect, a greater cause for dissention has arisen since they are suitors for the same maiden. Such a turn might be expected to give rise to the complications of intrigue Plautus and Terence would have revelled in, with confoundings, suspense, the humour of words saying one thing and being taken differently, innumerable difficulties and reversals. A succession of incidents, following each other in a chain, is what anyone might expect from this beginning, but instead, for three acts in which there are only two or three scenes that set things in motion (in one, the unmasking of the plan for the elopement, in another, the plan to marry Silvia to Sir Thurio), we are presented with scene after scene in which we are chiefly intent upon persons coming to terms with their own feelings. In the fourth and fifth acts the nature of the drama changes and the action is crowded, but all that happens now is to prepare for a conclusion that will complete what was commenced in that very different kind of representation.

The incident in *Diana* that Shakespeare was making particular use of was that in which Felismena, in love with Felix but separated from him, in the likeness of a page becomes a go-between in Felix's affair with Celia. She carries messages between the two and to each of them she interprets the other's response. The narrator also acquaints us with her feelings as after each exchange she reflects upon her own changing situation. The narrative is interesting of course as a story, we want to know how it is all going to work out, but before long it becomes clear that our greatest interest is in Felismena. Externally her thoughts take account of all the courtly mannerisms and proprieties, but we come to feel behind the words a grave and tender being. And as she comes to win our sympathy we begin to want answers to the questions she is asking, or is else afraid to ask—how constant is Felix in his new love? How does he take Celia's repulses? What does he think has happened to Felismena? What are his feelings towards this page in whom he has put such trust? What is in Celia's mind? What is she up to in leading Felix on? What is her feeling towards the page?

The writing is so fine it does indeed hold our attention, for the style and for the sensitivity and sensibility it expresses, but even more it holds us as we begin to sympathize with the changes these young people are going through. The affection, the uncertainty, the fear, the impulses, the self-questionings, take now one form, now another, and we become fascinated by the sense that if we could only put our finger on it we should discover a principle at work in the feelings of these three persons, a force common to all three directing and shaping their relations to each other. We are held, too, by the sense that they are all being carried along to an end they are coming to see less and less clearly.

The situation of a young girl disguised as a page was one of the stocks-in-trade of Renaissance drama, susceptible of poetic and ironic interest in a multitude of ways, although not commonly developed in so sensitive an exploration of character as in Montemayor's narrative. Shakespeare of course in other plays will be ringing many changes on the convention, and not least when the disguised maiden becomes the object of unwanted attentions, as she does in *Diana*. He forgoes almost all these opportunities here, and while he is taking the lead from Montemayor in giving so much over to explorations of feeling, instead of concentrating on the state of one of the young people he will bring forward four, one after another, the two young lords and the two ladies, as circumstances lead them from security and happiness into insecurity and trouble. The changes in Proteus are the most striking, and they are the mainspring of the action of the play, but no one of the characters so fully concentrates our interest as Felismena had in *Diana*.

Having altered the focus, Shakespeare kept the scenes separate, so to speak; for some time they are anything but closely knit in a continuing connection of cause and effect, and this was in part made possible because the role of Julia as the go-between had become minor. Accordingly Shakespeare could allow the patterns of parallel and contrast even greater scope as the situation now of one and now another was put forward. He could thereby expand the emphasis on the representation of the states of feeling and consciousness of the characters and defer interest on the sequences of events until, when this did take over, it would develop and sustain rather than replace the initial interest. He will need to achieve this effect because the play in the end will be asking us to accept a resolution that we can accept, not so much as one that accords with probability in the world as we know it, but for what it tells us of another order of reality, one we have come to reflect upon in observing the alterations love and unfaithfulness have made in these young nobles.

Many of the scenes themselves, particularly in the first three acts, are so constituted that they set other restraints upon any forward emphasis. Quite a number lead up to an extended soliloquy, in summary or in expatiation. A few commence with soliloquies. In the first scene, for example, Valentine and Proteus have been speaking among other things about the way love can take over a man's life, and after Valentine leaves we hear Proteus in his reflections on the current state of his own affairs and on his particular relations with Julia. In the middle of the next scene, after her companion's departure, we hear Julia grieving to herself over her failure to read the letter from her suitor that had been brought to her. She had asked Lucetta to return it as something she owed her modesty. When Lucetta comes back, still bearing the letter, Julia tears it up without reading it and, left alone again, again complains about her foolishness and about the love she is reluctant to confess. In the next scene we learn that the father and uncle of Proteus have decided he must go abroad in order to improve himself. Acquainted with the plan, we hear Proteus soliloquize on the ruin he thinks this will bring him to.

Shakespeare uses still other means of establishing a character and rhythm to the scenes in which something quite different than the ends of a comedy of imbroglio are in view. Scene after scene builds up if not into a formal song, into some most musical speech portraying the feeling of love—Julia's 'I would I had o'erlooked the letter' (I, ii, 50); and 'O hateful hands, to tear such loving words!' (I, ii, 105); Proteus' 'Thus have I shunned the fire for fear of burning' (I, iii, 78); and his 'Here is my hand for my true constancy' (II, ii, 8) and his 'Even as one heat another heat expels' (II, iv, 191). The whole sixth scene of the second act is Proteus' soliloquy, and the scene Julia herself ends with the plaintive—

> Only deserve my love by loving him,
> And presently go with me to my chamber
> To take a note of what I stand in need of
> To furnish me upon my longing journey. (II, vii, 82–5)

Some of the scenes have the character of *vaudeville*, or of an early Lyly play, the most charming, certainly, the scene of Launce and his dog. There are what appear to be deliberate discontinuities—the failure to follow up the unmasking of Valentine's plan for an elopement except in setting the stage for Proteus' plots, and after that there is an elaborately picturesque scene in which Valentine finds a place among the brigands. In their sum the scenes seem to be increasing our sense of waves of feeling carrying and tossing now this one and now that. Although we observe and take pleasure in some of the features that remind us of the Roman models, we are not being led to expect surprising events, rather we are being inducted into a growing comprehension of the extent and depth of the confusions men and women are prey to when love loses touch with reason.

Whatever other effects of these ways of ordering the play, they are also the means of bringing forward meanings that lie below the surface. Sometimes of course there are quite full expressions pointing to these underlying ideas, but quite as often they come out indirectly, even through the apparent discontinuity. The ideas are profound and powerful, they contribute a life of their own to the play, they provide the conception in which ultimately all the other interests are joined. They present a conception of a power changing the course of lives in ways that are unforeseeable and yet that come to seem inevitable. The play will unfold so that we may at least partly understand the forces that are at work in change and in the resistance to it. Not all will be explained, and at the end wonder will be as much the effect as understanding, but we shall at least see that love and constancy and alteration appear as strangely to those they rule as they do to us who are observing them. In this view the name of Proteus would be the key to the form and substance of much of the play —to the discontinuity as well as to certain significances—embodying the idea of the force so mysteriously working in the god. It is a force effecting transformations and metamorphoses, changes the sea-god could not have accounted for to himself as he became now a lion, now a dragon.

In *The Two Gentlemen of Verona* the young lover who bears this name is moved in an instant to transfer his affections, and thereafter to pursue a dishonourable course of a kind one supposes previously unthinkable to him. There is no accounting for the change any more than those we are later to meet with in the young Romeo or in Hamlet or in Leontes, passion suddenly re-directed and as authentic in its new form as in its old. Once it has asserted its authority in Proteus, the others in the play attempt to cope with it as best they can, and in the conventionally unlikely circumstances the world of courtly romances provides. They make their own adjustments, sometimes, also, at least appearing to take on another nature, Julia taking the form of a pageboy, Valentine of an exile from civilization. Quite apart from any idea of a divinely mysterious power at work, the kinds of changes that follow in the development of this drama relate to different ideas than the transformations and accommodations of *The Comedy of Errors*, where infants have grown into men, and a wife, redeemed from the sea, has become an abbess. And different from the changes of the princely following in *Love's Labour's Lost* where there are also alterations in the men's dispositions. Some of these are in themselves not wholly explicable no doubt, but they are at least intelligible. Similarly, the plots in those plays, having to do with changed appearances and the confusions attending on them, follow connectedly, one event succeeding another not only to represent the inevitable consequences of the initial events but also to develop the issues that have been brought forward so that we may recognize in the happy unions in prospect at the end a logic and meaning in the ways of life itself. But in this play the sense of the strange if not of the inexplicable in the ways of love is as powerful in the conclusion as it was in the initial changes in Proteus. We are of course pleased with the reuniting of Valentine and Silvia and Proteus and Julia. and there have been enough of the conventions of romantic comedy to lead us to expect such an ending. But the particular character of this play requires something else as well. It has proceeded so much in the representation of states of feeling, there has been so little emphasis upon incident and suspense, and we have been led into so much reflection on transcendent excellence, that the conclusion must satisfy expectations of a special kind. The happy ending here depends upon radical changes and the settling of deep disturbances, and accordingly the required metamorphoses must be understood as manifesting the strangeness in all change. Moreover, the dramatic means of effecting the transformations must be in harmony with the conventions governing the play from the beginning.

Accordingly one may wish to characterize the effects of the various patterns as relatively static. Such suspense and liveliness as there is, is largely confined within the individual scenes. But as these scenes succeed each other, as sometimes the same idea appears in different manifestations, or as situations are contrasted, a theme begins to become known. As the ramifications of this become clearer we begin to see how the theme is throwing light upon the situations in which the persons find themselves, as their circumstances in turn extend the references of the theme. When a certain kind of suspense does grow, we become interested in discovering the fuller import of certain suggestions. Above all, we are being held by the hope of discovering the principle that it seems enables individuals to perfect themselves, to establish constancy in their relationships, a principle that has a directing power over the life of any individual who consults with it. And in the contrary, as we see Proteus taking to troubled ways, we become anxious to discover what he might have done differently, what the error was that misled him, and how the principle that directs men to grow towards perfection, in the misguided destroys them. At the end of *Love's Labour's Lost* we were told that men must accommodate themselves to a salutary principle in the rhythm of nature. Here, we are not so much being told, as we are being shown, how a quite other principle is setting the terms for happiness and unhappiness. The example of Montemayor is the key, I think—we are being inducted into the ways of growth in the consciousness of those who in loving follow, or fall off from, the knowledge that alone sustains love.

There is in this manner of proceeding a marked likeness to the history plays Shakespeare is writing in these first years, where also the plays present a variety of persons in their relation to each other and where in the progression within a scene we discover ideas and sometimes themes taking form. Obviously chronology there sets a form, although it often provides less interest and less control than one expects. I believe it is not alone our modern interest in character that leads us to regard the *Henry VI* plays in this way as we reflect upon the terms on which various persons are living with each other. The plays themselves offer too many scenes in which only the slightest interest in eventualities is encouraged, in some it is even repressed, for again and again the mere vividness or the mere symbolism of a scene is what matters most—Margaret treating with a sorcerer, Henry alone in an open field, Mortimer relating genealogy on his death bed. In these plays, of course, the sense of the passing of time, and to change the figure, of the womb of time, overlays almost all, but it is true of many parts, as it is true of the whole, that our overriding concern is with the significance of the events rather than in them as causes or consequences.

With respect to *The Two Gentlemen of Verona* the likeness is, I think, in this succession of scenes in which one is more drawn to reflection than led into suspense, the pairings and the contrasts of the pairings, Proteus leaving Julia to go abroad, Launce parting from his dog. There is never any crowding of scene upon scene in some rush of action, nor is there an edict as in *Love's Labour's Lost* to get things moving towards a cumulative action, there are no contretemps to set everything topsy-turvy.

The complications follow as a result of Proteus' abandonment of one young woman and his suit for another, and what continues to be at question is the possibility of lasting attachments. Once the play has brought forth fully enough what these young people think the nature of love to be, and has developed a full enough representation of the value set upon constancy, the action of the drama can advance, and the issues that are being raised may be worked out in the progress of the plot.

There is the sweetness of a child in those first words of Valentine to his friend:

> Were't not affection chains thy tender days
> To the sweet glances of thy honored love,
> I rather would entreat thy company
> To see the wonders of the world abroad,
> Than, living dully sluggardized at home,
> Wear out thy youth with shapeless idleness.
> But since thou lov'st, love still, and thrive therein,
> Even as I would, when I to love begin. (I, i, 3–10)

And Proteus responds in carrying on the identical tone:

> Think on thy Proteus when thou haply seest
> Some rare noteworthy object in thy travel:
> Wish me partaker in thy happiness
> When thou dost meet good hap; and in thy danger,
> If ever danger do environ thee,
> Commend thy grievance to my holy prayers,
> For I will be thy beadsman, Valentine. (I, i, 12–18)

Thus at the beginning of the play, by the very charm of the language, we see that we are being brought into accord with the simplicity of the young in their happiness, their air of perfect trust. The warmth of their words is such we have no choice but to accept them as they are uttered, and as unselfconsciously as Valentine we are attracted to this apparently untried innocence. The words reveal no tension to strain our sympathy, and as the play proceeds we come to understand as well as to feel that what we are recognizing here is a sound that will persist through the entire work:

> from our infancy
> We have conversed and spent our hours together;
> And though myself have been an idle truant
> Omitting the sweet benefit of time

125

To clothe mine age with angel-like perfection,
Yet hath Sir Proteus, for that's his name,
Made use and fair advantage of his days;
His years but young, but his experience old;
His head unmellowed, but his judgment ripe.

(II, iv, 61–9)

This simplicity, this air of gentleness and idealism, is carried forward into the view of a kind of perfection in life, as if perfection were attainable and the barriers in its way not insurmountable. Valentine has suggested that love may be too demanding, that it may get in the way of men's proper ambitions, encouraging 'shapeless idleness' (I, i, 8), and the father of Proteus goes further:

I have considered well his loss of time,
And how he cannot be a perfect man,
Not being tried and tutored in the world.
Experience is by industry achieved,
And perfected by the swift course of time.

(I, iii, 19–23)

But most striking of all is the character of Silvia—

She excels each mortal thing
Upon the dull earth dwelling. (IV, ii, 50–1)

What is in one view a delightful simplicity, in another is affectation and exaggeration, and the Petrarchan and Platonic conventions in the mouths of the untried may simply be foretelling the disasters the innocents are thereby asking for. It is charming to joke about love in the language of religion, to talk of replacing the holy book of Christendom with the holy book of love, but the fashionable exaggerations may signify that neither the claims of religion nor of love are taken seriously enough, and that there may be a deep misunderstanding of the demands that love can make as well as of the requirements for perfection of any kind.

The virtues of simplicity and affection are real enough, and these young people are far more genuine than false and they are right in recognizing the all but supernal charm of Silvia. But even in loving her, Proteus certainly and Valentine pretty certainly, are seeing through a glass darkly. Their virtues by their limitations become faults.

It is the same with the cardinal virtue of generosity, as much the hall-mark of their gentility as of the young gentlemen of *The Merchant of Venice*. When Valentine learned that Proteus was to join him in Milan, no praise could go farther—

> for far behind his worth
> Comes all the praises that I now bestow.
> (II, iv, 70–1)

Julia similarly—

> His words are bonds, his oaths are oracles.
> (II, vii, 75)

When even Proteus obtains such praise, we can not be surprised to learn that these are the very coins of conversation in such a society, and of course in general the praise is only excessive, and not misdirected. It takes Launce to put it all in the right light—

> She hath more qualities than a water-spaniel,
> which is much in a bare Christian—
> (III, i, 270–1)

The excellence is there, the qualities are indeed sometimes 'angel-like' (II, iv, 65), but the fallings-off are terrible and in the cult of perfection as in the exaggerations of generosity there is much of the seed of the grief to come.

No one could be more free in his giving than Proteus in his service of Julia and in his admiration of Silvia, and not even those young courtiers in *Love's Labour's Lost* committing themselves to the masked ladies. There is no winter in the bounty of any of these young people, yet somehow this is not enough.

They themselves of course recognize the other side of the ambition for perfection, the completeness of failure. Almost every move that is being made is a wager on the absolute value of every undertaking and every attachment; every disappointment threatens to be fatally discouraging. As the play develops, the idea of becoming a perfect man in the world is displaced by the idea of perfection in love, although at the end something of that first concern will return in Valentine's demonstration of sovereign power. But in the interim the claims of love, both justified and exaggerated, will be asserted many times, and it will come to seem that the roots of the claim for perfection in this are much as they are in the exaggerations of generosity and ambition generally. It might seem for a while, as it is once said in *Diana*, that there is a virtuous and a vicious love. Both appear to demand the same service, perfect constancy, and it is with difficulty if it is not impossible to say, except as the deeds show, who is loving virtuously and who not. But the truth is something else. In the words of the Lady Felicia,

'Some saie there is no other difference betweene vertuous and vicious love, but that the one is governed by reason, and the other not: but they are deceived; because excesse and force is no lesse proper to dishonest, then to honest love, which is rather a qualitie incident to everie kinde of love, saving the one doth make vertue the greater by it, and the other doth the more encrease vice. Who can denie, but that in true and honest love excessive and strange effects are oftentimes founde?'[1]

Valentine, Proteus, and Julia all admit excess, even Silvia is fearful of it, all are enthralled, but only Proteus knows of another fault in what he has to offer:

> But Silvia is too fair, too true, too holy
> To be corrupted with my worthless gifts.
>
> (IV, ii, 5–6)

Before it has run its course, he was carried by the passion 'to so foule an extreme, as with violent hands, and such unseemly force to sease upon his beloved.'[2] Unlike the savages in *Diana* he knew he was corrupted and he knew the very character of the act he contemplated—

> [I shall] love you 'gainst the nature
> of love—force ye. (V, iv, 58)

Throughout the play it is not an idea of nature but an idea of reason at work in the very whirlwind of the passions that will be known to be the counter to excess, but more even than that, a principle with a life of its own. Excess is a manifestation of the disposition to unreason, it unbalances and it unmoors, whereas the prosperity of life as of love depends on constancy, a still and unwavering obedience to reason. What reason is and what it holds to will be the key business of the play to unfold. It will do this not as *Il Candelaio* does in making its point about the unity of vice, nor as *Love's Labour's Lost*, with argument and emblem. Rather, the philosophic reasoning of this play will be carried as a burden making itself known to us sometimes in metaphysical and theological statement, sometimes indirectly as in the song to Silvia, but mostly through the sense the play is able to communicate that these young people in their encounters with each other and in their thoughts reveal what we all know to be the stuff of consciousness and that this itself is the demonstration of whatever principles may be said to be real.

As the play begins, two friends are taking leave of each other talking about love and honour, but already they are being carried along by more than talk. Soon their affairs become complicated and troubled, and love and the problems it brings are at the heart of it. Distress follows upon distress until finally nothing can compose the dismay and confusion except something very like a miracle. And so it goes, the tangled problems of these young people holding us as many another comedy does about love and beauty and mischief. But all the while a certain intellectuality is making itself known, a certain idea is seen to comprehend vast implications, and the issues of the plot come to be known as the pieces of a game, the game being the life of love and the rules that govern it. When it is over, someone or something will have won, and we shall want to know what that is to be, but our chief content will be in seeing that what is presented to us as a play and an imitation of persons in life is in its very form and being a manifestation of an intelligible principle at work in guiding human affairs.

All comes to centre about what is true and what is false, and it is Proteus at every point who leads the reasoning into the complexities of the issue. He does not appear to doubt that his new love, for Silvia, is lasting, and the audience is given no sign to the contrary, yet Proteus is struck by the change that has come over him and he is puzzled—

> Is it mine eye, or Valentine's praise,
> Her true perfection, or my false transgression,
> That makes me reasonless to reason thus?
>
> (II, iv, 195-7)

The terms are pointed, and one hears in them the echoes of innumerable debates—about the nature of love, devoted to perfection or inspired by rage, occasioned by a being beyond wonder or by a treacherous passion. But the tone of Proteus expresses his unquestioning acceptance of the new state as permanent— right or wrong the power to which he is now subject will permit no rejection. Reason can offer nothing to lead him to change this allegiance, and he is unable or unwilling to conceive of any inducement to another falsehood.[3]

He does however know he has forsworn himself, and so he follows a way of thinking he now calls 'reasonless', he has recourse to equivocation knowing it to be that:

To leave my Julia shall I be forsworn;
To love fair Silvia shall I be forsworn.
To wrong my friend, I shall be much forsworn;
And ev'n that pow'r which gave me first my oath
Provokes me to this threefold perjury.

(II, vi, 1–5)

The difficulty, he sees, goes deeper than that of finding excuses,
the power of love is too much for reason:

I cannot leave to love, and yet I do;
But there I leave to love where I should love.
Julia I lose, and Valentine I lose.
If I keep them, I needs must lose myself;
If I lose them, thus find I by their loss
For Valentine, myself, for Julia, Silvia.⁴
I to myself am dearer than a friend,
For love is still most precious in itself;
And Silvia—witness Heaven, that made her fair!—
Shows Julia but a swarthy Ethiope.
I will forget that Julia is alive,
Rememb'ring that my love to her is dead;
And Valentine I'll hold an enemy,
Aiming at Silvia as a sweeter friend.
I cannot now prove constant to myself,
Without some treachery used to Valentine.

(II, vi, 17–32)

In some ways this hodge-podge of distinctions is no more confused, and cherishing of confusion, than that Petrarchan-
Platonic language with which he and Valentine were playing in
the first scene of the play, and if this is 'reasonless', it is a fine-
spun substitute for reason. Nevertheless, it does express some
truths, and this above all, that he still loves Julia and Valentine.
He has as vivid a sense of their worth as ever, but the new feeling
that has swept over him is so powerful he comes to speak of

them as if they were either his enemies or else dead to him. To be 'reasonless' now means to submit himself to mere power, to submit in mere subjection, and Proteus will even become forgetful of Silvia as someone good and holy and to be honoured:

> For love is still most precious in itself. (II, vi, 24)

He thinks he has no choice but to conspire with this force and he finds authority for his state and his behaviour in interpreting his subjection to love as obedience to himself and to truth. Even perfidy becomes the witness of his faith. If he remains by the side of Julia and Valentine he is 'constant'. He must value 'himself' above all else, and to secure that he will abandon all friends and all other claims. He turns the words about as if contradictions were irrelevant. The more the reasoning becomes obscure the more he returns to the assertion he must be 'constant' to himself. All he is really saying is that the wind may bear him where it will and he will call his compliance constancy.

Proteus speaks more of the power of love than of Silvia. One may think that it was something in her that effected the change, a loveliness that would have won anyone over, that it was her 'true perfection', not his 'false transgression' that was to be held to account. But in an important sense this is not true, for neither now nor later does Proteus give any indication that he thinks of Silvia as Valentine does and as the lovely song causes us to think of her. For him her 'true perfection' means something he can ignore in entertaining the thought of a good deal less:

> For since the substance of your perfect self
> Is else devoted, I am but a shadow,
> And to your shadow will I make true love.
> (IV, ii, 121–3)

He knows the language of philosophy and he can speak and think of her as of the transcendental, he can think of himself as but the semblance of an equal excellence, and with the same kind of fooling with paradoxes as in speaking of his constancy to himself he can use equivocations to justify the betrayal of all he appears to be honouring.

As we shall see, the conceits are pointing to the traditional oppositions of body and soul and they will turn out to be central to the themes that are developing in the play. Julia, for example, will be using the same language in reflecting upon the 'falsehood' in Proteus' love, and although here, and elsewhere, we shall be struck by the interest of these young persons in developing conceits, we must also recognize the depth of the thought the language is preparing us for:

> And, were there sense in his idolatry,
> My substance should be statue in thy [Silvia's] stead.[5]
>
> (IV, iv, 200–1)

For his part, Proteus knows that this power which has such complete control of him does not guarantee the success he must have, Silvia's submission. And he begins to think of the dilemma in a very strange way. His true self should obtain the love her true self could give, but since she rejects him he will cease to be his true self—'I am but a shadow'—and but the shadow of himself must be satisfied with the shadow of her. This can only mean, however he is perverting the words he uses, that he will now identify himself with that which can possess Silvia physically, as if body could possess body and be possessing truth, shadow making love with shadow, and the love thereof being 'true'.

In this play as in other of the early writings there appears from time to time the idea that truth harbours in the soul, or in the self. We have seen how both Valentine and Proteus ring many changes, on the need to be true to the self and the danger of losing touch with the self. In the simplest interpretation the idea seems to be that an individual, when neither observation nor argument offers answers to vital questions, may have recourse to an inner sense, a sort of oracular authority that provides answers.[6]

Or it may mean that an individual, reflecting on the relationships of love, for example, will suppose that he is responding to another with all that he values most in himself, and he may call this his very identity, his inmost being, some constant and most precious consciousness. He will suppose he is sharing with another all he values most in himself and what he would share only with that one who could be trusted to value this as he does.[7]

These paraphrases are vague partly because the idea is difficult to fix, and partly because in its simplest sense the self is a concept pointing to what is anything but a clearly designated faculty in men. The concept refers in fact to what ought not to be defined except in the most general way, perhaps only as the power in an individual that treats with truth as nothing else does.

In *The Two Gentlemen of Verona* the various persons appeal to the self with some such meaning as often as they do because the play has so much to do with constancy, in love and in friendship. Constancy can only exist between what is conceivably unchanging in individuals, and this always comes down to what can be thought of as truth, to what by nature and definition would be unchanging.[8]

So much might be said and the matter left at that if it were not that Valentine, for one, at several places uses the word *self* in conjunction with terms of necessarily metaphysical significance, and also if it were not evident that elsewhere in Shakespeare's early writings the word and the idea are at the centre of the meaning they are developing.

Proteus had said,

> I cannot now prove constant to myself,
> Without some treachery used to Valentine.
>
> (II, vi, 31–2)

Valentine developed a similarly negative doctrine;

> To die is to be banished from myself;
> And Silvia is myself. Banished from her
> Is self from self. (III, i, 171–3)

In *The Comedy of Errors* a more positive application included an idea of purity demanding to be preserved:

> Teach me, dear creature, how to think and speak;
> Lay open to my earthly-gross conceit,
> Smoth'red in errors, feeble, shallow, weak,
> The folded meaning of your words' deceit.
> Against my soul's pure truth[9] why labour you
> To make it wander in an unknown field?
> (III, ii, 33–8)

When Valentine says of Silvia, 'She is my essence' (III, i, 182), elaborating on 'Silvia is myself' (172), he is including this sense of the invaluable, what is to be cherished at all costs, but in introducing the philosophical term he is extending the reference to include a conception of reality, a conception both Proteus and Julia also have in mind in using the philosophical term *substance* in speaking of the self. Proteus was expressing resignation at his inability to obtain what Silvia could best give—

> For since the substance of your perfect self
> Is else devoted, I am but a shadow,
> And to your shadow will I make true love.
> (IV, ii, 121–3)

'Substance' is what is real and good, the reality underlying the self, and as Julia takes up the term this comes to signify divinity:

> And, were there sense in his idolatry,
> My substance should be statue in thy [Silvia's] stead.
> (IV, iv, 200–1)

Thus with the words *self, substance, essence*, we are being inducted into a view of the reality underlying appearances, divine in nature and of absorbing interest to humans. The contexts of the different speeches generally have to do with love and friendship, with kinds of union. And by the oppositions of *self* and *substance* with *shadow*, *death*, and *falseness*, we find that the life love hopes to share is something other than in an embrace:

> your falsehood shall become you well
> To worship shadows and adore false shapes.
>
> (IV, ii, 127–8)

'Substance' in the play certainly bears the theological meaning given in the Oxford Dictionary—essential nature, essence, or, as in Forcellini, *quo quid substat et consistit, sive essentia, natura, qua quaeque res est.*

How dense the texture of philosophical and theological thinking here is we see best in Valentine's sustained relation of Silvia to truth and divinity:

> And why not death rather than living torment?
> To die is to be banished from myself;
> And Silvia is myself. Banished from her
> Is self from self: a deadly banishment!
> What light is light, if Silvia be not seen?
> What joy is joy, if Silvia be not by?
> Unless it be to think that she is by,
> And feed upon the shadow of perfection.[10]
> Except I be by Silvia in the night,
> There is no music in the nightingale;
> Unless I look on Silvia in the day,
> There is no day for me to look upon.
> She is my essence, and I leave to be
> If I be not by her fair influence
> Fostered, illumined, cherished, kept alive.[11]
>
> (III, i, 170–84)

Mr. J. V. Cunningham has related this speech to the Scholastics and to Neo-Platonism, and he very aptly quotes Hooker:

'God hath his influence into the very essence of all things, without which influence of Deity supporting them their utter annihilation could not choose but follow. Of Him all things have both received their being and their continuance to be that which they are.'[12]

He then took up the term *essence* and through its use identified Silvia with the Christian God: 'Silvia . . . is regarded as perfection, as Love in the absolute sense, as the ultimate principle of the lover's being, as that by which he is fostered, illumined, cherished, sustained. She is God. She is immanent and transcendent, and the lover's relation to her is that of scholastic creature to scholastic Creator.'[13]

The point is clear, but putting aside for the moment the question of precise theological orientation, one may observe that in this conception the self, the repository of truth and participant in reality and in divinity, is not static, or passive, but is, rather, a form of perfection, sharing in the character of life. The self is an unfolding, perfection is a process of growth in the truth. In a rudimentary way this was in Antonio's mind in sending Proteus abroad:

> he cannot be a perfect man,
> Not being tried and tutored in the world.
>
> (I, iii, 20–1)

Valentine, under Silvia's influence, is 'kept alive'. Proteus himself emphasizes the apparent paradox:

> O heaven, were man
> But constant, he were perfect! (V, iv, 110–11)

Adonis, in Shakespeare's poem, put it most forcefully, relating what the individual appeals to in himself as the arbiter of truth to the processes of growth:

> Measure my strangeness with my unripe years.
> Before I know myself, seek not to know me.[14]
>
> (*Venus and Adonis*, 524–5)

At the beginning of the play Valentine, long before the issue arose, remarked on the way that untimely love, making a man foolish, could so distort his growth that he would come to nothing:

> as the most forward bud
> Is eaten by the canker ere it blow,
> Even so by love the young and tender wit
> Is turned to folly, blasting in the bud,
> Losing his verdure even in the prime,
> And all the fair effects of future hopes.
> (I, i, 45–50)

If one pursued the matter abstractly it would follow that a failure in the knowledge of oneself, or a failure to permit that self to flourish in the only way it can, in growing towards perfection, would be inconstancy. In the terms of the play, this would be the state of one who followed shadow instead of substance, either mistaking or preferring it. This might be a failure of knowledge, or of reason—that is, either in ignorance of the truth or through permitting reason to be overruled. And it is here that, as so often elsewhere, it is love in one or another of its infinite forms that overpowers reason. In these early writings all those whom love endangers believe themselves to be moving towards perfection, none of them lacks that fundamental faith, in his truth, in the power of knowing it, and in the proper inviolability of the self. The failures are always the failures of reason. Antipholus of Syracuse resolved to resist one of the loveliest of creatures because her power threatened his sovereignty over himself, blinding his reason, inducing him to betray himself:

> her fair sister,
> Possessed with such a gentle sovereign grace,
> Of such enchanting presence and discourse,
> Hath almost made me traitor to myself.

But, lest myself be guilty to self-wrong,
I'll stop mine ears against the mermaid's song.
(III, ii, 164-9)

It is a short step from relating the idea of obeying the principle within oneself that is leading one to perfection to submitting oneself to another in love when that other embodies just
such perfection as one's self. The conventions of the lover suing
to his sovereign mistress are at hand for Valentine, he becomes
such a servant, yet he may do it proudly, for in taking over the
language of philosophy and theology—'she is my essence, myself'
—there is no subjection and no loss of identity, she comes to
share in that which makes him perfect. Constancy therefore is
one and the same in being true to oneself and to that other who is
true to herself, constancy is the relation to substance or essence
by that in an individual which alone knows essence, participating
in it and knowing himself in his primary being and worth.

Deceptions arise from the very character of the thought which
speaks of love and knowledge as of like nature, the love and
knowledge of persons as of truth. Valentine says of Silvia, 'speak
the truth by her' (II, iv, 150), but he also said of Proteus, before
the betrayal, 'I knew him as myself' (II, iv, 61). Such a use of
words and the union of love with knowledge may be in the
nature of things but here there is the extension of the belief in
identifying truth with reality and essence, and in identifying love
and knowledge of a person with the love of perfection and the
divine. Neo-Platonism and Christian belief and perhaps Scho-
lasticism as well are therefore being drawn on to support the
ambitiousness in the love of these courtiers and ladies and to help
account for the fallings off as well.

The inconstancy of Proteus is all but spelled out as the errant
conduct of a man mistaking shadow for substance, knowing he
is thereby untrue to himself, wasting his life, deliberately doing
wrong. Love, leading him to embrace shadows, confuses the
power in him that seeks perfection. He knows he is no longer
himself, or so he thinks of it, he knows he is using reason foolishly

—which is to say, in treating shadow as substance, in dis-
honouring the divine which is alone reality. What Proteus is
doing is what the Neo-Platonists will always say of those who
seek for good outside intellect or reason, and the character of his
behaviour is very well accounted for by Montemayor when
expatiating on the turmoil of lovers:

'It is strange (faire Nymph) to see what a sorrowfull hart (that is
subject to the traunces of impatient love) doth suffer, because
the lest ill, that it causeth in us, is the deprivation of our judge-
ment, the losse of our memorie, and the surcharging of our
imaginations with his onelie objects, making every one to alienate
himselfe from himselfe, and to impropriate himselfe in the
person of his beloved. . . . Beholde heere am I, in whom there is
nothing, that can be governed by reason; neither can he have it,
that is so much without his libertie as I am, because all corporall
subjections do suffer the will (at the least) to be free, but the
bondage of love is such, that the first thing it takes in hand, is to
constraine one, to make a profession of it.'[15]

The specially significant idea is that love owes its very being
to reason: 'They do all affirme (that would seeme to know something) *That true Love doth spring of reason*: which if it be so,
what is the reason, that there is not a more temerous and unruly
thing in the worlde then love, and which is lest of all governed by
it? . . . I am of a contrarie opinion, affirming that Love, though
it hath Reason for his mother, is not therefore limited or governed
by it. But it is rather to be supposed, that after reason of knowledge and understanding hath engendred it, it will suffer it selfe
to be governed but fewe times by it. And it is so unruly, that it
resultes oftentimes to the hurt and prejudice of the lover: since true
lovers for the most part fall to hate and neglect themselves, which
is not onely contrarie to reason, but also to the lawe of nature.'[16]

As long as he is 'banished from himself', 'alienated' from
himself, Proteus cannot in the nature of things be constant. In
that long casuistical speech in which he acknowledged that he
had become 'reasonless', that he had 'lost' himself, he took the

responsibility for it all, not in the usual way saying merely that
love had overcome reason. He has turned to Julia not because
she means more to him than Silvia or Valentine or himself, all of
whom he must betray, knowing it is betrayal, but because love
has persuaded him that love in itself counts for more than that to
which it is given—

> For love is still most precious in itself. (II, vi, 24)

Love replaces truth and substance and self as his lord, and being
itself unruly, even though the child of reason, forces its subject
to reason in defence of all that is unruly. Proteus has fallen into
the trap the Neo-Platonists argued against unceasingly, turning
away from the source and foundation of truth within himself:
'Admiring pursuit of the external is a confession of inferiority;
and nothing thus holding itself inferior to things that rise and
perish, nothing counting itself less honourable and less enduring
than all else it admires could ever form any notion of either the
nature or the power of God' (*Enneads*, V, 1, 1—MacKenna).

Proteus understands and agrees with all that Valentine or
anyone would say about self and truth and perfection, and his
obsession with the word *constancy* reveals his understanding that
constancy is determined by the nature of that to which the
individual is devoted. It is love as love, the wayward, not Julia or
Silvia or truth Proteus is serving—constrained 'to make a profession of it'. Once a lover is unfaithful, until he returns to that
faith, if he still loves he must love shadow instead of substance.
Proteus knew this well as he juggled his contradictions, justifying
treachery, and Silvia knew it quite as well, putting it accurately
when she agreed to give him her portrait:

> I am very loath to be your idol, sir;
> But since your falsehood shall become you well
> To worship shadows and adore false shapes,
> Send to me in the morning, and I'll send it.
> (IV, ii, 126–9)

Proteus has given himself to love, and love is making him over into such an ever-changing thing as itself:

> This weak impress of love is as a figure
> Trenchèd in ice, which with an hour's heat
> Dissolves to water, and doth lose his form.[17]
>
> (III, ii, 6–8)

Proteus demonstrates the truth of the doctrine of Plato and Petrarch and so many Neo-Platonists, that the lover becomes what he loves.[18] The words are Bruno's but they could as well be Petrarch's or Ficino's or innumerable others', 'the ultimate and last end of the chase is the capture of a fugitive and wild prey, through which the hunter becomes the hunted, the pillager becomes the pillaged.'[19]

I believe one must always resist the interpretation of individual characters in the Shakespeare plays as either allegorical or symbolic representations, just as no single play can be usefully thought of as an allegory. We always recognize, of course, predominant traits or biases in tragic as well as comic figures, and the traditional likening of Falstaff to the *miles gloriosus* as many another of this order is very useful for criticism. On the other hand, there are times in *The Merchant of Venice*, for example, when Portia at certain moments might seem Mercy herself, although it is only at certain moments, and for the rest she may be all too human. But in *The Two Gentlemen of Verona* there are weavings of ideas that bring forth a comparable view of Silvia where it may be permitted to believe that she is to be likened to a certain part of that complex weaving. As I think the glorious song in her praise attests sufficiently, she is such a person as life can produce, but the emphasis also on her more-than-mortal fineness obliges us to discover as clearly as we may what that more-than-mortal character is. We do this in part by relating those epithets of holy, wise and fair to what else is said of her, relating them as abstractions to the ideas developed in the praise of constancy and truth. The meanings in the song more than conform to the central Platonic and Christian affirmations that are made so much of in the play, they contribute a certain authority to them.

It is almost as difficult to relate philosophy to poetry as poetry to life and when the question arises, does the characterization of Silvia correspond in our understanding to what is said of her, we must appeal to one hardly knows what as the adjudicator. The characterizations of this play are relatively thin but I think we have a sense of Julia, for example, as a young woman of spark and vivacity, easily and deeply hurt, yet in her faithfulness something a good deal less than abject. I think Silvia is not that vivid, but we very much need to have a clear sense of her, for the character of the impression she makes upon us strikes at the question of the validity of the philosophy the play forwards. Does she come across as a person at once human and possessing a more than human beauty?

We know her to be loving and modest, enterprising and delicate in expressing her feeling for Valentine, brave and strong enough to follow him against her father's wishes. When approached by the unfaithful and presumptuous Proteus, she dismisses him with indignation, although not with the vehemence of the Lady in *Comus*—she is scornful but without wrath:

> And by and by [I] intend to chide myself
> Even for this time I spend in talking to thee.
>
> (IV, ii, 100–1)

Similarly, in her appeal to Sir Eglamour the words are feeling and earnest, and though the flight to the forest is the conventionally desperate one of romances the words are far from desperate:

> And, for the ways are dangerous to pass,
> I do desire thy worthy company,
> Upon whose faith and honour I repose.
> Urge not my father's anger, Eglamour,

But think upon my grief, a lady's grief,
And on the justice of my flying hence
To keep me from a most unholy match,
Which heaven and fortune still rewards with plagues.
I do desire thee, even from a heart
As full of sorrows as the sea of sands,
To bear me company, and go with me:
If not, to hide what I have said to thee,
That I may venture to depart alone.

(IV, iii, 25–37)

Almost her last words in the play, as Proteus is assaulting her, are as much a plea for his good as they are a repulse:

Read over Julia's heart, thy first, best love,
For whose dear sake thou didst then rend thy faith
Into a thousand oaths; and all those oaths
Descended into perjury, to love me.
Thou hast no faith left now, unless thou'dst two,
And that's far worse than none; better have none
Than plural faith, which is too much by one.
Thou counterfeit to thy true friend!

(V, iv, 46–53)

These are remarkable words, at once tender, strong, and just, although curiously scholastic-like in making distinctions. But in their tone there is not only the assurance of steadfastness, there is something queenly and noble, a sense, even in rebuke, of an untroubled peace.

In the rest of the play she says little, and when we put it all together we are not able to have as clear an image of her and of her quality as we have, say, of Kate, in *The Taming of the Shrew*, or the heroines of the middle comedies. The characterization is not filled out, one is tempted to say, enough—it is more as it is with Helena and Hermione in *A Midsummer Night's Dream*. Although we know her in the essentials, the character of a living being as that can be created in drama is missing.

We do, of course, relate the impression she makes upon us to what is said of her because in the matter of verisimilitude is the crux of the play. A question is put forward—is this superlative being the proof that the right honouring of the truth within an individual is the key to constancy and serenity and the requital of love? The characterization itself does not give a clear answer, although in a certain remoteness as well as strength and clarity, Silvia gives us something to go on. On the other hand, when we examine her function in the play, it is evident that she is serving as a model for the philosophizing, and if it is not accurate to speak of her as an embodiment of the truths the Neo-Platonists suppose to be at issue in the relationship between God and humans, she yet possesses the quality that alone would lead any-one to respect the doctrines, the serenity that lends assurance to admiration.

She is said to be perfection, and in the text we take this to mean that she is conversant with the divine. As remark follows upon remark we learn how much the play and her role in it are developing ideas about the nature of love that derive from Plato and Plotinus. The reasoning in the play is so much of a piece that we find ourselves taking a song, which is from one point of view of incomparable simplicity, as an expression infinitely rich with thought.

The song is saying that Silvia is in the midst of the world and yet apart from it, content as those are whose thoughts are with God—

> [her] worth makes other worthies nothing;
> She is alone. (II, iv, 164-5)

The singer speaks of her as if he too were seeking recourse with the divine. And so when there are the words—

> Is she kind as she is fair?
> For beauty lives with kindness.
> Love doth to her eyes repair,
> To help him of his blindness,
> And, being helped, inhabits there—(IV, ii, 43-7)

we are taken back to the conceit in *Diana*, to the verses on those ladies

> whose starlike eies doe threate
> Despaire and death, to those that view them well:
> For there sits *Cupid* in his proper seate,[20]

and back to Valentine's words,

> What light is light, if Silvia be not seen? (III, i, 174)

We take these words in conjunction with all those that speak of the fulfilment of love, some power, some understanding humans follow and hold to, moving towards such perfection as Silvia illustrates, holy, wise, and fair,[21]

> if not divine,
> Yet let her be a principality,
> Sovereign to all the creatures on the earth.
>   (II, iv, 150–2)

In these early writings there is again and again the most thoughtful and even intricate speculation on the perfection so many hope for. The poems and the plays represent many of the conditions that encourage as well as those that defeat the aspiration. The King of Navarre, Antipholus of Syracuse, Adonis, all those for whom the idea is the very star of their being, are shown to be less skilled in argument than clear in their faith. Only Valentine is able to follow the reasoning through, and I think that in the word 'inhabit' of the unknown singer of this song, Shakespeare is underwriting the final Platonic implications of the doctrines so many in the play have drawn on. But for such indications we might give more weight to the mere conventions of romantic adulation.

I believe we are to refer the sense here to the meanings in Valentine's words about Silvia, that she is the very sustenance of his life, the light by which he sees, what gives wonder and beauty to the world. Holy, fair, and wise, in her presence he is repaired. The language, which expresses the idea of the closest union one can conceive of—'she is myself'—never gives the sense of that phrase from *Diana*, that the lover lives 'in the body of the beloved'.[22] Loving is not only embracing, it is seeing and knowing and above all being, the being that is shared through the knowledge of reality. The doctrine from the Neo-Platonists, that 'true Love doth spring of reason',[23] that *Diana* emphasizes is, I think, being illustrated in the love this play tells of. Silvia gives light to see by—in her presence music, the creatures of the earth, all life become themselves. Whatever this suggests of some more than earthly influence is reinforced by the idea that love 'inhabits' with her, for in this word is just such a meaning as the Neo-Platonists used in speaking of the relationship of the soul to the One. The suggestion is that in loving Silvia one exists in that very relationship that hers is with the source of light and music and life.

The word 'inhabit' points to that distinction Plotinus laboured to make between identification and participation with the One, for there were many reasons why it appeared to him necessary to believe that even in divine union individuality was preserved. According to this philosophy, substance and being are in the One, which imparts its power to all things. In the mere statement of the doctrine we see the grounds for an analogy with Valentine's words on essence and on light.

As the argument proceeds, Plotinus says that love longs for simplicity yet the individual desires to remain himself, in the presence of the source of good retaining his identity. Plotinus speaks of the lover as 'stationed' (ἐνιδρύμεθα) in the One: 'Many times it has happened: lifted out of the body into myself; becoming external to all other things and self-encentrcd; beholding a marvellous beauty; then, more than ever, assured of community with the loftiest order; enacting the noblest life, acquiring identity with the divine; stationing within It by having attained that activity; poised above whatsoever within the Intellectual is less than the Supreme, (IV, 8, 1—MacKenna).[24]

While the words of the song lead us to the thought of such contemplation as this speaks of, they also keep before us the picture of garlands and the sound of music in praise of a maiden. I think we may never think of Silvia as simply an embodiment of any aspect of the philosophy she is helping the play to illustrate, never to identify her either with Deity or with abstraction. We are being asked, I think, to accept her as we accept all in the Shakespearean creation, as a person, and we are being asked to discover whether in this instance philosophy may bring forward such analogies and even doctrines that common sense may accept in honouring whatever we do honour in admiring an individual.[25] It is not the truth as such but the aptness of Neo-Platonic reasoning we are being asked to acknowledge:

'And as to our own Soul we are to hold that it stands, in part, always in the presence of the Divine Beings, while in part it is concerned with the things of this sphere and in part occupies a middle ground. It is one nature in graded powers; and sometimes the Soul in its entirety is borne along by the loftiest in itself and in the Authentic Existent; sometimes the less noble part is dragged down and drags the mid-soul with it, though the law is that the Soul may never succumb entire.

'The Soul's disaster falls upon it when it ceases to dwell in the perfect Beauty—the appropriate dwelling-place of that Soul which is no part and of which we too are no part—thence to pour forth into the frame of the All whatsoever the All can hold of good and beauty. There that Soul rests, free from all solicitude, not ruling by plan or policy, not redressing, but establishing order by the marvellous efficacy of its contemplation of the things above it' (II, 9, 2—MacKenna).

So when we return to the question, is Silvia really like this?— I think all we can answer is, she may be. To put the answer another way, Marina in *Pericles*, does seem to be such a person as Silvia is said to be. She comes across more clearly. By that token, one may at least believe that characterization in drama is equal to philosophizing of this nature. This lack of dimension in

Silvia's characterization may give warrant to Mr. John Vyvyan in identifying her with 'the Uranian Aphrodite',[26] and in believing that she 'reveal[s] the celestial Love and Beauty',[27] as if to signify emanations in the Neo-Platonic scheme. For my part, I do not think this takes enough account of the image of a young girl about to elope, devising subterfuges with a friend of the family, speaking to a would-be ravisher with pointed criticism. 'Angel-like' and 'holy' seem to me to set the limits within which we must fit the ideas and beliefs that her character as a human being may be thought to illustrate and certify.

So much of what we take to be Platonism in this play comes from explicit statements, what amount to expressions of doctrine. Putting these together we observe coherence and in effect the accumulations of argument. The play itself we continue to accept as a certain kind of romantic comedy, in which the central business is the loves of some young aristocrats taken up with all sorts of courtly concerns and conventions. There are also fantastic adventures as well as reminders of life lived in the light of common day. But we are not allowed to remain only with drama of that order, the drift of the ideas that come forward is causing us to be intent on another kind of action simultaneously, the processes of existence in humans. We are being held by two matters at once but differently than in allegory, although as there the two interests frequently coincide not only in the characterization but in the plot—for example, the thwarting of Proteus' attack upon Silvia is accompanied by the revelation of the manner in which good may overcome evil. Yet even though no character has such vividness as to threaten, as Shakespeare's characters so generally do, to walk off the stage into life, neither does any one perform simply as an abstraction in an argument.

The play centres upon the character and situation of Silvia and Proteus. In a manner of speaking Silvia is put upon a pedestal to show us all what perfection is like. Proteus, the chief instigator of the trouble, is similarly always before us, and it is from him that we learn most about the ways of love and what happens to those who in loving fail to honour truth. Again, we need to make a distinction between what the characterization communicates to us and what Proteus' function is in the unfolding of the argument.

At the very beginning Valentine calls his friend, 'my loving Proteus', not only to allude to his devotion to Julia but in fondness, calling attention to the affection he too enjoys. Proteus is naturally loving. One does not know how seriously to take the remark that he is 'a votary of fond desire' (I, i, 52), in the midst of the high-flown language of the religion of love the two friends are casting back and forth, nor if one is to make anything of the complacency with which Proteus observes—

> as in the sweetest bud
> The eating canker dwells, so eating love
> Inhabits in the finest wits of all. (I, i, 42–4)

But there are one or two remarks early in the play that suggest he has some sense of the ways of his nature. Julia, he says, has 'metamorphized' him (I, i, 66), reminding us of the ancient Proteus and transformations as complete as his, the demon-like god turning into fire or fleeting water. The suggestion is reinforced when he thinks of the change that has come over him in leaving Julia—

> for now my love is thawed,
> Which, like a waxen image 'gainst a fire,
> Bears no impression of the thing it was.
> (II, iv, 199–201)

How susceptible to change, how defenseless before the claims of reason, he himself acknowledges after the merest glimpse of Silvia and after hearing Valentine's praise of her:

> How shall I dote on her with more advice,
> That thus without advice begin to love her!
> 'Tis but her picture I have yet beheld,

And that hath dazzled my reason's light;
But when I look on her perfections,
There is no reason but I shall be blind.

(II, iv, 206–11)

What might be simply hyperbole—that his reason is overthrown —cannot be only that for he takes up immediately with the notion that he is moving in the dark, a state he accepts so readily that it appears he is already resigned to an act in which he will both betray himself and go against nature:

> If I can check my erring love, I will;
> If not, to compass her I'll use my skill. (212–13)

His mind grows darker and in his perversity he reasons about the loss of reason, or its misdirection. He is evidently as committed to ideas of transcendence and immanence as Valentine and so in judging his own behaviour he does not hold back from calling it mad and corrupt. He remains courtly almost to the end but I think there is cyncism in what he says as he asks for Silvia's portrait.

His skill in reasoning never leaves him, and at the end he will still be twisting words even in straightening his course:

> What is in Silvia's face, but I may spy
> More fresh in Julia's with a constant eye?

(V, iv, 114–15)

The duplicity in that use of the word 'constant' is so consistent with his usual turning of words inside out that it may divert us from recognizing what must be a more important point that is being made. The mind intent on that which makes constancy possible will indeed discover that essence in Julia, it is the very truth Proteus was on the way to knowing earlier, and it is everywhere the same. But he would spy it more freshly now in her for in renewed faithfulness to her he would be repairing the faith he owed to himself that he had weakened in leaving her. He would be 'returning to himself' as he could not otherwise.

The reasoning in the play requires us to extricate such a meaning from these words although as elsewhere in this scene we are not well enough prepared either for the sudden turn of events or for the reversals of purpose and changes of mind. But we do need to hold on to the thought that in times past Proteus had won golden opinions for himself, and he always showed he knew wherein honour lay. Julia herself was in danger of idolizing him, at least if one were to take her words in full seriousness, but she who 'gave aim to all his oaths' (V, iv, 101) surely had something to go by for her praise—

> His words are bonds, his oaths are oracles;
> His love sincere, his thoughts immaculate.
> (II, vii, 75–6)

Anticipating his return to her, the term she uses for his faithlessness shows her belief in his ability to distinguish truth from falsehood and the insubstantial from the real:

> And, were there sense in his idolatry,
> My substance should be statue in thy stead.
> (IV, iv, 200–1)

It is because Proteus retains his understanding of the meaning of constancy that he can repent, he understands its rewards. He is brought to repent when he sees how faithful Julia has been, struck by the sharpness of her words—

> It is the lesser blot, modesty finds,
> Women to change their shapes than men their minds.
> (V, iv, 108–9)

We are to understand that he knows the cost as well as the nature of his transgression, we guess that he knows what he needs to regain:

My shame and guilt confounds me. (V, iv, 73)

Pursuing his confession, he makes the statement that, had the context been fuller, we should accept as reasoning developing the full meaning of the play:

> O heaven, were man
> But constant, he were perfect! That one error
> Fills him with faults, makes him run through all th'
>   sins:
> Inconstancy falls off ere it begins. (V, iv, 110–13)

Again he is being too clever with words but the thought could only have arisen in one who had a just perception of the wrong:

> If hearty sorrow
> Be a sufficient ransom for offense,
> I tender 't here; I do as truly suffer
> As e'er I did commit. (V, iv, 74–7)

Unfortunately the scene does not express the depth of the suffering and a quality to the contrition that would justify Valentine in words so serious that they seem to be speaking of the ransoming of sinners by divinity:

> Then I am paid;
> And once again I do receive thee honest.
> Who by repentance is not satisfied
> Is nor of heaven nor earth, for these are pleased,
> By penitence th' Eternal Wrath's appeased.
>   (V, iv, 77–81)

The meaning is clear enough but the play has not prepared us for the full weight of the contrast—if the love of the angel-like be light and life, transgression is the way of everlasting death.

Consequently, we may not think of Proteus as a true embodiment of the fires running in the veins of his namesake although

Shakespeare will show us well enough what that is like, in Hamlet and Leontes and many another. In *The Two Gentlemen of Verona*, as generally in the early writing, Shakespeare has less to do with the passions than with the love of God.

In *Henry VI*, however, the feelings are profoundly engaged and in a matter where we understand that the issue has once again to do with the power of love to take over a life. Suffolk in his love for Margaret capitulated to the god as Proteus never did. Before there was any indication his love might be returned, Suffolk recognized the attraction of Margaret as a 'labyrinth' where 'Minotaurs and ugly treasons lurk' (*I Henry VI*, V, iii, 188–9). But later, when she became Elysium to him, the thought of leaving her was as a death, not as Valentine spoke of absence from Silvia, but as absence from her embrace. Elysium is her body and Elysium is breathing with her breath.

> If I depart from thee I cannot live;
> And in thy sight to die, what were it else
> But like a pleasant slumber in thy lap?
> Here could I breathe my soul into the air,
> As mild and gentle as the cradle-babe
> Dying with mother's dug between its lips;
> Where, from thy sight, I should be raging mad,
> And cry out for thee to close up mine eyes,
> To have thee with thy lips to stop my mouth:
> So shouldst thou either turn my flying soul,
> Or I should breathe it so into thy body,
> And then it lived in sweet Elysium.[28]
>
> (*IIHenry VI*, *III*, ii, 388–99)

I take it that in this way of thinking the loss of the soul would be complete only in such a metamorphosis and such a sub-ordination as Suffolk entertains the thought of. To put it another way, in all such loves as Shakespeare tells about in these early plays the idea of a loving union is always being illustrated by the traditional idea of the love becoming the very person of the beloved—as Petrarch puts it, of being transformed into the other. There will be ideally—Valentine says it clearly—a union of such sympathy that one might think of it as a sharing of identity—'She is my essence'—although it will not be exactly that. To be lost in the body of the beloved is neither what Petrarch had in mind nor Valentine:

> O thou that dost inhabit in my breast,
> Leave not the mansion so long tenantless,
> Lest, growing ruinous, the building fall,
> And leave no memory of what it was!
> Repair me with thy presence, Silvia. (V, iv, 7–11)

It appears that love, surrendered to as love, as it is with Proteus, displaces the self as the power does that transformed the god into beast and monster, reasonless and unconfinable.[29] That power is tyrannic, and it is reasonless because it seeks its forms only within bodies, themselves by nature mortal and ever changing. The god could not escape change ever, but Proteus the man, we discover, may, for there remains with him the knowledge of that which allows for constancy.[30]

In these early works certainly, and I think always, Shakespeare was enraptured with the idea of an inherent purity men know to be such. In crises, particularly, they would appeal to this as the justification of their being. When we examine the idea carefully we discover, I think, a foundation in Platonic and Christian beliefs, and we also discover something about the nature of the evil that comes about in the loss of that central integrity.

As the reasoning that sustains this notion is reconstructed, the clear meaning that is, however perfection is to be defined, in striving for it, whether in maturing or in love, an individual must make the right choices freely. Doing so he preserves his purity, which I understand to be the potentiality of his being as a rational creature. The King of Navarre proposed study, 'still and contemplative', as the supreme good—as Dumaine put it, 'living in philosophy'. Berowne, taking another tack, argued that love would lead to heavenly knowledge, and the rapture of the soul:

> If knowledge be the mark, to know thee shall suffice:
> Well learnèd is that tongue that well can thee commend,
> All ignorant that soul that sees thee without wonder.[31]
>
> *(Love's Labour's Lost*, IV, ii, 113–15)

These are but other ways of pointing to what is being repeated again and again, that there is indeed a supreme satisfaction, and that it may be attainable.

The plots in the plays and poems have much to do with what endangers such fulfilments, and in them it is often love in one form or another that misleads or destroys men. Antipholus of Syracuse, Adonis, Lucrece, Silvia, all must resist the unwanted offering of love or the attacks of lust. All make their resistance in the name of freedom, not condemning love itself, but insisting on the need to receive it freely and in season, receiving freely when able to give it freely. All contemplate with horror the damage done when love is not returned as love and the damage of violation of any kind. It must be that all these lords and ladies believe themselves stewards of a precious treasure whose safety is in part within the keeping of the will. This precious possession they will speak of as 'self' or 'truth' or 'troth'—the words may be interchangeable. Proteus could be using any of them when he said—

> I leave my self, my friends, and all for love. (I, i, 65)

Or the terms could be kept distinct, as with Berowne—

> We to ourselves prove false,
> By being once false forever to be true
> To those that make us both.
>
> *(Love's Labour's Lost*, V, ii, 773–5)

156

But whatever the discriminations, this self, this truth, whether the knower or the known, must avoid expropriation, must exist on its own terms in order to confer and to receive. In so doing it does not live to itself alone but in its relation to a sovereign power:

were man
But constant, he were perfect!
(*The Two Gentlemen of Verona*, V, iv, 110–11)

Through the relationship of cognition, constant to substance, to essence, to that perfection which sustains and forms the reason that perceives it, perfection is a sovereign who is not a tyrant to the freely serving subject. By Silvia truth itself is known—

if not divine,
Yet let her be a principality,
Sovereign to all the creatures on the earth.
(II, iv, 150–2)

In this emphasis on knowledge and the means of it we perceive reasoning of a Neo-Platonic character, so different from the modern Gnostic modes: 'The soul of the philosopher [for Plotinus] has achieved the independence . . . for which all Greek thinkers sought. There is a recognition here that each man is ultimately responsible for himself, that each man's troubles are his own and each man's decision can only be made by himself. And each man, for Plotinus, has the *power* to make his own decisions. His soul has been providentially designed to be of such a kind as to be able to make the journey back without any additional help from the One.'[32]

In these early writings, in all the ways of flourishing—in the service of the fair and holy, in the pursuit of wisdom, in the contemplation of being—the individual retains his identity. If he loses freedom he loses himself, and he may be irretrievably lost, as it is in death, when the boar kills Adonis or when Lucrece kills herself or when Suffolk surrenders to Margaret. But the self can allow no expropriation other than death's, it cannot permit a wrong against it that would oblige the individual to an act he has not freely chosen, and is not free to reverse. Silvia's defiance is a sufficient example of the definitive doctrine:

> Had I been seizèd by a hungry lion,
> I would have been a breakfast to the beast,
> Rather than have false Proteus rescue me.
>
> (V, iv, 33–5)

The root of the matter seems to be that wrong—breaking or violating trust—harms through depriving the individual of the freedom to choose to serve that to which it is necessary to be constant—truth, being, good. The wrong against the Princess of France—

> Your oath I will not trust;
> (*Love's Labour's Lost*, V, ii, 795)

against Julia—

> Thou has no faith left now, unless thou 'dst two,
> And that's far worse than none; better have none
> Than plural faith, which is too much by one;
> (*The Two Gentlemen of Verona*, V, iv, 50–2)

against Adonis, is the interruption of the love of that to which alone it would be possible to be constant, that constancy itself possible only in the freely giving of one's own 'truth', one's 'self', that identity which remains itself even in 'inhabiting' within the light—

> What light is light, if Silvia be not seen?
> What joy is joy, if Silvia be not by?
> Unless it be to think that she is by,
> And feed upon the shadow of perfection.
> Except I be by Silvia in the night,
> There is no music in the nightingale;

Unless I look on Silvia in the day,
There is no day for me to look upon.
She is my essence, and I leave to be,
If I be not by her fair influence
Fostered, illumined, cherished, kept alive.

(III, i, 174–84)

This is why the word sin comes into frequent use—the wrong is disobedience to divine injunction. The violation of another is the betrayal of the self, whose life as light exists in order to serve perfectly that which gave it being—

that pow'r which gave me first my oath. (II, vi, 4)

Proteus is referring to love and also, I think, to the power behind love.

In *Love's Labour's Lost* as in this play the perfidies and crimes are to be redeemed by contrition, penance, the traditional sacrifices, and as in *The Comedy of Errors*, specific, unmistakably Christian allusions, coherent enough with much that is romantic and idyllic, underly and sustain the words truth, love, constancy, and the rest. In most of this early writing it is love and lust that bring the greatest dangers, doing harm that even the betrayal of trust does not do. The expropriation of the person in defiance of his wishes and will touches upon that individual's very being in what he judges to be a sacreligious way. From the examples of Lucrece, Adonis, Julia, Silvia, it is clear that it is not physical union itself that does the harm. The corruption of the soul's pure truth is in the complicity with the overthrow of reason:

O sweet-suggesting Love, if thou hast sinned,
Teach me, thy tempted subject, to excuse it!

(II, vi, 7–8)

The sticking point in the last scene, more even than the haste with which the denouement is effected, the instant changes of feeling, the instant transfers of love, the immediate removal of resentment, is Valentine's act in surrendering Silvia and as it were consigning her to Proteus.

It seems to be fair to put it this way, and, if it is, one would be saying this is as foolish and offensive a trick-ending as one would find in the crudest of writers. Since it is Shakespeare's, with all the faults there must be something more to it than this. For whatever it is worth, the ending, following upon the preposterous adventures in the forest, need not meet all the requirements of verisimilitude. There is this, too, that following the initial concern with engagements, elopements, plans for education, the practical interests were increasingly swallowed up in fantasies and in the speculations of philosophy, so much so that a conclusion was required in which there would be marvellous rescues in company with the triumph of idealism. If enough is to be made of the theme that constancy shares in the character of divinity, it would be right for a sovereign to illustrate the very power of divinity, even in apotheosis to come down and manifest his efficacy in this troubled world.

Valentine has indeed taken on the manner of sovereignty, he has evidently attained that poise his father sent him abroad to attain, and his first act is king-like and even god-like, for he not only proposes that hereafter all shall be

One house, one feast, one mutual happiness,

he proclaims it. He is enjoining not a domestic accommodation but a state of harmony and joy in which the requirements of friendship as well as the demands of love are fulfilled. The demands of constancy in the terms in which the play has presented them are being met. Ficino said that the end of friendship is a communion of life (*Amicitiæ finis est uitæ communio*).[33] For all those truly intent upon reality and divinity there can be no rivalries, lovers and friends all share in the one good and there are no exclusions of any true loving, 'all their minds transfigured so together.' (*A Midsummer Night's Dream*, V, i, 24)

Having said this, one wonders how a scene could have been devised that would bring the idea off. The few lines allowed to carry such a heavy burden, the brief time to dispose of all the questions the characters in their life-likeness are asking, are not enough. But the failure may be as much in the philosophy as in the art. The difficulty the problem of evil poses for Neo-Platonism is notorious, and the dilemma that faces Valentine may be showing itself to be insuperable. I think there is some sense of this we get through his use of words that remind us of Christian belief and the authority of a priest to absolve sin. It is as if Shakespeare in defeat fell back upon the thought of sacraments and true miracles. But this too was not enough, for Valentine, after all, was but a young courtier, handsomely come into manhood and power, but neither priest nor divinity.

The final question then becomes—is the failure of the ending evidence that Shakespeare realized that the philosophy he was exploiting was inadequate in the face of the issues? The works that follow would lead us to answer that question affirmatively.

NOTES

1 *A Critical Edition of Yong's Translation of George of Montemayor's Diana and Gil Polo's Enamoured Diana*, by J. M. Kennedy, Oxford, 1968, Book IV, p. 157.
Bruno provides a discussion of love and irrational behaviour in the First Dialogue of the First Part of the *Heroici Furori* but it is in the Fifth Dialogue of the same Part that there is the remarkable characterization of all love as troubled: 'Love becomes debased and flies close to the ground when it is attached to base things; it flies high when it is intent upon the more noble enterprises. In conclusion, then, whatever it may be, love is always afflicted and tortured, so that it cannot avoid becoming material for Vulcan; for the soul, a divine thing and by its nature not the slave but the lord of the material body, is thrown into painful disturbance while it voluntarily serves the body where it does not find that which satisfies it. And no matter how much it may fix itself upon the beloved object, the soul cannot avoid being sometimes agitated and shaken' (*Giordano Bruno's The Heroic Frenzies*, edited and translated by P. E. Memmo, Jr., Chapel Hill, 1964, pp. 166–7).

It is possible that Shakespeare holds the same idea, and that in this play Silvia and Valentine are in the nature of love only less troubled than Proteus and Julia.

2 *Diana*, Book II, p. 76.

3 Drawing on traditional sources, including the Scholastics, one may define constancy as the virtue which sustains the individual in his attachment to the good in the face of difficulties acting upon him from without. Inconstancy is a vice, causing him to abandon the good without a reasonable cause.

For the Stoics this virtue is of course made possible as an individual succeeds in becoming passionless, and in the Renaissance that view was influentially developed by Justus Lipsius. This philosophy cannot be the background of the honouring of constancy in *The Two Gentlemen of Verona* for here it is love, entertaining 'honest' passion, that proves itself in constancy. Nor can Bruno's conception of love, by nature troubled, account for the serenity Shakespeare's faithful lovers are assured of in their fulfilments. The Scholastic conception, with what it brings of Christian values to the classical idea of inner composure, more nearly accords with the state of being of Silvia, more especially, and of Julia and Valentine as well—at the end certainly—and even of Proteus as he conceives of the satisfaction he pursues. But Proteus, inconstant in loving, unstable in his attachment to good, is necessarily in turmoil: 'Robert Grosseteste et saint Thomas d'Aquin insistent tout particulièrement sur cette idée, la paix étant pour eux, non point l'immobilité du non vivant, mais la possession active, vivante, parfaite d'un être par lui-même. Un être est beau, dit Grosseteste, dans la mesure où il est identique à lui-même, il est comme il doit être, *il est en paix avec lui-même*. Le beau 'en accordant le divers, pacifie les oppositions'. C'est pourquoi la beauté parfaite des statues gothiques exprime une sérénité totale qui, dans l'ordre morale, traduit la "constance" de l'être' (Edgar de Bruyne, *L'Esthétique du Moyen Age*, Louvain, 1947, p. 131).

4 Berowne in less danger plays with the same equivocation:

> Let us once lose our oaths to find ourselves,
> Or else we lose ourselves to keep our oaths.
>
> (*Love's Labour's Lost*, IV, iii, 360–1)

5 Compare:

> I am but a shadow of myself:
> You are deceived, my substance is not here.
>
> (*I Henry VI*, II, iii, 50–1)

Love like a shadow flies when substance love pursues,
Pursuing that that flies, and flying what pursues.
(The Merry Wives of Windsor, II, ii, 215-16)

The very substance of the ambitious is merely the shadow of a dream.
(Hamlet, II, ii, 263-4)

E. I. Fripp notices other references to this idea in *Shakespeare, Man and Artist*, London, 1938, I, 287.

6 In a certain respect this is the sense of Plotinus:

'The souls go forth neither under compulsion nor of freewill; or, at least, freedom, here, is not to be regarded as action upon preference; it is more like such a leap of nature as moves men into the instinctive desire of sexual union, or, in the case of some, to fine conduct; the motive lies elsewhere than in the reason: like is destined unfailingly to like, and each moves hither or thither at its fixed moment' (IV, 3, 13—MacKenna).

7 The matters broached here are discussed in a wider context in note 14.

8 One of Ficino's definitions is: 'Veritas est naturae cuiusque pura integritas, et integra puritas' (*Theologia Platonica*, IX, vi [*Opera*, Basel, 1576, I, 261]).

9 Compare *The Two Gentlemen of Verona*, IV, ii, 85, 'his pure heart's truth'.

10 The phrasing is conventional: '. . . si anima nostra, solam intellectus umbram haberet, non intelligeret defineretue unquam formam et substantiam intellectus, sed accidentia tantum confuse prospiceret' (Ficino, *Theologia Platonica*, XIV, ii [*Opera*, I, 309]).

11 Bruno makes use of the figure of nourishment in speaking of love: 'And just as by its essence the mind is in God who is its life, similarly by its intellectual operation and the consequent operation of the will, the mind refers itself to its own light and its beatific object. It is therefore with dignity that this passion of the heroic frenzy feeds itself [*si pasce*] upon so high an emprise' (*The Heroic Frenzies*, Part I, Dialogue III, p. 116).

12 ' "Essence" and *The Phoenix and Turtle*', *English Literary History*, XIX (1952), 267. The reference is to Hooker's *Works*, 7th ed., edited by R. W. Church and F. Paget, Oxford, 1888, II, 247-8.
    Underlying the conception of feeding upon 'the shadow of perfection' is of course the Platonic idea of transcendent reality and the imperfections

of all else, but in the sense Valentine has of the dreariness of his life when deprived of the perfection, we observe a sensibility the Renaissance Neo-Platonists contributed to the idea.

The oppositions of *substance* and *shadow* are metaphysical and as such they here become extensions of the Petrarchan manner. The Petrarchan antitheses are congenial to Platonism, if they are not rooted in it, and in such expressions as these of Valentine praising Silvia they are particularly useful to the philosophical direction of the play.

In this respect a comment that has been made upon Bruno seems to me to be relevant. Professor Memmo observed that in writing of Diana as the most noble object of love Bruno was carrying 'the Petrarchan dialectic to its metaphysical end'. Diana, he indicated, 'is not of the same lineage as Beatrice and Laura. Diana is closer to the Platonic idea and the Plotinian νοῦς than to the angelic nature of Beatrice' (P. E. Memmo, *The Heroic Frenzies*, p. 45).

In Valentine's thought Silvia is also at the apex of a hierarchy of some sort, 'closer', I think, to Bruno's Diana than to Beatrice, but also more human.

---

[13] J. V. Cunningham, ' "Essence" and *The Phoenix and Turtle*,' *English Literary History*, XIX (1952), 268. Mr. Cunningham goes on to argue that Valentine's relation to Silvia is to be construed in Neo-Platonic terms, 'worldly Neo-Platonism, precipitated out of the latent Neo-Platonism of Christian dogma.' There is a certain point to this, but I think we must also suppose that Neo-Platonism came to Shakespeare directly through, for example, such a source as the *Diana*. One may take into account all that gives Miss Kennedy grounds for this comment: '*The fourth Booke*, which is devoted to considerations of beauty, wisdom, virtue, and the nature of love in the setting of the Temple of Diana presided over by Felicia, is the philosophic core of the novel. Chastity is here represented as loyalty in love. . . . The choice of Diana as goddess of chastely loyal lovers was probably suggested by such Neoplatonic allegorizations of the classical myths concerning Diana as are found, for example, in Leone Ebreo, and in Cartari, who discusses Diana as she appears in her more fruitful identities such as Lucina and Isis (*Le Imagini con la Spositione de i Dei de Gliantichi*, Venetia, 1556, ff.xxiii–xxviii). Felicia's name is probably intended to suggest the happiness achieved in that union with the highest beauty and wisdom which is the ultimate end of love according to Renaissance Neoplatonic theory (see, for example, Leone Ebreo's third dialogue). Ideally Montemayor's lovers are presented as seeking happiness in the chastely fruitful union of marriage with those they love because they see in them some reflections of the divine beauty and wisdom' (*Diana*, p. 433, note for p. 131. 8).

The reasoning in this speech certainly corresponds to traditional Neo-Platonism, but I think one may be allowed to take the phrase 'She is my essence' in a sense differently than Mr. Cunningham does. In the controlling sense of the speech that has to do with the fulfilment of the self, and where it is said that 'Silvia is myself', 'essence' may be a synonym for 'myself'. This would remove the difficulty Mr. Cunningham points to: 'Apart from the blasphemy involved, there is only one difficulty in the passage: this resides in the proposition, *She is my essence.* The proposition is technically incorrect with regard to the relation of creature and Creator in the scholastic system, for it is manifestly false to say that the soul is of the substance of God. Although the soul is a simple form in its essence, it is not its own being but is a being by participation' (p. 268).

Valentine's rhetoric proceeds first in setting forth the nature of his deprivation in being exiled from Silvia. This would be torment and death, for it would be the loss of his 'self', his identity, his being. Then, still negatively, and through the key question—what good is the light of the sun if the light that Silvia gives is not here to light my mind?—he goes on to say that the life of common day, of the senses, holds nothing for him. The implication is that he in his true nature can see truly, that is to say in the spirit, only when she is by.

Up to a point this argument is proceeding as Bruno's Tansillo presents his, characterizing the deprivation and explaining the necessity of union with the loved one: '. . . every lover who is separated from the beloved (to which, joined by his desire, he would also be joined in act) finds himself in anguish and pain, crucifies himself and torments himself. He is so tormented, not only because he loves and is conscious that his love is most worthily and nobly employed, but because his love is deprived of that fruition which it would attain if it had arrived at the end toward which it tends. He does not suffer because of that desire which enlivens him, but because of the difficulty of the labor which martyrs him [*per la difficultá del studio ch'il martora*]. Thus others consider him as being in an unhappy condition because of the fate which seems to have condemned him to these torments; as for himself, despite these torments, he will not fail to recognize his debt to Love and will not fail to render thanks to it, because it has brought an intelligible form before his mind. For in that intelligible form, although he is enclosed within the prison of the flesh during this earthly life, bound by his sinews and confined by his very bones, he has been permitted to contemplate an image of the divinity more exalted than would have been possible had some other species and similitude of it been offered him' (*The Heroic Frenzies*, Part I, Dialogue III, pp. 114-15—Memmo).

It remains for Tansillo somewhat later to include the idea that seems to be the foundation of Valentine's reasoning, that that which is peculiarly

his—whether to be spoken of as self or essence or life—is only to be perfected when she is by: 'for in this condition of ours we cannot desire or
attain greater perfection than that which is ours when our intellect
through the medium of some noble intelligible species is united either
to the separate substances, as some say, or to the divine mind, if we employ
the idiom of the Platonists' (p. 117). It works both ways—the noble object is the means of his own perfection and only by virtue of his perfection
can he participate in its being: 'And just as by its essence the mind is in
God who is its life, similarly by its intellectual operation and the consequent operation of the will, the mind refers itself to its own light and its
beatific object' (p. 116). '. . . the divinity can be the object only in similitude, and not a similitude abstracted and acquired from corporeal beauty
and excellence by virtue of the senses, but a similitude the mind can dis-
cern by virtue of the intellect. When it has reached this state, the mind
begins to lose love and affection for every other sensible as well as intelligible object, for joined to that light it becomes that light, and consequently becomes a god' (p. 115).

In *The Expulsion of the Triumphant Beast* there is this: '[Providence]
is not Truth, herself, but is truthful and partakes of Truth; she is not the
sun, but the moon, the earth, and the star which shine because of another.
So she is Sophia, not in essence, but by participation; and she is an eye
which receives light and is illuminated by an external, wandering light; she
is not an eye in herself, but through another. . . . Just as there is no one
who can touch her at all, so there is not found here below anyone who can
perfectly understand her; because she is understood and equaled only by
that [being] in whom she dwells as essence, and this is none other than she
herself.' (Translated by A. D. Imerti, New Brunswick, 1964, pp. 142–3
[Second Dialogue, First Part])

Valentine ends by speaking of Silvia as if she were a star, raining influence upon him, nourishing, loving, and keeping him alive. She is himself and other than himself, not his creator but his sustainer. It is up to
him to be where she can shine upon him. All this way of speaking seems
to me to rule out the possibility that he is identifying her with God, and
to say rather that her relationship to God is like his to her, moving towards union with divinity without becoming one with God. The distinction is one of the prime cruxes of Neo-Platonism, as such most profoundly
insisted on by Plotinus, and it is a distinction Bruno is as familiar with as
Ficino. One of the great virtues of the distinction is that it allows dignity
to all things, all persons, it deprives nothing in the creation of its essence,
no identity is lost even within the divine. In Bruno this opens the way for
his naturalism, for his identification of body and soul. I think Shakespeare
was never attracted by this view, and at any rate that Valentine is not
expressing it. In this speech Silvia, too, remains herself, and like the

nightingale's music and the light of the sun they are all united not in essence but in participation, and the nearest analogy I can come upon is in Plotinus: 'The gods belonging to that higher Heaven itself, they whose station is upon it and in it, see and know in virtue of their omnipresence to it. For all There is heaven; earth is heaven, and sea heaven; and animal and plant and man; all is the heavenly content of that heaven: and the gods in it, despising neither men nor anything else that is there where all is of the heavenly order, traverse all that country and all space in peace' (V, 8, 3—MacKenna).

As for the identification of Silvia with God, or as 'love in the absolute sense', or anything comparable, I think this does injustice to the play, where Silvia is a charming person with something of the imperfections as well as the ordinariness of humans. There is much sense in the common notion, and certainly a notion Christianity would support, that one might love the divine and love the human also, and in loving the human be loving the human for its relation to the divine: 'L'amour s'adresse à l'existant (non pas à l'existence, qui n'est qu'un abstrait), à cet existant-ci comme tel, non pas à ses qualités seules (quoi qu'en pense Pascal) ou à sa nature seule' (J. de Finance, *Essai sur l'Agir Humain*, Rome, 1962, p. 152 [*Analecta Gregoriana*, Vol. 126]).

14 These words recall the command of the Delphic oracle, and the sense Shakespeare gives to them shows how extensively in his Platonizing he makes use of the interpretations of this injunction that the Platonists and the Christian theologians worked out.

The *Charmides* is mainly occupied with explaining what it means to know oneself and why this is so important. Two of the chief problems are, first, discovering what knowledge of itself is (165E and 166C), and second, discovering what a man knows and what he does not know (167A). The discussion is developed with the subtlety the problems require and one of the main directions that develops has to do with the usefulness of knowledge of the self.

The Delphic command is deceptively simple, but Socrates marks out what were to be for later thinkers the main lines of interpretation and argument. He once asserted that if we have knowledge of ourselves 'we are likely to know what pains to take over ourselves; but if we have it not we never can' (*Alcibiades* I, 129A). In taking care of ourselves this knowledge helps to keep harm at a distance (132A–C). What we attempt to know in knowing ourselves is not easily singled out in a word or a phrase, but it seems to be what the words wisdom and reason allude to, the principle or pattern of conduct and of life implanted within the soul, and which the person would follow in moving towards his perfection: 'And if the soul, too, my dear Alcibiades, is to know herself, she must surely look at a

soul, and especially at that region of it in which occurs the virtue of a soul
—wisdom, and at any other part of a soul which resembles this?' (133B,
translated by W. R. M. Lamb). Within the soul reason (φρνεῖν) is said
to be the most divine part (133C), and in this resides the understanding of
the principles governing the proper relations between the soul and the
body.

In some aspect of this idea Ficino keeps close to Socrates but in others
he develops it, while consistently enough, into implications Socrates and
Plato held back from. At one point, in speaking of adolescence, Ficino
says that by looking inward the soul may learn what providence has in
store for it: 'Vbi apparet quanta sit animæ cum cœlestibus concordia,
quanta cum Deo cognatio, quæ quotiens in se redit, cœlestium arcanorum,
et diuinæ fit prouidentiæ particeps' (*Theologia Platonica*, XIII, ii [I,
295]). '[Socrates] Putat enim animo uerorum lumina omnium innato fuisse
ideóque si in seipsum prorsus inspiciat, uera in se omnia conspecturum'
(*In Charmidem, uel de temperantia, epitome* [*Opera*, II, 1305]). Bruno en-
larges upon the idea: '. . . the Pythagoreans and the Platonists hold that
souls, not only by a spontaneous will which brings them to an understanding of natures, but also by the necessity of an inward law written and
recorded by a fatal decree [*della necessità d'una legge interna scritta et
registrata dal decreto fatale*], at certain times set out to seek their own des-
tinies' (*The Heroic Frenzies*, Part I, Dialogue III, p. 120). See also Hélène
Védrine, *La Conception de la Nature chez Giordano Bruno*, Paris, 1967, p.
343 especially.

All this that is involved in the idea of the knowledge of the self, the
self being the very touchstone of truth and the guide for the future, is
sometimes characterized in its later development as 'le Socratisme
chrétien', and I think Shakespeare depends upon the approach not only
in these early writings but always. (One phase of this, with respect to his
mode of characterization, is pointed to in my *The Art of Shakespeare*,
London, 1964, pp. 20–7.)

As I see it, it is generally not so much the supporting doctrine that is
important for the poetry of the Middle Ages and the Renaissance as the
fact of its attractiveness to the imagination. Though a most complex
belief, it invites instant and feeling subscription, in its mere statement it
appears to communicate the authority of a common insight. The appeal
to something other than the exclusively rational, the resistance to critical
analysis, makes the injunction and the dogma attractive to whoever needs
to appeal to feeling or love, or sometimes even appetite, as authority and
sanction. Properly, of course, the doctrine keeps clear of the easy abuses
of appeals to the senses and sentiments, and keeps clearly in view, if not a
mystical certainty, a profoundly religious conviction that, as the source of
the command is divine, the object of the knowledge is divinity. In Augus-

tine and many another the study of the self is the study of the image of God, and Socrates and Plato have plainly prepared the way for this development. (See, for example, P. Courcelle, '*Nosce teipsum* du Bas-Empire au Haut Moyen Age. L'heritage profane et les développements chrétiens', in *Il Passaggio dall'antichità al Medioevo in Occidente* [*Settimane di Studio del Centro Italiano di Studi sull'Alto Medioevo*. April, 1961], t. IX, Spoleto, 1962, pp. 265–95.)

Medieval theologians expanded upon the idea of the relationship of self-knowledge to constancy in a variety of ways, and much of this is outlined in Edgar de Bruyne, *Études d'Esthétique Médiévale*, Bruges, 1946 (for example, in II, 273; III, 37, 40, 129).

The potential ambiguity of the doctrine is laid out by Pascal in distinguishing between *l'amour propre* and *l'amour de soi*, a distinction well known to Petrarch. (See Anders Nygren, *Eros et Agape*, Paris, 1952, II, 97.) And of course, in the Renaissance there is the return to the most significant issue, the determination of what the dogma can be in its most responsible senses.

With Petrarch there is the complex matter of relating all that the knowledge of the self can signify to the self in loving, and his thinking on the matter passed through many phases. Something of the comprehensiveness and subtlety of his reflection may be indicated by this penetrating observation: 'Chez Pétrarque, la question de savoir qui je suis, peut aussi bien revenir à m'interroger sur ce que je vaux. Le *moi* se demande, *à chaque instant*, dans quelle mesure il est ou il n'est pas admirable, s'il est vrai, comme nous l'avons vu, que le sentiment de la *permanence* pétrarquienne se fonde sur le sentiment fondamental d'une innocence originelle et qui demeure sous-jacente en dépit des aléas qu'elle semble éprouver au cours de l'existence' (Arnaud Tripet, *Pétrarque ou La Connaissance de Soi*, Geneva, 1967, p. 169 [*Travaux d'Humanisme et Renaissance*, XCI]). This 'innocence' may be the state Christian theology would certify, or it may be that 'pudor ingenitus' Ficino discovers in Platonic philosophy (*In Protagoram Epitome* [*Opera*, II, 1299]).

There are many phrases and statements in these early writings of Shakespeare (and more illustrations will be brought forward in the present study) that lead us to work out whatever there is that approaches a philosophic attitude in the writer, and this inevitably obliges us to relate that attitude to contemporary philosophical writing as well as to traditional Christianity. There are some points on which we are certain— Platonic and Christian ideas and beliefs are being exploited. But we always need to discover how much method there is in this exploitation at a particular place, and further, we need to ask if we can learn whether Shakespeare's art rests on particular beliefs. Without attempting a definitive conclusion at this point, I think one must agree that the indications point to the serious acceptance by Shakespeare of philosophical if not theological support of the injunction to self-knowledge.

It is difficult, and often, I suppose, it will remain impossible, to say that at such and such a point Shakespeare is at one with Bruno, or with Ficino as opposed to Castiglione, with the Scholastics, or with a tradition deriving from the School of Chartres. One thing is evident, that his thought is as complex and subtle as his poetry, he is thinking for himself, his conclusions are his own. It is this very independence that makes it so necessary to explore the full range of the traditions in which Platonism and Christianity are engaged with each other, for Shakespeare evidently knows the main lines. Whatever he absorbed from his reading and his associates, he was certainly absorbing the fruits of the speculation of Petrarch and the Platonists and the theologians. His commitments as well as his withholding of commitment are to be understood in the light of the state of thought in Europe. Accordingly, one is not suggesting recondite sources when one surveys writers who may now be almost lost to sight, one is merely attempting to point to the limits of the definition of the general issues. Two works that help greatly may be named: Etienne Gilson, *L'Esprit de la Philosophie Médiévale*, Paris, 1948; and Edgar de Bruyne, *Études d'Esthétique Médiévale*, Bruges, 1946.

It is precisely because such ideas as I am here discussing have been commonplaces in medieval and Renaissance writing that I think it proper to quote a modern writer who, in debating with Sartre and Merleau-Ponty among others, develops something much in harmony with these traditions. I think it important to do this because it is not only the historic context of Shakespeare's use of such ideas that is at issue, it is the question of their philosophic soundness: 'Du premier point de vue, le sujet a pour lui-même un amour d'une qualité unique, fondée sur la perfection incommunicable de son ipséité: il s'aime dans sa subsistence et sa différence, d'un amour qui persiste au milieu des pires désordres et des pires désastres. Si déchu, si avili qu'il puisse être, il reste pour lui-même cet *unique*, que nul autre ne peut remplacer. ("Mon unique," dit l'hébreu, pour dire "mon âme," ce qui équivaut à "moi-même", *myself*.) Du second point di vue, le sujet s'aime lui-même en tant que, ordonné a l'Idéal, il en participe déjà d'une certaine manière. Il habite déjà par l'amour cet Idéal qui le hante et c'est de là qu'il juge et apprécie son moi actuellement donné. Pour l'adolescent, la vraie vie, c'est cette vie encore, "absente" de l'homme qu'il rêve de devenir. L'intervalle qui l'en sépare lui apparaît comme un temps sans valeur, un temps mort.

'Sous l'une et l'autre forme, l'amour de soi—d'un soi qui n'est pas nécessairement celui de l'égoïsme—est à l'horizon . . . de la volonté considerée comme la nature, vérifiant, sur son mode et avec ses ressources propres, la loi de toute nature, qui la fait chercher à être plus et mieux.

Et l'on ne franchit pas cet horizon, on ne passe pas de l'amour de soi à l'amour désintéressé des autres et de Dieu, sans an acte qui nous élève à un niveau supérieur de conscience spirituelle—un acte de libre dilection.

'Ce qu'on retiendra surtout de ces analyses, c'est le rôle de l'idée de perfection dans la philosophie de la valeur. La perfection est vraiment à la charnière de l'ontologie et de l'axiologie. Car le parfait est ce qui accomplit son essence, ce qui est pleinement ce qu'il est—et ceci relève de l'ordre de l'être. Mais le parfait comme tel est désirable, animable et ceci relève de l'ordre du bien' (J. de Finance, *Essai sur l'Agir Humain*, Rome, 1962, pp. 89–90 [*Analecta Gregoriana*, Vol. 126]).

[15] *Diana*, Book IV, pp. 158–9.

[16] *Ibid.*, Book IV, pp. 156–7.

[17] Montemayor uses comparable analogies: 'But what wilt thou have me do, since absence hath frozen the former love, and the continuall presence of a peerelesse beautie rekindled another more hot and fervent in me?' (*Diana*, Book II, p. 97).

[18]   E s'io non posso transformarmi in lei
        Più ch' i' mi sia. . . . (Sonetto LI)
Bruno also has the words 'la cosa amata l'amore converte ne l'amante' (*De gl' Heroici Furori*, edited by P. H. Michel, Paris, 1954, Prima Parte, Dialogo 1, p. 141).
    Something of the range of meaning the Neo-Platonists developed with this figure is indicated in my *Dante, Michangelo and Milton*, London, 1963, pp. 62–5.

[19] *The Heroic Frenzies*, Part II, Dialogue II, p. 225.

[20] *Diana*, Book IV, p. 150.

[21] In the *Diana* Orpheus sings a song in praise of a number of Spanish ladies, and while no one of the stanzas devoted to the individual persons includes all the attributes that are designated as Silvia's in the song heard at the inn in Milan, it may be worth observing that holiness, wisdom, grace, perfection, are terms used again and again, and the superlatives several times suggest the more than mortal—

    Whose grace and beautie hath this day a seate,
    Where humane thought could never reach at all.

That matchlesse beautie sweete and peregrine,
Not seene in any, but in her alone,
Which every wit and soule doth so refine
With holy love, as like was never none.

The light of all the world, the flowre of *Spaine*,
The end of perfect beautie, and of grace.

The Lady Isabell Borja here doth stand
Perfect and absolute in every thing.
                              (*Diana*, Book IV, pp. 145–53)

22 *Ibid.*, p. 157.

23 *Ibid.*, p. 156.

24 This problem is examined by G. J. P. O'Daly, 'The Presence of the One in Plotinus', in *Atti dell' Accademia Nazionale dei Lincei*, October, 1970.

25 I again find the analysis of J. de Finance precisely to the point: 'Je ne puis aimer, en esprit, l'existant que dans son rapport à l'Idéal, mais je ne puis aimer en vérité l'Idéal qu'en l'aimant dans l'existant' (*Essai sur l'Agir Humain*, p. 323).

26 *Shakespeare and Platonic Beauty*, London, 1961, p. 70.

27 *Ibid.*, p. 69.

28 The language with which Julia expresses her longings is much like this and yet the words have so much less of sensual urgency that by contrast at least there seems to arise the suggestion of something like spirituality:

I'll be as patient as a gentle stream,
And make a pastime of each weary step,
Till the last step have brought me to my love;
And there I'll rest, as after much turmoil
A blessèd soul doth in Elysium. (II, vii, 34–8)

29 Bruno brings forward the idea of the metamorphoses of the ancient gods in supporting the idea of Plotinus that the transformation into lower forms was not permanent and that the deities would return to their previous excellent state. A similar question needs to be answered for Shakespeare's Proteus, whether he will be condemned to change after change, or whether, as we hope at the end, he will come to rest in his best existence: '. . . because of the sense of their own dignity, [the gods] recover their

own divine forms; just as the heroic lover, raising himself by his conception of the species of divine beauty and goodness upon the wings of his intellect and intellectual will exalts himself toward the divinity, abandoning the form of [the] more ignoble thing' (*The Heroic Frenzies*, Book I, Dialogue III, pp. 121–2).

30 'Amor enim liber est, ac sua spontè in libera oritur uoluntate: quam neque Deus etiam coget, qui ab initio liberam forè decreuit. Quo fit, ut amor, qui uim omnibus infert, omnium effugiat uiolentiam' (*In Convivium Platonis De Amore Commentarium Oratio Quinta*, cap. VIII [*Opera*, II, 1339]).

31 Berowne is developing the meaning of his earlier phrase, 'angel knowledge' (I, i, 113).

32 J. M. Rist, *Plotinus: The Road to Reality*, Cambridge, 1967, p. 163.

33 *Proœmium in Platonicam Theologiæ Platonicæ*, XVIII, viii (*Opera*, I, 319).

The Henry VI Plays

When Jusserand said of Shakespeare, 'Le beau domine l'œuvre entière', I think he had in mind a purpose as well as an effect, the intent of informing every scene and every word with beauty. We all feel this and we have come to know that we shall meet with it whatever the circumstance—in the scenes of Launcelot Gobbo with his father, of Caliban and Sebastian, of Kate and Petruchio, of Antipholus of Ephesus locked out of doors by a loving wife, of Lear upon the heath. There is such wonder in every naming and in the words given to each character as they become his own that whatever the world they are a part of, it is a brave world, the thought of the day's glorious walk and peaceful night is present in the naming of every day and night, we are taken with beauty in the dungeons of Dunsinane, in the halls of drunkenness in Denmark, in the repulsiveness of Edgar's disguise. This is the same point Geoffrey Bickersteff made about *Lear*, whatever the horror, whatever the slightness, it is a golden world.

> O happy living things! no tongue
> Their beauty might declare:
> A spring of love gush'd from my heart,
> And I bless'd them unaware.

The stamp of Shakespeare is not quite this, although we sense in the imagination and mind and spirit in his words some lucidity we might not mind calling love or even beatitude, but whatever it is it has something to do with the honour paid to things as they

174

are. The teeth of serpents and the wombs of vipers, likenesses stigmatizing the rottenness of humans, always express in whatever they name the character of wonder that alone supports thought. As an Elizabethan might have said, no vapours or exhalations stain the light of his mind, as unimpeded as the Attic light and as lovely.

The words themselves bear every sign of temporality—the fashionable, the archaic, the ornate, the rag-tags of street-talk, the detritus of history and the magnificence of tradition, the savour of politics and theology, and even as they are telling of the actual and the contemporary the thought is as unconfined as air or fire. Having said this one must still believe that over all the words there hovers at least the shadow of their author, for we know of no human work that is free of the character of the one who gave it its form, the bird brooding upon the abyss has left the trace of its passing. It may be God's plenty it has given a life to, but it is less than God's creation. Shakespeare's imagination is immaculate, but to that it adds still another authority, the integrity of the thought of the individual he was. The charm of the work ultimately lies not in its prophetic but in its human character.

The Comedy of Errors, on the face of it so transparent an enterprise, is for just that reason extremely useful in helping us appreciate the generosity with which Shakespeare will let us enjoy what he brings of himself to all he imitates. The play is remarkable in retaining as much of the character of antiquity as it does, so brilliant in the representation of events and particulars, its attention to the external world so faithful that even men's feelings appear to be represented as it were from the outside, with no effort to explain them away, accepting complacently what cannot be explained. These men and women almost come before us without an interpreter as if Shakespeare like the ancients was able to think of the overshadowing sky and the powers above and below the earth more accountable for arranging men's fortunes than the powers within. But this play, of course, as an imitation of an ancient, participating in the humanist aspiration, was inevitably self-conscious and as such it inevitably brought with it some special concerns of the author. Far from disguising this intrusion Shakespeare made a great deal of it, overlaying the yearning in the search for lost kin with nostalgia, introducing into the idea of the happiness of reunion the idea of lasting solace, introducing into the character of the women a marvellous purity.

Being in the English vernacular the play took the opportunity for topical reference. It exploited English folklore to contrast it ironically and poetically with the ancient setting and nonsense, and in the Dromio's in particular, the predecessors of Launce and Speed and so many others, we hear the hubbub of Shoreditch and Cheapside. We get the sense of the vitality of quite a different city than Ephesus even while we think we are also getting a little of the sense of the coast of Asia Minor and an alien and exotic world. And flourishing words as they do, one after another of these ill-disguised Englishmen opens up another life, there are new varieties of mountebank, town fools, spirits out of old wives' tales, neighbourhood witches—common, superstitious, Christian England. All this writing illustrates something that Henri Foçillon spoke of so well, a sense of humanity that is the peculiar achievement of medieval culture: 'There is, of course, a humanism of the humanists, but there is also another, wider in scope, and, one may perhaps say, more sincere, since it owes little to tradition and much more to life itself. The grandeur of its vision of man and of his relationship with the universe is revealed to us in medieval art. It does not present man in isolation. It shows him at grips with the exigencies, the miseries, and the splendours of his destiny. It does not dwell on the bloom of his youth—save when it lays him at last upon his tomb—but shows him at every age, in every condition, toiling, and enduring. The blind man high on Reims cathedral proclaims the twin glories of divine justice and human patience. To the sweetness of the Gospels, to the majesty of theology, the humanism of the images adds the strength of its sympathy for all things living, a wonderful compassion and sincerity and openness of heart. It encompasses all things and sets man in the centre, and this image of God is all humanity.'[1]

I think this is what Dryden had in mind when he spoke of the God's plenty of Chaucer; it is Langland's as well, as comprehensive a sense of creation as in any cathedral; and this is Shakespeare's inheritance, endowing and forming his imagination.

When Shakespeare took to the new ways of thinking and writing—imitating the ancients, absorbing the manners of the Petrarchans and the reasoning of the Neo-Platonists—he found as much that was congenial to his heritage as he found what would transform or erode it. The ancient comedies provided him above all else with a way of plotting. With that he necessarily adopted a manner of detachment inherent in the process of dramatizing the alien and unlikely. As time passed and he absorbed the lessons of the Italian story writers, their secularity gave him the lead to extend the range and implications of the criticisms the act of imitation compounded. The idea of the alien—whether in Ephesus or Navarre or Verona—encouraged when it did not require an unending exploitation of contrasts. In the exchange of one vernacular for another, classical street scenes for familiar ones, ancient romanticism and pieties and allegiances for his own, the very richness of his exploitation of this other world required an equal vitality in putting the ways of the past into a light in which his audience could find its way. His own endowments, theatrical as well as intellectual and religious, the immediate resources of the morality and mystery plays, the jest-books, and any number of literary traditions, all that fed the life of his mind joined with what he was getting from the ancient works, and it was of course modernity that was determining the direction all was to take finally.

As everywhere, the Petrarchan inspiration was fundamental. This gave Shakespeare the impetus towards amplification that countless writers were to explore and extend in the development of style after style, in this century and the next. There was at work in the assimilation of the figures and devices central to Petrarch's love poetry a mentality that was discovering in the plurality of interminable contrasts what might turn out to be the entire province of thought, and indeed what might be equal to the representation of the world of experience, even equal to offering a model of the world itself. It supplied the bridge between the oppositions of experience in the sensations of lovers and the conviction of God's presence in the copiousness of all things—'Dio è nella pienezza della realtà'. In the unending oppositions of hot and cold and day and night and red and white, all that made up nature and experience, reality revealed itself in correspondence with the infinite variety of the life of the soul.[2]

Shakespeare took to this way of thinking and writing from the very beginning. The Petrarchan conventions were to be of primary use in opening the vast conceptions of the sonnets, they were able to introduce him so to speak into the depths of thought precisely because they offered the means of sounding the quality of individual experience. Petrarch exploited the appeal to experience most searchingly in love lyrics, and even as the writers of *novelle* and dramas assimilated what he had taught them in their own forms the fundamental character of lyrical expression asserted itself in their relations of the struggles and joys of love. So the lords and ladies of Montemayor and Sidney and Shakespeare are, as it were, always removing themselves from the currents of their adventures to come forth singly upon the scene to utter in some self-dramatizing way the correspondence of their feelings to the world in which they are enmeshed.

The Petrarchan method was evidently the means of releasing a sustaining and productive energy of extraordinary authority. When in succeeding years the Neo-Platonists contributed their enthusiasm and understanding to the newly forming civilization, effecting, as Garin put it, the renewal of the inner life, they were in effect renewing for poetry and thought the Petrarchan inspiration.

So I think we may look at the first comedies particularly to learn how Shakespeare was bringing together what he had learned at his mother's knee, as Professor H. T. Price used to speak of it, with the new learning and the new society. Whatever the accommodation, the fundamental conflict between Christian faith and pagan pessimism would continue to erupt. Thought was not to be pursued very far by him before the inadequacies of both medieval and Platonic philosophy made themselves known, not so much when confronted with new forms of materialism and even a secular temper as in meeting with the problem of evil. The elaborations of Platonic reasoning were not making up for the deficiencies they exposed in scholastic thinking, and if anything the grounds for despair grew in the face of this inadequate optimism, inadequate to account for the fallings-off of men as well as for the violations of body and soul the universe itself so casually and unceasingly contrived. But until the collapse, or the rejuvenation, the new ways filled thought with enthusiasm and the imagination with all but inexhaustible joy.

We see Shakespeare in these first years taken up with the example of Roman comedy, the beauty of music and of masque-like entertainments, with romances, with the delights of philosophy, and then we see him at the same time intent upon the meanest as well as the grandest details in the matter of England, intent upon what the historic past meant for the life of his own people. We see many of the same matters—perfidy and perjury, the mistaking of love, the failure to deserve trust, the quest for perfection. In the actions of the histories, however, rather than love, the thirst for power is the governing impetus. The relatively small crises of groups of young people and a couple of families give way to the conflicts of a people at war with itself. The matter of history is putting the new culture to a test.

As the writings accumulate we begin to believe that the character of the beauty of it all is implicit in each fragment, the beauty of the fullness of the creation is the same beauty we meet with in the accent of every speech. We understand very well that in his embrace Shakespeare was taking in more and more as time went on, but we see, too, that even what was most comprehending was present in the tone of the beginning. We see his thought taking different forms and we see the truths in them changing as they remain themselves. When Valentine, in the

forest of the brigands, speaks these lovely words in which he
dreams of a pastoral happiness—

> This shadowy desert, unfrequented woods,
> I better brook than flourishing peopled towns—
> (*The Two Gentlemen of Verona*, V, iv, 2-3)

we are reminded of Henry's longing for a shepherd's life and all
that the words express of the Christian's contempt for the
world—

> O God! methinks it were a happy life,
> To be no better than a homely swain.
> (*III Henry VI*, II, v, 21-3)

So much that is the same, and yet in those different 'betters',
different worlds. The likenesses proceed almost as if by rote, and
yet the range of meaning expands apparently endlessly—something like Nemesis taking different forms and yet recognizably
itself in Berowne's humour, in Julia's trusting, in Gloucester's
virtuousness, in Joan of Arc where vilest things become themselves.

Accordingly, we continually return to the conviction that this
elaborate achievement is as much of a piece in the variety as in
the likenesses, in the sense of the expansiveness of life, and as
much in the juggling with words in *The Comedy of Errors* as in
the scope of *Henry VI*. The innumerable echoes as words and
ideas sound back and forth tell us of the richness of texture that
belongs to every word. We see variations on the same themes,
the origin and character of evil and suffering, the fineness and
tenacity of love—but it is the variety in the representation that
counts for as much, the variety and what we make of it as variety.
I think Jusserand is right in speaking of the beauty of this work
as residing in the bounteousness of imagination the drama of the
Middle Ages expressed: 'on est frappé de l'incroyable vie et du
sentiment qui animent ce théâtre. Dans la boue et la poussière,

d'un éclat aussi vif que celle d'aucun théâtre et d'aucune littérature. Ni Shakespeare, ni personne, n'a fait mieux.'³ In Shakespeare there is something more as well, this also owing much to the Middle Ages and the philosophy of creation although the aesthetics is ultimately Aristotle's: 'Every realm of nature is marvellous: and as Heraclitus, when the strangers who came to visit him found him warming himself at the furnace in the kitchen and hesitated to go in, is reported to have bidden them not to be afraid to enter, as even in that kitchen divinities were present, so we should venture on the study of every kind of living thing without distaste; for each and all will reveal to us something natural and something beautiful. Absence of haphazard and conduciveness of everything to an end are to be found in Nature's works in the highest degree, and the end that results from her generations and combinations is a form of the beautiful.'⁴

The difference was always to be as it was with the imitation of Plautus, in the charm of Christianity, in the idea of a world held together not only by purpose in all its parts and their harmony with each other but where the parts are transfigured by their participation in still another concert. Such a sense, I believe, informs the naming of every particular, unlike the naming of the flowers and stones and men and women in Greek poetry and in Catullus and that whole other world. The naming of

> daisies pale and violets blue,
> And lady-smocks all silver white,

brings with it the same wonder and something of the same strange splendour of

> To her let us garlands bring;

something of the wonder of Richard's

> like one lost in a thorny wood,
> That rends the thorns and is rent with the thorns.
> (*III Henry VI*, III, ii, 174–5)

In every word there is the sense of a lovely seamless world abiding the most horrible intrusions.

MAN BORN TO RENOWN BY LIFE OR DEATH

If Shakespeare began with comedy, he would have been turning away from that from time to time to writing the histories. Or it might have been the other way around, but whichever it was, in view of the scope of the plays that were to be treating of the story of England from the death of Henry V to the ruin of Richard III, one knows that his mind was continuously absorbed in this ambitious enterprise, the dramatization of the full sweep of the struggle for power in England for more than half a century.

In important ways the histories would be preparing Shakespeare for the tragedies to come, although the form he was finding for the comedies would be contributing to all his dramatic work, and the Ovidian poetry he was writing at this time would also be pointing towards the tragedies. One might go farther, blessed as we are with hindsight, to believe that his imagination in its earliest life was already carrying the burden not only of the tragedies but of the final comedies, and indeed the points of similarity between *The Comedy of Errors* and *The Tempest*, to mention only one matter, are truly astonishing. It is not so much that his like anyone's work can be shown to grow from embryos harbouring the future. This universal judgment is rewarding although dangerously misleading when we apply it to a work where the scope is so vast. Yet there is a certain need to understand how Shakespeare, in turning from comedy to history to mythological poetry to love poems, was fired not only by the sense of the wealth of life and of thought but also by the sense of the relations among all the things that were attracting him and leading him on, by the sense not only of variety but of unfolding. His thought was advancing, his perceptions were going deeper, he was mastering more and more skills, and all this was not merely accretion. His thought was growing into new forms, and even when he returned to a device or a technique or a theme or even an image, it became something else as well. And all the while he was discovering with each change whole worlds he could not have guessed were there.

As we try to discover what there is of unity in this vast achievement we take up certain likenesses in the handling of forms, certain similar and sometimes identical expressions and ideas, certain comparable effects, but even as we examine the smallest detail it turns out to be so rich and many-sided we arc almost prevented at the start from going farther. Nevertheless, we progress. The Henry VI plays, for example, bring so much before us that we are tempted to believe they make almost everything that can be made of the idea of kingship and of the ferocity and intricacy of ambition, matching the all but inexhaustible life in the ambition of humanity with the sense of the greater power of death. One may not wish to call these plays tragedies, and it may be that it is not until *Romeo and Juliet* and *Julius Caesar* that we have the economy that term seems to call for. But we do know that even in those works in which the ordering is apparently the simplest—*Titus Andronicus*, say—the apparently simple is accompanied by a luxuriance that we take for profligacy itself. And when, in *A Midsummer Night's Dream*, or *Lear*, we find elaborate, manifold plotting, the humorous mingled with the terrible, the unearthly with the commonplace, we know we shall soon be discovering that somehow all is under control, there is a principle at work, not so clearly to be defined as Hamlet's 'temperance in the very whirlwind of the passions', but certainly in command. It does not lead to the close and visible articulation of many a dramatic action, but it would be a mistake to suppose that it is not providing a form for the Henry VI plays, a life-giving form. In *The Comedy of Errors* there comes a time when we almost despair of coming upon anything that could bring order into the confusion overwhelming everyone, but the means of clearing it up were always present and when the time was ripe they were brought to bear and all confusion vanished. We in the audience are delighted with the resolution, for we are persuaded that the very surprise in the untangling belongs with the wonder with which it all began. In a less formalized way, the idea of a shaping power at work in the phantasmagoria of the Henry VI plays makes itself known to us thematically and also through the resolutions appropriate to drama. The effect in the conclusion we recognize also as having its origin in the way in which it began, led up to unforeseeably and yet as it had to be. Whether the threee plays make a trilogy, or whether they require *Richard III* as their conclusion, they present themselves as a single co-ordinated movement ending in satisfaction.

If there are commonnesses between the comedies and the history plays there are also interactions, and it is probably impossible to say which is an outgrowth of the other. In *Love's Labour's Lost* one may properly assert that Armado, Coster, and Moth owe their presence in the play in part to Lyly's example, who introduced into his comedies not only members of contrasting classes but persons engaged in minor actions that reflected upon as well as merely reflected the interests of the chief persons. In the Henry VI plays there are many comparable contrasts, persons and entire episodes set off against each other. The introduction of twin servants into *The Comedy of Errors* may have owed to Plautus and Terence and Lyly and it may have owed to certain pairings in the history plays. Much of course is free invention, and similar practices may have come from wholly unlikely suggestions. The main point, of course, is that they are being put to widely different uses. But in the long run we are probably justified in believing that the Plautine form is everywhere asserting its usefulness, and that it will take hold in the histories wherever intrigue is sustained, that it will contribute to the management of *Lear* as well as to *Twelfth Night* and *The Tempest*. It will help serve the richest interests of all, and even as one says this one is reminded that the distinctive conception of the history play as such will contribute its value to the later works, and we remember, for an instance, the very title, *The History of Hamlet, Prince of Denmark*.

There is an interesting comparison to be made in the ways in which the comedies and the histories commence.

The first comedies begin with scenes in the life of noblemen— a place of judgment, a palace where a king is determining policy, a place in which gentlemen speak of preparing for life at the Court of the Emperor. (*The Taming of the Shrew* stands out by contrast for the outrageous Plautus-like raucousness—'I'll pheeze you, in faith!') The speech is formal, the manners elevated. What follows, however, has relatively little to do with majesty and power, and the plays are soon treating chiefly with matters of private concern. Though the circumstances are sometimes strange and wonderful, our interest is directed towards the personal affairs of young people not much out of the ordinary.

Their business becomes so complicated, however, that it can hardly be straightened out by ordinary means. We are forced to hope that the troubles and confusions will be cleared up, and they are such that we cannot expect a simply arbitrary intercession to bring this off, so we find ourselves looking for some other means of rectification, and these, it turns out, only fancy can provide. In no time at all we become convinced that we shall not be able to rely on likely consequences to save these baffled and troubled persons caught up in their entanglements, but we are being so driven to hope for a happy outcome that we become disposed to accept any logic however preposterous that will shape events to the conclusions our sympathies require. In short, even though these plays commence with scenes stamped with a certain authenticity, as if we were to be concerned with affairs in the great world where justice and truth and honour receive their full due, we are very shortly demanding the satisfactions that only fiction can supply. And this even though these plays continue to owe something to that initial authorization of events supposed to be indeed taking place in Ephesus and Navarre and Verona. The suggestion of historicity will beguile us throughout the plays, the more so since the scenes are often splendid with the splendour of truth and true nobility, a loveliness that as it persists will even help give credence to the splendour of the happiness with which the fanciful conclusions end.

Something gets under way as it were understandably, in circumstances not too far from actual happenings, but the final events include not only what could not have been foreseen but suggestions of something like magic, or at least of another kind of life than the play has shown us heretofore. In the course of things there have been many twists and turns to surprise us, but nothing so strange as those at the end that alone, it appears, could have enabled the lost to be restored, love to become happily established, and peace to reign. The plots, it seems, have to do not merely with love but with romantic love, and not only with marriages but with aspirations bordering on the eternal, and the happy endings sometimes bring before us vistas not only of larks at heaven's gate but of felicity itself. The satisfactions are sometimes those of the Patient Griselda and Giletta of Narbonne and Daphnis, and they are sometimes those of Cupid and Psyche.

Yet the nature of the concluding happiness also owes significantly to the character of the feeling in the beginning scenes, incidents in which there is mentioned the possibility of eternal doom effected through the execution of justice on earth; or in which thought is being given to setting up something like a society for the preparation of philosopher-kings in the refusal of all diversion; or we are induced to picture a life of perfection and imperial power. As events followed, the majestic and the noble gave place to the common and even the profane, philosophy gave way to common sense, ambition gave way to resignation, and yet the air of splendour and greatness and even of the holy was maintained.

The early histories begin similarly with formalities of at least as great importance for the effects to be attained finally. The First Part of *Henry VI* opens with the funeral of Henry V, and some substantial part of the ceremony would be enacted. The Second Part opens with a magnificent scene in which in the presence of all the Court Gloucester begins the reading of the articles of the marriage contract of Henry and Margaret. The

Third Part opens with York moving forward to take his seat upon the throne in Parliament House. All these beginnings are emphatic in calling attention to the plays as re-enactments of history, that is, as the representation of what indeed did take place, and in this of course is their radical difference from the comedies. In those the opening is to lead into matters that accord with the intention of the author as a writer of fiction. In the histories the openings prepare for conclusions that follow in accord with patterns thrown up out of the very processes of time itself, the patterns of doom, with whatever of general import accompanies them in the faithfulness of their imitation. Set beside each other, the two kinds of openings give the other a new dimension.

There is a special character to the formality in the introduction to the histories that is peculiarly significant and this by virtue of the representation of ceremony. Ceremonies are by nature deliberate, slow, and complete. They are useless unless they are perfect, in form and in meaning. The last thing they can tolerate is interruption. Neither can they permit extrinsic appeals—beauty as such, or drama—to divert attention from their movement towards completion, and even their conclusion, as a climax, may not detract from the demonstration of continuity. All must be unfaltering, and as it were a halting of time.

True ceremony cannot be incorporated in drama for it exists only for itself, but a replica, a representation of a particular ceremonial act, one that has been performed in the past in particular circumstances, can be, and, inevitably, will be re-enacted ironically for it is known as an imitation and as such it demands to become part of another action in time that has not been stopped. The remembrance of the particular occasion must intrude upon it, even interrupting it, for our interest in the re-enactment is focused not on the ceremony but on the circumstances it was originally devised to meet with.

True ceremony arrests time while it brings to fruition the efforts of man or nature or God. It plots the future as it sanctifies the present. But in the re-enactment the irony changes all, for in light of subsequent circumstances, which are so much in our minds as we watch the reconstruction, we are certain above all else that time was not stopped, the future was not well enough plotted, and in fact time has defied what would have confined it. The fact of re-enactment is a sign that what we are now to behold is what the womb of time brought forth to honour and dishonour the ceremony. The re-enactment points to what is to happen to the ministers and the objects of the celebration, and in effect it brings scorn upon the Prometheus-like claims that were made. And whereas in the comedies the beginning in the representation of pretension at the centre of power prepares us for a certain splendour and seriousness in the ending, in the histories the magnificent pretensions of ceremony by the irony of its re-enactment prepare us for the folly of all pretension that the drama will have demonstrated as it comes to its end. Edward, newly King, concludes the Third Part of *Henry VI* with words we know to be the perfection of ignorance—

> For here, I hope, begins our lasting joy.

The conclusion of *Richard III* with its call to a sacrament—

> And then, as we have ta'en the sacrament,
> We will unite the White Rose and the Red—
> (V, v, 18–19)

but renews our knowledge of the impermanence of peace and comfort. Yet there also persists something of the solemnity and religious awe of the original ceremoniousness, not everything is obliterated in the irony, for time has not ended in complete destruction, what was celebrated continues to demand to be recognized, and hope continues to make ordinary men feel like anointed kings.

Another important practice the histories and comedies share is the alternation of persons in succeeding scenes. Accustomed as we are to the device, it is nevertheless worth remarking on. In

188

The Two Gentlemen of Verona, for example, after the scene between Valentine and Proteus, there is one with Julia and Lucetta. In the First Part of *Henry VI*, after the scene in London following the funeral of Henry V, the next scene is in France where the French and English are warring. Shakespeare habitually exploits disjunction as preparation for an eventual focus on many matters at once. He very often avoids presenting scenes that follow in causal necessity from the immediately preceding, and he uses many pretexts to introduce more and more persons and matters of different substance, as it were to forestall too direct an approach to the resolution of the central action. No doubt this is the way of a writer who wishes nothing to come before us that is not resonant with the richest effects, and he takes the risk of causing us to lose our way before he lets us know that everything is indeed in its proper place and that, as we learn what is following, we shall welcome it as falling into the place in which it belongs. Each play of course will have its own order for filling out the complexities of relationship that are the drama, and accordingly the specific function the second scene serves will vary from play to play. But in observing this practice here as elsewhere we are observing what is central to Shakespeare's style and art—variety, complication, and, through disjunction, irony. The first scene in *The Two Gentlemen of Verona* shows us two friends expressing different attitudes towards love. The second shows us a young woman whose behaviour is revealing love's power over her. It is as important as it can be that very quickly we shall understand the nature of what is possessing Julia to her very being, and how that differs from the manner of love's possession of Proteus, but it will not be till towards the end that we shall understand the import of that difference, for we shall also need to know what love means to Silvia and Valentine and Sir Eglamour and Launce. The varieties and complications of the relationships and actions create as it were a succession of ideas each more comprehensive than the last until finally all comes to the completion of an idea that is rounded off in conjunction with the ending of the action.

At the beginning of the First Part of *Henry VI* we see the English leaders falling out among themselves as they learn of the defeats being inflicted upon their forces in France. In the second scene we see the French in disarray, taking up in desperation with a sorceress. We can anticipate that both scenes must lead to other tests of strength between opponents, but what Bedford or Gloucester or Regnier or Alençon or Joan is to have to do with all that is going on we cannot guess. We are particularly uncertain how the rivalries among the English that are so much stressed are to influence not only the war but the holding of the crown. Yet before the play ends we shall understand that every one of these persons is contributing to a single, embracing movement, and that here too everything is falling into its place, the beginning scene being what it was. It may be that we shall decide that here or there a scene could be dispensed with, and certainly in the histories there is a greater danger of the superfluous than in the comedies. But the modifications of chronology—for example, advancing the siege of Orleans by seven years, the anticipation of Suffolk's wooing of Margaret—as well as pure invention—the Iden story—are indications enough of Shakespeare's ordering of the whole, that limits are being placed upon what in life itself might have seemed impertinent.

As it happens, in these two plays the third scene introduced still other matters and persons also in a not uncharacteristic way, but sooner or later a deed here, a word there, a decision, the return of one of the persons we have already met will pick up from something brought before us earlier, and more and more consequences will become evident as such and will be pointing to still others on the threshold, some of them implicit and foreseeable, until finally there will come a scene in which the fortunes of all the major persons are coming to a head. In *The Two Gentlemen of Verona* this occurred in the last scene when Julia's disguise is discovered and the final match-making takes place. In the First Part of *Henry VI* this occurs in the last two scenes when the English and the French make their treaty and the King agrees to the marriage with Margaret.

The great difference in the management of the so similar methods is that in one the playwright makes his controlling intention known to us, and his doing so is part of the interest and amusement. In the other, the intention is concealed, with the result that any pattern that does come forward, of disconnectedness, of the unexpected, of confusion, will take on only such meaning as the flux of time itself might be thought to justify.

The comedies present us with events falling into patterns, whether in causal sequence or in pointed contrasts, or according to any number of principles that serve the purposes of drama. Ideas and their inner coherence, the play and variety of character itself, spectacle and music all contribute to the pleasure we take in seeing how all belongs together. In these first comedies the patterns often call themselves to our attention as obviously formalized, and in any event they are seldom lost sight of however attractive the play of life and thought and colour. And indeed it may be that comedy as such will normally depend on maintaining for us a sharply distinct idea of the very form the action is taking, distinct in order that at one and the same moment we may observe the degree to which what is before us is both conforming and failing to conform to the way events occur in the world we live in. In short, the early comedies are like most others in making claims for verisimilitude even while they are otherwise delighting fancy.

Which is to say that the matter of the plays is limited in order that it may be conducive to this kind of management. As we know, the plays are mainly concerned with love and friendship, to a less extent with family affection, and chiefly among the young. The key limitation set upon these concerns derives from the all but complete exclusion of the claims of power and ambition upon men and women in the actual world. By and large the young persons of the comedies are leading charmed lives.

Yet there will be pointed reminders of the claims life itself is always making. In the last comedies of all the romantic matter will be penetrated through and through with the most serious concerns there are, but in these early ones the claims of the world itself will be represented, chiefly through philosophy and through the frame in which we are to be contemplating the patterns of comedy. The world of a comprehensive actuality is acknowledged in the scene of judgment in *The Comedy of Errors*, in the edict of the King as King in *Love's Labour's Lost*, in the background of the Emperor's Court in *The Two Gentlemen of Verona*. After the initial reminder the world of authority and rule is essentially excluded from the main body of the plays, to return only in the conclusion, to remind us once more of all that is determining the limits in the matter before us.

As we know, even actions so circumscribed by artifice can raise issues and concerns of the greatest interest, but even when the full resources of the Greek and medieval romances and *novelle* are drawn on, the kinds of events comedy offers are inevitably so limited, the imbroglios, the intrigues, the separations and reunions among friends and lovers allow for such restricted possibilities, that ideas of pattern and form can be clearly maintained, as they must be, and they can therefore dominate attention and achieve clearly definable effects.

In the histories, however, rule and the ambition to rule are the major concerns of the chief persons, who are generally grown men and women in fullest vigour. All else—love, friendship, religion—is incorporated in the more comprehensive interests and passions required for obtaining and maintaining power. In the representation of consuming ambitions thought and policy are laid before us as required by philosophy as well as practice, lives are at stake, death is the common lot, and rivalries without end are passed on from generation to generation. The strife is so fierce, so unceasing, the violence so unending, that no law whatever seems to be setting any limit upon the struggles. Failure succeeds failure, all successes are temporary. In retrospect the audience, as many of the persons caught up in the action, is led to think that this is as it is fated to be, although the dreams and prophecies and premonitions never themselves convince us that a pattern of fate is truly manifest in the turmoil. What we at least become sure of is that time appears to be passing endlessly, that multitudes of persons of the greatest stature and energy give their full strength to manage fortune, and that for all their greatness and even splendour they are like those other great ones that ebb and flow by the moon, in themselves no more capable of being trammelled up than time itself, the most elusive energy of all.

So, for the writer of drama, the problem becomes one of discovering, if not a pattern within this flood, the basis for at least an idea of order in reality, coherent within itself in measuring the apparently endless and formless flow of human life:

> The gaudy, blabbing and remorseful day
> Is crept into the bosom of the sea,
> And now loud-howling wolves arouse the jades,
> That drag the tragic melancholy night;
> Who, with their drowsy, slow, and flagging wings
> Clip dead men's graves, and from their misty jaws
> Breathe foul contagious darkness in the air.
>
> (*II Henry VI*, IV, i, 1–7)

To give the effect of form, history presenting him with the material it does and allowing him but limited license, Shakespeare draws on the full resources of irony, no doubt the single instrument adequate to the demands of probability that arise when form is imposed upon the formless. Certainly in drama this was the hallowed means of revealing patterns within the inchoate. The point and the tone are set immediately. The moment the funeral is ended Bedford breaks forth with words that repudiate the spirit of the ceremony he has just witnessed, opposing to that effort, to certify Heaven's blessing upon the dynasty, a call for a revolt in Heaven against the powers that have brought this terrible change to England, calling in blind rage for other changes:

Hung be the heavens with black, yield day to night!
Comets, importing change of times and states,
Brandish your crystal tresses in the sky,
And with them scourge the bad revolting stars
That have consented unto Henry's death!

(I Henry VI, I, i, 1–5)

Whirl is to be king. Fate follows no law, only passion; fury springs from ceremony; what has no end forms a pattern that is repeated endlessly.

But just as the early comedies differ in their ordering in accord with their matter, so the histories, at one time proceed in presenting a mosaic of parallel and contrasting scenes, at another a series of consecutive events; at another a whole drama in little is permitted to interrupt the rest. I think it is impossible to detect in these a unifying structural principle as one may even in so unorthodox a work as *Julius Caesar*, yet anyone who has seen the series in the theatre is aware of an effect that can only be ascribed to a unifying conception. It would be pleasant to be able to appeal to Bishop Hurd's notion of unity of design, the principle in Gothic art he opposed to the classical idea of unity, but this calls for a symmetrical ordering not to be discovered in this work. The idea of the *non finito* in one or another interpretation might also be proposed, not as characterizing a work whose perfection is supplied through suggestion but as one deliberately distorted in order to bring to mind the idea of reality as similarly imperfect. For my part I think the most reasonable way of accounting for a certain failure in co-ordination is to suppose that the work outgrew itself so to speak, that it took on a larger burden of meaning than Shakespeare anticipated, and that as its burden grew larger, as events came to throw light on wider and wider prospects, he was obliged to bring into play techniques and conventions other than those he began with, that in themselves might have been adequate to a more limited drama. Whole blocks of scenes would have been composed before the possibilities of this growing conception became clear and before they were subjected to the discipline it called for. There are, then, incoherences, irrelevances, awkwardnesses, most noticeably in the first two parts, although nothing, I think, alien to the final conception and indeed serving it well enough. So that when—certainly not later than Henry's sacrifice of his son's claim to the throne—the work moves forward to conclude in the irony of Edward's last words the drama has attained such impetus that the earlier hesitancies are lost sight of.

But however one approaches this question, one characteristic of the ending effect is certain—for all the crowding and horror and the demonstration of the tireless energy of evil, we have come to rest in awe. Had this been largely inchoate and predominantly sensational we should have been depleted and depressed. Instead we are as it were sustained, even elevated. We have supped on horror, and yet the conviction of dignity and greatness survives to put the rest in the shade. Something abides the sound and fury, the infinite variety being something other than chaos even as the idea of the infinitude of horror persists.

For one thing, at the centre of works about men struggling to get and hold power, there is the representation of men of almost unimaginable energy. And when at the very beginning the action explodes, we discover as powerful an energy in the language and in the thought. There is no more restraint to the imagining than to the events as first Bedford, then Gloucester and Exeter and Winchester, and then the Dauphin and Alençon and Regnier and Joan come striding like colossi into the theatre. The crowding of the scene, the changes from Court to battlefield, from England to France and back, quarrels pouring over the stage, tirades, conspiracies, pantomimes even, nothing it appears will restrict this bodying forth of half the creatures of earth and hell, as if Shakespeare were no more fearful of what a stage could hold than of the world. It is as if he were luxuriating in his power to conceive, as if his imagination were as vast as the spirit in the race of England in its unending enterprise of quarrel and slaughter and dignity, as if it dared him to make it known for what it was. The bounty of his conception is such, the power over thought and language so magnanimous in its prodigality, discovering within himself the power of a giant he endows his images with that same power.

Bedford's first words pour drapes in great black folds from the sky, blotting out the stars; Gloucester conjures up a history of the dead King,

> His arms spread wider than a dragon's wings;
> (*I Henry VI*, I, i, 11)

and Exeter meets that language by magnifying it—

> We mourn in black; why mourn we not in blood? (17)

We may call it rant, we may withhold credit in the grief and passion of men speaking in this way, but we must not overlook the main matter, that nothing is being thought of in anything but the largest terms, that these are giants speaking the language of giants:

> Instead of gold we'll offer up our arms,
> Since arms avail not now that Henry's dead.
> Posterity, await for wretched years,
> When at their mothers' moistened eyes babes shall suck,
> Our isle be made a nourish of salt tears,
> And none but women left to wail the dead. (47–51)

With the third act the action moves forward with the power of a flood, the culmination is preparing, and the language matches it with still more force. York is at bay, his enemies are coming in for the kill. Thought could not be more crowded with images than this is—

> Now Phaëton hath tumbled from his car,
> And made an evening at the noontide prick.

My ashes, as the phoenix, may bring forth
A bird that will revenge upon you all;
And in that hope I throw mine eyes to heaven.

So cowards fight when they can fly no further;
So doves do peck the falcon's piercing talons.

Come, make him stand upon this molehill here
That raught at mountains with outstretchèd arms.

What, hath thy fiery heart so parched thine entrails
That not a tear can fall for Rutland's death?

O tiger's heart wrapped in a woman's hide!
How couldst thou drain the lifeblood of the child,
To bid the father wipe his eyes withal,
And yet be seen to bear a woman's face?

Off with his head, and set it on York gates,
So York may overlook the town of York.
                    (*III Henry VI*, I, iv)

In all the turmoil there will now and then come a moment
when we feel we have got at the heart of it all. Queen Margaret is
exhorting her followers to make the last effort as failure reaches
out for her. She speaks clearly and deliberately but fiercely,
betraying no uncertainty, even relishing the humour of disaster:

And what is Edward but a ruthless sea?
What Clarence but a quicksand of deceit?
And Richard but a ragged fatal rock?
All these the enemies to our poor bark.
Say you can swim—alas, 'tis but a while!
Tread on the sand—why, there you quickly sink!
Bestride the rock—the tide will wash you off,
Or else you famish: that's a threefold death.
This speak I, lords, to let you understand,
If case some one of you would fly from us,

That there's no hoped-for mercy with the brothers
More than with ruthless waves, with sands and rocks.
Why, courage then! What cannot be avoided
'Twere childish weakness to lament or fear.

The young Prince Edward takes it all in. The words have kindled him even though he recognizes he is not yet the man he needs to be. He sees what there is of device in what she is saying, but he sees in it too what the hunchback could not have seen any more clearly as he hits upon the one word, magnanimity, that distinguishes her ferocity:

Methinks a woman of this valiant spirit
Should, if a coward heard her speak these words,
Infuse his breast with magnanimity,
And make him, naked, foil a man at arms.
(*III Henry VI*, V, iv, 25–42)

With such words the very image of fierceness takes on body and breath; as it is again and again, the least particular brings with it such force and life that we come to appreciate the effectiveness of the work in the crowding of energy, so like the crowding of chaos we hardly ask for a more shaping pattern.

In the comedies it is mostly young men and women who hold the stage, here it is grown men and women in their pride who bring their resources into play. We have before us always the character of tested bravery exerting itself against greater and greater strength, weighing choices as those prepared to pay the heaviest prices, never hesitating to wager the highest stakes. When in the First Part Talbot tears the garter from Falstaff—

this fact was infamous
And ill beseeming any common man,
Much more a knight, a captain, and a leader—
(*I Henry VI*, IV, i, 30–2)

we are breathing the air of those whose deeds match their words, who bring all their force to bear as if there were no such thing as fear. Even the King, himself no warrior, must honour this tone in life—

> Be packing, therefore, thou that was a knight. (46)

The plays make all they can of the manner of men accustomed to power, as men exulting in their manhood, as commanders, sure of the authority of race, joying in insolence. They can and do descend to bickering, they can justly accuse each other of pettiness, quarrelling over a straw, and in intrigue every meanness hostility can invent will dishonour them as it will even in combat where at least some of them will slay children. But even at their ugliest they retain the manner of royalty, hate itself never destroys their grace, and they are never more graceful than in the hatred of death. I think that throughout it is the constant presence of men of large spirit that as such accounts not only for the interest of these plays but for the satisfaction they give us. The idea of what deserves to be indomitable continues to hold us in admiration even as all ends in the foolish vaunting of a clan who in themselves increasingly inspire contempt.

> My sons, God knows that hath bechancèd them:
> But this I know, they have demeaned themselves
> Like men born to renown by life or death.
> Three times did Richard make a lane to me,
> And thrice cried, 'Courage, father! fight it out!'
> And full as oft came Edward to my side,
> With purple falchion painted to the hilt
> In blood of those that had encountered him:
> And when the hardiest warriors did retire,
> Richard cried, 'Charge! and give no foot of ground!'
> And cried, 'A crown, or else a glorious tomb!
> A scepter, or an earthly sepulcher!'
>
> *(III Henry VI*, I, iv, 6–17)

When Margaret comes to taunt York, the language brings even more of the universe—moles reach at mountains, the heat in the body dries up the very entrails, a woman becomes a tiger, the gates of mercy open. Heaven takes its place beside Hell.

Largeness of spirit and vision is the phrase one continually falls back on, every one of these power-mad and Christian warriors has it, their God is the God of majesty not least in His mercy, but most of all the poet himself is endowing the entire representation with this sense of his own magnificent power, bringing forth one after another of the figures from history, from the laboured writing of the chronicles, into the fully peopled world, their own minds themselves peopled with all the creatures, all the memories, all the thoughts of Christendom.[5]

In this one scene, as in any number of others, we get the sense of 'the vast variety of hell' and of the earth. There is nowhere a comparable sense of the energy of the love of the Christian God even though Henry would appeal to Him, but there is a light shed upon this infinity of detail that owes more to religion than to understanding. If the mere energy of war redeems war, some love of splendour in the language redeems the horror. Nothing is cold or bare, nothing is merely lucid, there is none of the cold particularity we have come to know through Stendahl and Flaubert—

> That face of his the hungry cannibals
> Would not have touched, would not have stained with
>   blood.
> (*III Henry VI*, I, iv, 152–5)

> Look, as I blow this feather from my face,
> And as the air blows it to me again,
> Obeying with my wind when I do blow,
> And yielding to another when it blows,
> Commanded always by the greater gust—
> (*III Henry VI*, III, i, 84–8)

In the first parts the artifice is often bare, the language plain and bold, but there too it is as if all it speaks of is cherished simply because it exists:

> Myself, as far as I could well discern
> For smoke and dusky vapors of the night,
> Am sure I scared the Dolphin and his trull,
> When arm in arm they both came swiftly running,
> Like to a pair of loving turtle-doves
> That could not live asunder day or night.
>
> (*I Henry VI*, II, ii, 26–31)

> My tongue should stumble in mine earnest words;
> Mine eyes should sparkle like the beaten flint;
> Mine hair be fixed an end, as one distract;
> Ay, every joint should seem to curse and ban:
> And even now my burdened heart would break,
> Should I not curse them. (*II Henry VI*, III, ii, 316–21)

There is a similar simplicity in some of the stage action, as when Margaret comes on the scene holding to her breast the severed head of Suffolk, and in the scene: 'Enter a Son that hath killed his father at one door; and a Father that has killed his Son at another door.' The effort is not to revolt us but to hold our attention with the respect passion as much as thought owes to all circumstance. The largeness of imagination that can pay such heed to the smallest particulars, daisies pied and Dick the shepherd and the face the hungry cannibals would not touch, like charity itself is not to be measured. Given its rein in the matter of history, imagination of this character can only be thought of as the imagination of charity.

By whatever means, the representation of historic events in which the great-souled oppose all their strength to fortune centres on civil conflict. The substantial matter is civil war, and whatever parts magnificence and magnanimity play in it, a world is being ravaged, families are torn apart, the mighty, the weak, the innocent are being destroyed. Piety and patriotism and religion are defamed, yet no more than the warriors themselves are we led to disprise virtue and beauty. The greatness, even in destruction and even in folly, we continue to love as greatness. Even Richard knows it is not all there is to honour, it is merely that life without greatness is unthinkable.

A single interest, ambition, is everywhere at work, insatiable. There are some who set restraints upon it, and these we recognize as virtuous men—Henry, Gloucester, Iden. In some the ambition that is limitless is for glory rather than for power, and sometimes it is for King and country and righteousness rather than aggrandizement, but in most it admits no such direction. In the many struggles defeats are inevitable, but for the virtuous, the ones who limit their ambitiousness, the defeats come more surely, as if the implacable processes of destruction had been set into motion earlier than they might have been by attempts at moderation.

But these are men, whatever is said of Richard and Margaret, this is not yet 'the wilderness of tigers' of *Titus Andronicus*, these men fight as the members of noble families. When Henry reminds Salisbury that in defecting he is violating the oath of allegiance, an oath made before God, the reply is something other than casuistry:

> It is great sin to swear unto a sin,
> But greater sin to keep a sinful oath.
> Who can be bound by any sinful vow
> To do a mur'drous deed, to rob a man,
> To force a spotless virgin's chastity,
> To reave the orphan of his patrimony,
> To wring the widow from her customed right,
> And have no other reason for this wrong
> But that he was bound by a solemn oath?
>
> (*II Henry VI*, V, i, 182–90)

He has been persuaded that Henry is not in the legitimate line of succession, and that he, as a true man, is bound to honour the ties of blood before all else. He changes masters because he now believes the line of legitimacy is York's, and this is no mere abstraction in his mind, it is a line of flesh and blood known as flesh and blood, the names of each parent and each child are the names he knows and has always known of, some of them he has known in life, and he himself is bound by just such ties to father and son, they all are, and the claims of kinship are the claims of earthly law:

> Edward the Third, my lords, had seven sons:
> The first, Edward the Black Prince, Prince of Wales;
> The second, William of Hatfield; and the third,
> Lionel Duke of Clarence. . . .
> (*II Henry VI*, II, ii, 10–13)

The assertion is clear, York claims his title by descent from the third son, the second having died without an heir. If blood means anything it means everything. So for York and his three sons, for Talbot and his son, for Clifford and his, for Margaret and hers, the assertion of the tyranny of kinship is impregnated with every idea that religion and the lust for power and for survival can produce. So in the judgment passed upon Suffolk by the mere lieutenant who will cut him down, the whole of the English people is avenging the single absolute principle guiding the conduct of life:

> And now the house of York, thrust from the crown
> By shameful murder of a guiltless king
> And lofty proud encroaching tyranny,
> Burns with revenging fire, whose hopeful colours
> Advance our half-faced sun, striving to shine,
> Under the which is writ *Invitis nubibus*.
> (*II Henry VI*, IV, i, 94–9)

By contrast with rivalries so inspired, the quarrels of Agamem-
non and Achilles and Hera herself are quarrels among strangers
and aliens, but in the fealties of these men, all is infused with the
sense of horror at the primal murder and the primal tie. Faction
is the fundamental betrayal, civil war the comprehending horror—

> a true-born gentleman
> . . . stands upon the honour of his birth.
> (*I Henry VI*, II, iv, 27–8)

Plantagenets and Lancastrians alike 'maintain the party of the
truth' (32). The son, resolute to die beside his father, invokes the
mother's name—

> O, if you love my mother,
> Dishonor not her honorable name,
> To make a bastard and a slave of me.
> (*I Henry VI*, IV, v, 13–15)

In the blood relationship is honour, patriotism, and religion. And
so the enchantment of the idea of the kingly is the witness of the
guiding aspiration of all, the power to rule and the honour of the
family. The highest praise is that which says a man is kingly in
thought (*II Henry V*, i, 29), and in act he who does not measure
up to that state is outside esteem:

> he that loves himself
> Hath not essentially, but by circumstance,
> The name of valour. (*II Henry VI*, V, ii, 37–9)

The kingly, the royal, is the character of the anointed and of the
patriarchal—

> And, Henry, hadst thou swayed as kings should do,
> And as thy father and his father did—
> (*III Henry VI*, II, vi, 14–15)

The family in its continuing descent is the foundation the King, all men, build on. The largeness of men who honour the claims of blood justifies, even sanctifies civil strife. The parties of Lancaster, of York, of England are the parties of truth, but they are also the parties of sanctity. In the wars of England we see put to the test such a sense of the preciousness of kin as drove Aegeon and his son to their desperate searches, and finally when a Richmond comes to heal the wounds he will look forward to just such a sacramental blessing as the Abbess in Ephesus offered her reunited family.

The infinite varieties of ambition are rooted in pride and love of family, there is no winter in the life in the blood. It is not only the love of honour, it is of glory, always behind it is the thought of 'the golden round which fate and metaphysical aid' hold out, as Lady Macbeth has it, the crown not only of England but of life. The claims of kin, the praise of the fathers who begat them, the dedication to the sons, this is the love that in the comedies was only beginning to come to grips with time and fortune. In the histories it is coping with time at the flood.

In the comedies a view of reality, however playfully meant, relates to conceptions of the immanent or the transcendent. The happy ending of *The Comedy of Errors* is made possible by what is indicated as a spirit moulding circumstance and influencing fortune. In *Love's Labour's Lost* nature, which wisdom recommends that men follow, is the body of divinity, and in consulting it and in communion with its life, men fulfil their most wideranging aspirations and make whatever accommodations they can with circumstance. In *The Two Gentlemen of Verona* some few order their being and life in honouring the transcendent, and others, ignorant of it, are lucky if they know they have been deprived of the knowledge of the good and the perfect and the everlasting. These conceptions are central although much of the action in these plays proceeds according to postulates not obviously metaphysical, but the philosophical and religious affirmations are central to the importance given to the claims of love which are the springs of so much of the action, and they engage the thought as well of the specially important persons of the plays. On the other hand, the Christian allusions that occur rather frequently and sometimes at crucial points indicate still another mentality contributing an important interest to the plays, matching the Platonism with an exuberant realism, and making possible the appeal to a special power when the grievous and the potentially tragic come too close.[6]

In the histories the appeal to the supernal is often in the terms of orthodox religion, but neither the words nor the action does much to certify a theological orientation to the plays. There is, however, so much use of magic and prophecy and premonition that we are bound to speculate that strange, perhaps spiritual, powers are at work in the horrors as well as splendours of English history. There are times when we think Shakespeare is following Hall in being persuaded that Providence is playing a part and also that some moral agency may be at work effecting retribution if not rewarding virtue. On the whole the drift is not that way, and there is at least this against the idea, that the richness of detail, the colour, the vividness of representation of character and of incidents of every kind, is such that no theory could be offered to account for it all unless, as is surely not so, all were being expounded in a coherent allegory. There are also the obvious contradictions to oppose such interpretations. We are invited to entertain the idea of magical powers in a most provocative way in the conjuring before the Duke of Gloucester, there is the suggestion of more power than we had come to credit Joan with when she dizzies Talbot—

> My thoughts are whirlèd like a potter's wheel;
> I know not what I am, not what I do.
> (*I Henry VI*, I, v, 19–20)

But all such suggestions are mocked by what we have heard at the beginning, that God fights on both sides, or when we remember the frauds perpetrated on Gloucester and his Duchess in the names of religion and witchcraft.

Ideas that destiny as such is at work in these events are somewhat more provocative, not so much because occasional prophecy or premonitory dream is borne out but because we know we are attending to the re-enactment of history and accordingly that doom is in the cards, that the war will spill over for years before a Richmond comes to put an end to it. Then, too, there is the strong patriotism and the feeling the play encourages in us that the best must come about for a nation that deserves the best. Then we add to this such evidence as there is that evil consumes itself, that murder will out, that the vicious do not prosper forever. Yet all this falls short of anything like an argument, and there is the fate of Henry if there is nothing else to remind us of the counter proposition, that in this England, for the good there is not even a haven to retire to. No one, not even Richard, can go far without calling on Heaven or Hell, and even act as confident of their aid, but if God or Providence or Fate is in control, their plans are certainly inscrutable, and too much evidence points the other way. And whereas in the comedies all is managed in order that sooner or later the audience will be brought into the secret and will learn the rhyme and reason of it all, in the histories affairs will be managed to a very different end, the disappointment of any such expectations. These will be aroused again and again, only to be dashed, and the only pattern of meaning to take and keep form is of regularity in the succession of disappointments, and the single meaning to keep coming out is that life and nature are incessantly at war with themselves. This is not all the plays have to tell us but it is almost all, and this comes out not simply in the representation of well laid plans that come to nothing—which might make the point more sharply—but in the representation of confusion, of sustained enterprises and casual interruptions, of strange concatenations, and above all, in the inclusion of such a variety of the noble and the ignoble in men, some of them of unlimited capacity, that we come to believe that it is not so much an idea and a meaning that is taking form in the succession of events as it is life itself in the forms that distinguish it from death.

So it appears that when we take all such matters as these into view—the re-enactment of the history of Courts and peoples, the magnitude of the persons, the nature of the struggles—we see that the discovery and management of adequate dramatic forms proceed variously.

After the first scenes of the First Part, in which the great lords on the English side and the French leaders move towards war, there is again an alternation of scenes, the first in which Gloucester's and Winchester's men scuffle before the Tower of London, followed by a scene in France where Talbot is preparing to join battle and there is a brief skirmish with Joan. The contrast here is not so pointed as in the first two scenes, and new matter is being brought forward, but the chief business is now evident, the war itself in its many phases. Then there comes a pair of scenes in which through the contrast a point is again being made, this time that fortune works equally unexpectedly on both sides. In one scene a Master-Gunner and his son shoot down two of the English lords standing on the turrets, and in the other, a surprise attack by night results in driving the French from Orleans.

The direction the play has been taking is now abruptly interrupted while our attention is focused on an extensive view of the rivalries among the British, and it is not until the third act that we are returned to the original matter when the British leaders agree to put aside their differences and to get on with the main job. But the play does not proceed now as it had at first. There are a number of remarkably vivid scenes—the by-play between Talbot and the Countess of Auvergne, the last days of Talbot, Mortimer's death, every one of them increasing our fascination in the succession of things as well, but none is necessary to the representation of the stages of the war itself, none is a necessary part of the ordering of incidents leading to the English success and the arrangements for the peace. Moreover, Shakespeare has given up the device of contrasting scenes. It appears he has abandoned any idea he may have had of setting up oppositions and arranging entanglements and manipulating consequences towards a resolution according to the method of *Love's Labour's Lost*, for example, where all follows in an orderly way as the terms of the contrasts in the first scenes set the pattern for.

Now the play advances in presenting a number of scenes that may even be superfluous, but they are so vividly conceived, the language so splendid, the invention so bold, that if anything they strengthen the play's hold on us. In the quarrel of Winchester and Gloucester, the anger is so hot we see and hear nothing else. In the scene of Joan on the walls with a burning torch, the mere spectacle is enough. And above all there is the continual display of heroism. So if now and then we think we can see a step ahead, we almost never see farther, and often we cannot see that far, and we begin to believe that what we are seeing is the mere limit a span of time, one king's reign, puts upon the energies of ambitious men. We are prepared for a conclusion to the mess, a kind of peace, we welcome the nonsense that a marriage can be expected to seal the peace, but even as we are commencing to make these habitual accommodations we are made queasy by some uncompleted details in the arrangements. It appears that even a formally composed ending to a particular strife only aggravates a conflict in which so many men are working at cross-purposes. We are being reminded that at the funeral of Henry V and the naming of the heir similar promises had been made, and the strife also only magnified.

So it does come about that we expect the next scenes to go on showing war and misery and courage and confusion continuing, and in the idea of lasting uncertainty and of the inability of men to control events we must entertain the suggestion that the inevitable is fated. It is not so much that we are persuaded of a pattern of cause and effect or of a law in nature. It is simply that our hopes are always being dashed. Each time the English, with whom our sympathies lie, are in a position to go forward, some terrible disappointment comes upon them. The ones who might have made all the difference, Salisbury and Talbot, are killed, and the gloom is only heightened by the treaty of peace Henry makes afterward. It is not even clear that men are the architects of their own failures.

But whatever we make of the ordering of scenes in this First Part, we shortly learn that the ordering of the next Parts are not only different but if anything less coherent. We are of course at a disadvantage, for we do not know that the plays were composed in this order. If we knew them to be composed in some other order, this would only make more difficult our efforts to discover a guiding plan for the whole in which the Parts in any event must succeed chronologically. At best we must work clumsily, but we have all the same the one necessary assurance, that produced in succession these plays achieve a magnificent effect. In some remarkable way this is a single work.

To a great degree the Second Part moves as though intent with purpose, as if each element were immediately directed to a resolution of conflicts and issues alike. The introduction with music, Henry's words to Margaret and Suffolk, the interrupted reading of the marriage contract, the *post mortem* in which Gloucester and Winchester and the others speak up, all begins to point to one result, the downfall of the King. Almost every incident—whether of Gloucester rebuking Suffolk, of the Cardinal taking exception to Gloucester, of Buckingham's compact with Somerset—advances the overthrow. The intrigues are more complex than simple, and there is more than one obstacle in the way, but it is certain that there is but one prize. Not all the plotters are working together but all are galvanized by the same intent.

The first scene ends with a soliloquy in which York makes just this point, and he almost makes another important one. The loss of Anjou and Maine, the grief and recriminations to follow will intensify the rivalries, all will weaken Henry's position, and he will stand by to turn one against another until he has destroyed them all. Then he will take over. So he sets to work, and the first step is to knock down Gloucester. The event will not be all of his making, but scene after scene now follows that will show how this is brought about. Others beside York had their parts to play, the Duchess of Gloucester in particular would become a ruinous pawn, and chance is important—the agent, John Hum, playing both sides, Simpcox the charlatan embarrassing the Protector, and there is the hint of something more awesome than such luck, Gloucester's premonitory dream and the prophecy that Suffolk will fall. It will be some time before York, intervening here and there, will himself be manipulating the events, but the fact that his analysis was right, and that events are playing into his hands begins to give his reasoning a strange authority. History it appears is on his side, and this means that his reasons are as important dramatically as his acts. His intelligence is prophet-like, events may be thought to follow such reasoning as his, the future it seems must bear him out. He has in effect said that the virtuous and the foolish can never hold power long. Gloucester would serve another in the name of a different cause than his. The Duchess will trust a servant. To put a limit upon ambition is to throw oneself away as surely as to let cunning doze. Winchester was ruthless enough but perhaps not diligent enough or canny enough, in any event he was the dupe of fortune.

A remarkable irony is now evident. A play that gives so many signs of an ordering to illustrate a process at work in human affairs is showing that process to be wholly without order, life being neither more nor less than what an opportunist can make of it. And once this point is made, the action may revert to an imitation of what we might just as well call the fog of war. The scenes can now proceed as drama and history simultaneously, *apparently* disconnectedly, *apparently* confusedly, resisting every proposal to impose upon them any end demanded by love or virtue or religion. As Gloucester will say,

> Virtue is choked with foul ambition,
> (*II Henry VI*, III, i, 143)

and York has said,

be still a while, till time do serve:
Watch thou and wake, when others be asleep,
To pry into the secrets of the state. (I, i, 248–50)

Berowne had also appealed to the need to work according to the
seasons, but in that play in following nature one obtained
nature's blessings. There is no blessing to be had from nature
here, all is dare and challenge and treacherous submission.

Gloucester has been ill-served by his Duchess, by the skill of
his enemies, and by his luck. On other counts as well he is probably no match for York, but his final and most terrible mistake
is to believe that God would not allow evil to prosper beyond a
certain point:

> I must offend before I be attainted;
> And had I twenty times so many foes,
> And each of them had twenty times their power,
> All these could not procure me any scathe,
> So long as I am loyal, true and crimeless. (II, iv, 59–63)

More than once he uses the appropriate words, 'So help me God',
but the time comes when he recognizes that God will not prevent 'the plotted tragedy' (III, i, 153), yet in an ironic contrast it
is he who arranges the trial by combat between the drunken
armourer and his apprentice in which the result seems to show
that God does support the side of justice in this world.

But even while this point is made, another one also is, for soon
it is Winchester's turn to die, at the peak of his greatness, just at
the moment York is making his advance. If fortune can make a
plaything of Winchester, then we may believe that York can
find no more help from that quarter than Gloucester had from
God.

So we may say that for nearly three acts the play unfolds as
brilliantly as complexly, in presenting the circumstances that led
to the destruction of one man and that at the very moment of his
downfall, which is also the demonstration of a certain erroneous

attitude in politics, an idea comes forward to go on from there to test another system. It is the same kind of re-direction we are to observe in *Julius Caesar*, where after Caesar's death other men and other ideas are to be put to the test, and finally, as that works out, we learn we have been attending to a single developing action, and that the death at half-way was merely the occasion for enlarging the scope of the theme. And the apparent breaking-off of the action, Gloucester's death, Caesar's death, this conclusion that is no conclusion is in part the means of re-informing our conception of the play before us as a re-creation of history in which all coherent formings are always being interrupted.

The next scene of this Second Part is stunning in this light. Suffolk, banished and in disguise, flees England by ship and is captured by marauders. An ordinary lieutenant, learning who he is and believing him to be Gloucester's murderer, beheads him in the name of all those who loved Duke Humphrey and love England. He damned him also as the lover of Margaret and the instrument of York. Evil, apparently, can as easily turn back upon its fosterers as not. A mere chance begins the undoing of complex plans.

The Third Part can stand on its own, yet in one aspect it is governed less than the others by anything resembling a plot or an articulated action. Its primary form is the simple moving back and forward between opposing camps. There are a few instances of another kind of continuity and of scenes opposing each other in contrast, but the main procedure is the simple one of showing the strength and capacities of the forces opposing each other, re-peating the point that fortune takes sides as she will. It comes out that men on both sides labour to identify their cause with right, as they use every means simply to impose themselves upon their enemies.

As this simple rhythm is pursued many contrasts and parallels are as it were thrown up. In the first scene York insolently takes his seat upon the throne as a persuasive case is made for the legitimacy of his claim. A few scenes later Margaret captures him and sets a paper crown on his head. On one side Clifford kills young Rutland, on the other Edward and his brothers murder the Prince. King Edward and King Henry have their victories, are taken prisoner, and escape. And there is of course the scene that is a paradigm of much, a man bringing in the body of a man he has just killed whom he discovers to be his father and another bringing in the son he has killed.

Now it is time to show Richard playing the game his father played before him, biding the time when it will be his turn to strike. With this parallel, as the most comprehensive comment of all, we are learning that in the course of the fury raging in England, in the rising and falling of the flood, in the coming to power and in failing, the energy of men will wear itself out, knowing no other way, taking no form except exhaustion. The process shows all the resources of fury, the strength and magnanimity and piety it can drink up as well as the lust and ambition, and it shows that there is nothing else to count on. That which arouses its full use also undermines it, the need for ambition to direct itself against the enemy of the moment. York we now know, Edward, too, and we may even think that Richard in the end will no more be able to impose a scheme upon events than Humphrey with his faith, or Henry with his good will.

There are suggestions of a pattern indeed existing in this raging back and forth that may be known of, at least in part, through mantic means—prophecies that bear repeating, premonitions that are borne out, the thought that good may come of evil and that in this England so many love so deeply, a glorious peace will come at last. But the abiding meaning is rather that as in the past, as these events testify, history comes into the present as the incessant struggle for power, power which sooner or later will slip away even from the indefatigable. In short, we are seeing in human affairs just such a process as we are reminded of in the Nature of *Love's Labour's Lost*, in the procession of the seasons. But because in the histories it is the procession of generations of men we are observing, we are not so ready to accept equably the recognition of the remorselessness of time and change. And the tenor of this history is such we are not being encouraged to.

Civil war and public tragedy make up the main matter of these plays, but the individual histories interest us nearly as much and in the lives of many we observe some of the same affirmations and beliefs Shakespeare was making so much of in the comedies. The scene of course is larger, there is a greater variety in the persons, the issues if not more complex are more complexly exposed, and probably the reasoning is developed more searchingly. It does not over-simplify, I think, to say that the failures of public policy are but different manifestations of the causes spoiling the individual lives. But as we see this happening we make still something else of it than a political tragedy, the private and religious concerns absorb us in their own right.

The general dismay with the conditions attending the marriage of Henry with the daughter of the King of Naples aggravates existing discontents and creates others. The party that Suffolk now makes with Margaret sets itself against Gloucester and his interest, and joins temporarily with York and Winchester in the growing struggle to get control over the weak King.

The plots increase, the fighting spreads. As civil war like a flood penetrates everywhere, a variety of incidents shows us now this or that great soldier meeting a crisis—in the field Salisbury and Talbot and a whole gallery of magnificent soldiers, at the Court, Warwick finding the ground cut out from under him as he is carrying out the mission assigned to him by Edward at the Court of France. A variety of small scenes of special horror passes before us, the slaughter of children, the outrages of Cade. But in the midst of what has the effect of illustrating how small things lead to great, a certain action deriving from the alliance of Suffolk and Margaret provides a focus and a means of ordering what might otherwise have become diffuse. That action is the rise and fall of Suffolk. In itself it is of extraordinary interest, as a miserable passion takes hold of the two and sustains them in their drive for power. It has a part, too, in the larger action for, with Gloucester disposed of and Winchester dead, Suffolk and Margaret are left alone to oppose the party of York. Then, when it is Suffolk's turn to die, the King is left to the kites. The King, whose recourse to religion was never enough to make up for his failures as a man, is kept in power now only by the talent and ferocity of his wife. Here and there a Clifford or a Warwick will fight for him, but their history illustrates on the face of it the inadequacy of men, however magnificent, who work outside the discipline of a party or a faction.

In the Third Part there is only the ebb and flow of battle to run its course until Margaret too goes under. We are learning that men in the whole spectrum of nobility and courage and righteousness are no match for the forces men more or less without principle can easily enlist. It appears that the conscienceless have more staying power. The King, and Gloucester as well, had believed in spite of what their senses told them that right and truth are invulnerable and invincible:

> What stronger breastplate than a heart untainted!
> Thrice is he armed that hath his quarrel just,
> And he but naked, though locked up in steel,
> Whose conscience with injustice is corrupted.
>
> (*II Henry VI*, III, ii, 232–5)

The King lacks, however, what a whole line of saints have maintained, faith that the power of virtue would bring to bear power in its full majesty—

> the uncontrouled worth
> Of this pure cause would kindle my rap't spirits
> To such a flame of sacred vehemence,
> That dumb things would be mov'd to sympathize,
> And the brute Earth would lend her nerves, and shake,
> Till all thy magic structures rear'd so high,
> Were shatter'd into heaps o're thy false head.
>
> (*Comus*, 793–9)

And even without that faith Henry lacks the character and perhaps the will to bring even earthly power to bear—being very much like the historic Henry, not so much a saint as, in the Pope's words, 'an innocent'—unable to provide also anything like Joan's or Talbot's ability to inspire an army:

> Sometime the flood prevails, and then the wind;
> Now one the better, then another best;
> Both tugging to be victors, breast to breast,
> Yet neither conqueror nor conquerèd:
> So is the equal poise of this fell war.
> Here on this molehill will I sit me down.
> To whom God will, there be the victory!
>
> (*III Henry VI*, II, v, 9-15)

Dying, even as he foresees the horror to come—

> Men for their sons, wives for their husbands,
> Orphans for their parents' timeless death—
> Shall rue the hour that ever thou wast born—

he can forgive the scourge of England while submitting to his knife—

> O God forgive my sins, and pardon thee!
>
> (V, vi, 41-3, 60)

Similarly, we cannot believe Joan's strength to have been God-given, although we must credit her ardour, and Gloucester is unable to obtain from God for himself what he calls for in ordering trial by combat for Horner and Peter.

Other brave and great men assert their strong and living faith in offering themselves as the executors of God's justice, Salisbury, Talbot, Warwick, Clifford, and, one senses, companies of such men, all dedicated, although sometimes some are confused or wayward. They do not appeal as Antipholus of Syracuse does to 'the soul's pure truth', or to any such authority as Adonis appealed to in begging Venus to allow him to take to what life offered him in its due season. They do not, that is, suppose that in preserving their integrity they are obtaining from circumstance and chance and God a guarantee of fulfilment. They are dedicated in the ancient sense, their integrity achieved only as they die.

Clifford and Warwick ask for no reward other than the consciousness of service and of having made the fullest use of their strength.

> Here burns my candle out; ay, here it dies,
> Which, whiles it lasted, gave King Henry light—

Clifford knows he is dying, and his grief is that the failure of the King as a man has brought and is continuing to bring mourning to England:

> And, Henry, hadst thou swayed as kings should do,
> Or as thy father and his father did,
> Giving no ground unto the house of York,
> They never then had sprung like summer flies;
> I and ten thousand in this luckless realm
> Had left no mourning widows for our death.
> *(III Henry VI*, II, vi, 1–2, 14–19)

He makes no pleas:

> The foe is merciless and will not pity;
> For at their hands I have deserved no pity. (25–6)

In slaughtering young Rutland he slew an enemy, but chiefly he avenged a father. Justice may inhere in revenge, but Clifford knows too that he is mad:

> Had I thy brethren here, their lives and thine
> Were not revenge sufficient for me;
> No, if I digged up thy forefathers' graves
> And hung their rotten coffins up in chains,

It could not slake mine ire, nor ease my heart.
The sight of any of the house of York
Is as a Fury to torment my soul;
And till I root out their accursèd line
And leave not one alive, I live in hell. (I, iii, 25–33)

He himself deserves no pity unless it should be from such as the King, but he served the King and his regrets were only for the King's and England's defeats. He deserved nobler enemies.

Warwick looms over the battle like a cedar among shrubs, but he too has been stained by confusion and, no doubt, shame. In his return to Henry's side he confesses an error in his defection, although how deeply weighed the play does not make plain. His is the full magnificence of mortal pride, one sees nothing of the devout in him as he dies, nothing of passion, no clinging to what he loves, no grief for what is lost or for what has not been accomplished, all there is is the recognition that his greatness is done with:

My mangled body shows,
My blood, my want of strength, my sick heart shows,
That I must yield my body to the earth
And, by my fall, the conquest to my foe.
Thus yields the cedar to the ax's edge,
Whose arms gave shelter to the princely eagle,
Under whose shade the ramping lion slept,
Whose top-branch overpeered Jove's spreading tree
And kept low shrubs from winter's pow'rful wind.
These eyes, that now are dimmed with death's black veil,
Have been as piercing as the mid-day sun
To search the secret treasons of the world.
The wrinkles in my brows, now filled with blood,
Were likened oft to kingly sepulchers;
For who lived king but I could dig his grave?
And who durst smile when Warwick bent his brow?
Lo, now my glory smeared in dust and blood!
My parks, my walks, my manors that I had,

Even now forsake me, and of all my lands
Is nothing left me but my body's length.
Why, what is pomp, rule, reign, but earth and dust?
And, live we how we can, yet die we must. (V, ii, 7–28)

A weak and Christian King, a devout and raging soldier, a self-sufficient lord, are joined in opposition to the faction of York by the corrupt. From the moment of her arrival in England Margaret had embarked upon the course that was as necessary to her as breath, to put herself in the King's place and with her tiger's heart to rule England. On first meeting her, Suffolk had felt her attraction, he recognized it immediately as the insidious appeal of adultery. The resistance was momentary. As for her, she seemed to know none. Fierce, conscienceless, habitually if not instinctively devious, she instantly made partners with one who responded to her as in a perfect team, adding little enough to her potentialities. He offered one more blade with which to strike down Gloucester, being on the spot he knew how to go about destroying the Duchess. How much Margaret needed him it is hard to say, though if he had continued to oppose her original suggestion to get rid of Gloucester (*II Henry VI*, III, i, 238–42) she would have had to proceed more slowly. They were close enough to know each other's thoughts, but when he was gone she fought as tirelessly and brilliantly as she had ever done.

This speak I, lords, to let you understand,
If case some one of you would fly from us,
That there's no hoped-for mercy with the brothers
More than with ruthless waves, with sands and rocks.
Why, courage then! What cannot be avoided
'Twere childish weakness to lament or fear.
(*III Henry VI*, V, iv, 33–8)

When Suffolk departs for exile, it appears her grief is less than it might be, assured in her own mind that in time she will have him back. Her language was surely comforting:

Away! Though parting be a fretful corrosive,
It is applièd to a deathful wound.
To France, sweet Suffolk: let me hear from thee;
For wheresoe'er thou art in this world's globe,
I'll have an Iris that shall find thee out.

(II Henry VI, III, ii, 403–7)

But she gives no sense of a certain meaning love has for him, who thinks and speaks of her as Paradise, damned though he knows their love is. Henry, Clifford, Warwick, were in their ways self-less—as young Clifford said of the men he admired,

> He that is truly dedicate to war
> Hath no self-love. (V, ii, 37–8)

Suffolk and Margaret were not such. Suffolk was dedicate to Margaret, and his words parody love and honour alike—

> For where thou art, there is the world itself,
> With every several pleasure in the world,
> And where thou art not, desolation. (III, ii, 362–4)

It is the same folly as Margaret's but more womanish:

> *Enter . . . the Queen with Suffolk's head . . .*
> But who can cease to weep and look on this?
> Here may his head lie on my throbbing breast;
> But where's the body that I should embrace?
> (IV, iv, 4–6)

In short, the varieties of loyalty are as pervaded with ambition and selfishness as disloyalty itself—all is consumed by 'the canker of ambitious thoughts' (I, ii, 18), compounded variously with the goadings of revenge and vainglory and lust and even love, and had there not been a Gloucester one would have thought virtue as Hydra-headed a monster as vice. York sees all this more clearly than Richard, and he is capable of seeing that it has gone so far with him he might be called mad:

> Faster than spring-time show'rs comes thought on thought,
> And not a thought but thinks on dignity.
> My brain more busy than the laboring spider
> Weaves tedious snares to trap mine enemies.
> Well, nobles, well: 'tis politicly done,
> To send me packing with an host of men:
> I fear me you but warm the starvèd snake,
> Who, cherished in your breasts, will sting your hearts.
> 'Twas men I lacked, and you will give them me:
> I take it kindly; yet be well assured
> You put sharp weapons in a madman's hands.
>
> (III, i, 337–47)

And it is with Richard as with them all, none has retained the assurance that will prevent him from inventing his own destruction. He puts it best:

> And I—like one lost in a thorny wood,
> That rends the thorns and is rent with the thorns,
> Seeking a way and straying from the way,
> Not knowing how to find the open air,
> But toiling desperately to find it out—
> Torment myself to catch the English crown:
> And from that torment I will free myself,
> Or hew my way out with a bloody axe.
>
> (*III Henry VI*, III, ii, 174–81)

The fate of Gloucester shows that a virtuous man in authority, however determined to make justice prevail, can in himself never outmatch persistent enmity. Envy and ambition are unresting, time itself is their ally, and, besides, sooner or later someone will be found to betray authority from within. Gloucester's fate shows this not only because envy and ambition are as they are but because in the uncertainty of human affairs not everything can be foreseen. If the downfall of Gloucester was inevitable for such reasons, the King, Salisbury, Stafford, Warwick, and many others had less call to count upon success in their cause, being less fixed in purpose to serve justice uncompromisingly, and besides they were submitting themselves more constantly to the hazards of war.

Malice and selfishness in authority is equally vulnerable. York, Edward, Richard, careless of justice and probity, will make enemies of friends, and indeed for them the idea of lasting alliance is a contradiction in terms. Moreover, ignorant of the resilience of virtue in men however oppressed, the malevolent exaggerate their own resources and undervalue the strength of what opposes them. Such men accordingly and inevitably fall back on force where force can never assure their aims.

Among all there is no one who has given himself to life with any fullness of heart except Suffolk and perhaps Margaret who is not ready to die. The young prince and one or two others who have not seen manhood may not want to, but they have not had time to learn what they would care to make of life. All those who have, when they know their time has come, may or may not have regret for what has happened, but they are not sorry to leave. For many—like Clifford—this was no doubt because their aspirations, even in revenge, were impossible to attain, but it is Warwick whose words are the most telling, for his desires were for nothing else than for what was in anyone's grasp, power and possession. We might put it as the King did in another sense— the balm is washed away (*III Henry VI*, III, i, 17), at the end the joy has gone out of life. It was the joy that had sustained them all; the energy, the ambition, the hate, the passion, were always exultant. The largeness of thought, the grandeur of the language, all this that went beyond the measure was the witness of their joy in living, life and joy were the same, and they signified rule. Margaret is like them all in the strength of the hatred with which she repells the onslaughts against her, as exultant in hate as in possession, for the loss of power is the loss of joy, and to be ruled is worse than death. The King and Gloucester may propose that true happiness is in serving a divine master and in fulfilling the law, but not knowing that law well enough they were unable to enforce it and accordingly they suffered as all do who find themselves without power. To be ruled is to be enslaved, and then death can only be welcomed:

> Be that thou hop'st to be, or what thou art
> Resign to death; it is not worth th' enjoying.
> (*II Henry VI*, III, i, 333-4)

Richard puts it most perfectly, he is truly himself when there is no one who can make a claim upon him. He is speaking of the claims of love, of the claims of brothers, and it might as well be of subjects:

> I have no brother, I am like no brother;
> And this word 'love', which graybeards call divine,
> Be resident in men like one another
> And not in me: I am myself alone.
> (*III Henry VI*, V, vi, 80-3)

Love says that men discover themselves, their 'truth', in others, Richard is sufficient to himself. To a degree Clifford and Warwick and Gloucester serve the truth that is in them in serving the King, or in revenging the harm done to kin or country, serving in love and with devotion, but there is not one of them who does not also serve ambition, and one after another puts himself first. This is Richard's point, and it refutes as the play refutes young Clifford's dogma that only those are essentially brave who have no self-love. He speaks as things should be, and might be, and are not.

Yet what he asserts, or rather, the order of thinking on which it is based, provides the standard by which the events beings placed before us are steadily judged. As Rutland says, greybeards call love divine, Clifford appeals to essence, and even

when such explicit assertions are lacking, the thought of everyone is pursued in the light of an unchanging and all-embracing
truth, at once residing in men and existing in itself. So the
inconstant Clarence:

> Pardon me, Edward! I will make amends;
> And, Richard, do not frown upon my faults,
> For I will henceforth be no more unconstant.
>
> (*III Henry VI*, V, i, 100–102)

So the exemplar of all ruinous behaviour:

> I'll drown more sailors than the mermaid shall;
> I'll slay more gazers than the basilisk;
> I'll play the orator as well as Nestor,
> Deceive more slily than Ulysses could,
> And, like a Sinon, take another Troy.
> I can add colours to the chameleon,
> Change shape like Proteus, for advantages,
> And set the murderous Machiavel to school.
>
> (III, ii, 186–93)

So Gloucester:

> Sorry I am to hear what I have heard;
> Noble she is; but if she have forgot
> Honor and virtue and conversed with such
> As, like the pitch, defile nobility,
> I banish her my bed and company.
>
> (*II Henry VI*, II, i, 192–6)

So the King:

> The Duke is virtuous, mild, and too well given
> To dream on evil. (III, i, 72–3)

So Lord Say:

Unless you be possessed with devilish spirits,
You cannot but forbear to murder me. (IV, vii, 77–8)

The light that lighteth each man that cometh into the world
is the light by which they judge the chaos that is theirs and of
their making; and the joy of power, without the idea that it is
true power and everlasting and invincible, would not be joy. It
is not only the loss of power but the loss of light that terrifies. It
terrifies Richard who will deliberately and systematically work
to cut free from any dependence upon any certitude whatever,
but even in his defiance he knows the darkness for what it is and
recoils from it, in his terror

> Not knowing how to find the open air.
> (*III Henry VI*, III, ii, 177)

The plays themselves, the re-creation of history, this effort
to bring it all back as it was, depend upon the continuous reference to a vision of reality, and the words forced upon us at every
step—love, truth, virtue, self, evil—and all the imagery and
reasoning that go with them demand that same reference from
us. The key words here and elsewhere in Shakespeare are *truth*
and *self*—*truth* as what is to be known, and *self*, as the self *esssen-
tially*, that is, in its relationship to truth. The conspiracies, the
plucking of the roses, all rest upon oaths, all men aspire to be
members of 'the party of the truth' (*I Henry VI*, II, iv, 32), and in
these plays as certainly as in the comedies this signifies participation in absolute being.

The remark was made in *The Two Gentlemen of Verona* that
oaths are 'servants to deceitful men' (II, vii, 72), but Julia judged
Proteus differently, and in a protestation that called on one
supernal authority after another she said his 'truth' derived unimpeded from that which presided over his entrance into life:

> . . . truer stars did govern Proteus' birth.
> His words are bonds, his oaths are oracles,
> His love sincere, his thoughts immaculate;

His tears pure messengers sent from his heart;
His heart as far from fraud as heaven from earth.

(74–8)

Like those in *Henry VI*, Proteus will swear feelingly and believe
he swears truth. The event proves otherwise—for him, for Henry
in being crowned, for Warwick, and of course for the 'deceitful
men'. The one who thought he needed be true to no one supposed he could make himself into another Proteus, changing
endlessly. That Richard saw himself thus, as one who would

Change shapes with Proteus for advantages—
(*III Henry VI*, III, ii, 192)

is the last conclusion Shakespeare draws through the characterization of men who play so desperately with life. As it is in
Spenser, change is known for what it is only in the thought of the
unchanging. Richard would identify himself with a deity whose
power to change is never circumscribed, and in this very aspiration he reveals the rigidity of the limits in his thought as in his
power. He is no more equal to circumstance than the others,
ultimately as untethered as inconstant.

I am not sure if Margaret's love for her son and for Suffolk
liberates her at all from such a wilderness as Richard would cut
free from if he could (*III Henry VI*, III, ii, 181), like Michael
Angelo's slaves, or the form that inheres within the rock, but
Suffolk certainly understood that there is a power in love that
frees the self, paradoxically, in sharing the company of another—
in Platonic language, retaining its identification even in participating in the being of another:

To have thee with thy lips to stop my mouth:
So shouldst thou either turn my flying soul,
Or I should breathe it so into thy body,
And then it lived in sweet Elysium.
To die by thee were but to die in jest.
(*II Henry VI*, III, ii, 396–400)

In the idea of the heavenly intermingling of bodies he wishes to believe that death becomes life, when the main point, to the thought he does have a glimmer of, is that whether in soul or body the individual remains himself even as he participates in such a light and reason and affection as Sylvia's. Richard, too, at least in his language, related his idea of love to a 'resident' (*III Henry VI*, V, vi, 82) in men, and so to a sense of being apart from the self to which the self might on occasion repair.

But apart from this perception of Suffolk's, in the world of *Henry VI* there is no evidence that men have access to a resource that would free them from the labyrinth and the canker, from mortality, from the loss of joy that is inevitably theirs as men who like all men never sufficiently honour the truth that is in them, incapable of constancy, with nothing to hold to. Yet it is in the light of the conviction of truth that Shakespeare is exultantly making these endless discriminations, that he pursues these characterizations in which no shading is too fine, no judgment too clear, in which there is never any doubt about what is evil and what is good—as Coleridge was to say of *Venus and Adonis*, no matter what the subject the author was never influenced by it.

NOTES

1 *The Art of the West*, translated by Jean Bony, London, 1963, I, 7–8.

2 On this matter I have found the criticism of Alonso Dámaso wonderfully illuminating, particularly in his 'La Poesia del Petrarca e il Petrarchismo', in *Studi Petrarcheschi*, VII (1961), 73–120. Another valuable essay is that of P. L. Valente, 'Petrarca e Shakespeare', *Studi Petrarcheschi*, I (1948), 195–211. Giuseppe Ungaretti's preface to his translation, *40 Sonetti di Shakespeare* (1946), though idiosyncratic, is perceptive and valuable.

3 *Le Théâtre en Angleterre depuis la Conquête*, Paris, 1878, p. 8.

4 *On the Parts of Animals*, I, 5, 645a.

5 I find the phrase 'magna, spatiosa, clara' which Edgar de Bruyne quotes

as the epitome of medieval aesthetics beautifully apposite (*Études d'Esthétiques Médiévale*, Brussels, 1946, II, 89).

6 Mr. Tom Driver has argued that the form of the history plays follows from Shakespeare's dependence upon an idea of time that the Christian consciousness developed. For example, in *Richard III* 'time in this play is not merely a quantity to be measured by the movement of stars or the flowing of sand in the glass. Time is laden with purpose, and therefore it tends to gather itself together, as it were, into certain particular moments when long-prepared actions are completed and great issues are decided. This quality is to be seen in small affairs as well as in the most consequential.' All the usual devices of drama are 'mere techniques . . . with which Shakespeare achieves variety and emphasis within the dominant framework of advance from incipient beginnings to what is essentially an eschatological fulfillment' (*The Sense of History in Greek and Shakespearean Drama*, New York, 1967, pp. 92–3 and 104).

The view partly harmonizes with my own, but as with others that relate the management of the drama to subconscious patterns, I think it does not make nearly enough of consciously formed patterns and meanings made explicit. I am glad for Mr. Driver's emphasis upon Richmond's specific appeal to a sacrament to seal the peace that has just been concluded, and I believe he would be right in pointing to this as not only significant in the culmination of the movement of *Richard III* but in the completion of the matter of the Henry VI plays. I should relate this conclusion, however, to the meaning the issues themselves have developed, which has so much to do with the endless repetition of defeated hopes. Were the religious ceremony Richmond has in mind enacted, not merely mentioned, I think it would make the point I should hold to, that in these plays the divine and natural worlds are kept separate, and that Shakespeare does not use his disposition to honour teleology if not eschatology to underwrite the meaning of the plays.

The same problem presents itself in Mr. Wilbur Sanders' *The Dramatist and the Received Idea* (Cambridge, 1968). I think he demonstrates the pervasiveness of the sense of the transcendent in Shakespeare's writing, but I cannot accept his idea that the particulars of experience, the things of nature, all the matter of observation, owe their authentically vivid character to 'the tension between the ideal and actual' (p. 355). This character I find in the naming and description of material objects in some mystical writing (in Vaughan's), but as I see it Shakespeare always keeps the distance between the immanent and the transcendent. Bruno had failed to do this, and Nature in *Love's Labour's Lost* as well as ceremony in the Henry VI plays illustrate neither the intercession of spirit nor of Providence in the world of men. If humans and their affairs are to work out well, it is because they use their freedom in the service of reason as well as of the divine, and if they are blessed it will not be through the instrumentation of the immanent but through the offices of the Christian church or Christian discipline. As in differing with Mr. Driver, I believe it right to stress the factor of rationality, partly because this enables us better to account for the tragic potentialities, the possibilities of utter defeat that are so certainly in view.

The Encounter with Rome

In these same years Shakespeare is writing *Venus and Adonis* and *Lucrece*. The poems are distinguished above all else by sophistication and finish. Coleridge's words on *Venus and Adonis* are as true of *Lucrece*—'An endless activity of thought in all the possible associations of thought with thought, thought with feeling or with words, of feelings with feelings . . . making everything present to the imagination. . . . You seem to be *told* nothing, but to see and hear everything.' The style of verse in the two poems is quite different but it is everywhere as polished as it is ornate, and the control of the thought is as perfect as the control of the manner. In obvious ways the poems are looking towards other effects than the dramatic writings, although they share a certain elevation and an interest in subject matter of the greatest import, and in the poems Shakespeare is exploring approaches that will be extremely useful to him in his management of drama thereafter.

The Comedy of Errors is of course based on an ancient play. No one has so far discovered a major source for *Love's Labour's Lost*, and although *The Two Gentlemen of Verona* is significantly indebted to Montemayor's *Diana* and Brooke's *Romeo and Juliet*, as a whole it derives from no particular model. There is much confusion and little certainty about the use Shakespeare made of other plays in relating the events of Henry VI's reign, but the chief obligations are clearly to the historical writings of Hall and Holinshed. This is to say that with the exception of the adaptation of Plautus he was not making use of material already in a finished dramatic form.

He was to remain peculiarly dependent upon narrative writing for sources. Both *Titus Andronicus* and *The Taming of the Shrew* at close to this time are made up from well narrated stories (if we suppose, as I think right, that Mr. Peter Alexander and others have disposed of the idea that in *The Taming of the Shrew* Shakespeare was rewriting an earlier play). Hereafter the greater number of Shakespeare's comedies will be derived from stories Boccaccio taught all Europe how to write, as sophisticated in articulation as in thought, treating underlying moral themes with the liveliest intelligence, and having everything lead to a point. The sources of *Venus and Adonis* and *Lucrece*—whether or not they came to Shakespeare through Painter or someone else who had taken lessons from Boccaccio and Bandello and the other great Italians—are not so complex as those superficially simple stories, Boccaccio's *Giletta of Narbonne*, Bandello's *Appolonius and Silla*, and Cinthio's *Othello*, but in Shakespeare's hands they take on characteristic complexity and irony. This is the more strange and the more effective for their possessing attributes that belong to mythological poetry and legends so hallowed they might be incorporated in the Lives of the Saints.

Anyone who has seen any of the countless Renaissance paintings on these subjects recognizes the attraction of legends that can be so fully expressed in a single image. Moral issues all but spell themselves out as two persons confront each other. The concentration of meaning is so obvious that it would be difficult if not impossible to subordinate the moral to the mere representation. It is the same when words tell the stories, the situations require that the moral dominate. But the way Shakespeare goes about developing the episodes is most unusual, and it involves attitudes and approaches that he will be experimenting with in drama. *Richard III* and *Titus Andronicus* are in certain respects quite unlike the plays that have gone before, some of the attributes new with them are made even more of in the masterpieces to come—*Romeo and Juliet* and *A Midsummer Night's Dream* for the nearest examples—and something of what we observe in the narratives may account for the innovations.

Shakespeare does not isolate the central figures in these poems quite so barely as Ovid and Livy do. There is in *Venus and Adonis*, for one thing, the elaborate background of nature illustrated by the meaningful incident of the jennet and the courser; in *Lucrece* there is not only the vivid account of the talk of soldiers, there is the detailed description of the tapestry. The language itself is all but overladen with images. At the same time there is a most uncharacteristic spareness in the concentration upon such few persons to the exclusion of the usual Shakespearean crowd. The characters are the fewest, the setting the simplest, there is but one issue. In both poems a moral choice is to be made, and morality rather than tragedy is the subject. The poems are designed to interest us in moral questions, to inform us of the consequences whatever the choice finally made, to acquaint us with the sacrifices inevitably to be called for, and to enlist our support for Adonis and Lucrece as they make their decisions.

In resisting compulsion each affirms an obligation to preserve and maintain a certain state of being—the integrity of the self, purity, whatever it was to be called:

> 'Fair queen,' quoth he, 'if any love you owe me,
> Measure my strangeness with my unripe years.
> Before I know myself, seek not to know me.'
> *(Venus and Adonis*, 523–5)

> 'Though my gross blood be stained with this abuse,
> Immaculate and spotless is my mind;
> That was not forced, that never was inclined
> To accessary yieldings, but still pure
> Doth in her poisoned closet yet endure.'
> *(Lucrece*, 1655–9)

Neither Adonis nor Lucrece ever questions the obligation as inherently sacred—the need to preserve something intact—and although there may be some thought of pragmatic values (in *Venus and Adonis*, that there is a time and place for all things; in

Lucrece, that where the will does not consent the person may not be held responsible), neither Adonis nor Lucrece conceives the issue to be thus. Each chooses to forgo all such calculation in order to serve an absolute good.

This need to know himself that Adonis appeals to is that same 'pure truth' Antipholus of Syracuse honoured, not only the touchstone of integrity but the principle of maturing:

> 'Who wears a garment shapeless and unfinished?
> Who plucks the bud before one leaf put forth? . . .
> Measure my strangeness with my unripe years.'[1]
>
> (415-16, 524)

He would violate his truth in allowing an appeal not properly respectful of nature.

Lucrece relates a whole catechism of sins to her defilement:

> 'O, that is gone for which I sought to live,
> And therefore now I need not fear to die . . .'
>
> (1051-2)

> 'Well, well, dear Collatine, thou shalt not know
> The stainèd taste of violated troth . . .' (1058-9)

> 'Ay me, the bark pilled from the lofty pine,
> His leaves will wither and his sap decay;
> So must my soul, her bark being pilled away.'
>
> (1167-9)

The body as the soul can only be bestowed honourably and religiously, and religion will not permit children to be born in impurity.

By concentrating on the danger compulsion represents for the need to preserve purity, Shakespeare is able to restrain his habitual disposition to elaborate through parallel actions and the display of varieties of experience, and only the stanza with its wealth of rhyme and the luxuriant rhetoric contrasts with the single fact, the single encounter, he is having us attend to, an encounter not between characters conceived in all the richness and splendour of human and divine natures that some of the paintings are but as between rather simple persons forced to a debate.

Even more significantly, the concentration on struggles within the minds of the main persons is carried out with different effects than in Shakespeare's most powerful work, where the relationship between the life within the mind and the interplay of forces in nature and the universe lead into the most powerful exploitation of our feelings, of sympathy and awe. Here the exclusion of such a context so limits the use of implications for sensibility that the chief persons—all of them—are as singled out as figures in a pantomime, so absorbed in thought and gesture they are cut off from the mere life of humanity.

Then, too, the conflicts in the two poems lead into crises of a kind unknown to the early comedies at least, for they admit of no compromise. The plays exploit accommodation, but here disaster is met full face, as it is in *Henry VI*. By the very nature of Venus' love it would not matter if Adonis had survived the hunt and had lived to be won over to her. She must possess for herself alone, and she could allow no claims another might have for himself. The idea of the seasonable would be intolerable to her. And ironically, it is not only what she represents that would stifle him, what else there is in the world will not assure his growing to perfection. Which is as much as to say that whereas reason, in the form of debate, has been employed to resolve issues that go to the heart of the idea of sacredness in human life, disaster comes forward in implacable mockery of the pretensions of thought to control events. One can only conclude that the occasion for the poem is horror.

The horror is front stage centre in *Lucrece*. As with the earlier poem Shakespeare is not trying to stir us, the arguments, the reasonings and rhetoric are even more elaborate, they so to speak encircle the encounter and the rape so that we are directed to concentrate almost exclusively on the issues, on the difficulties raised for thought as well as conduct, and even the self-murder with its pictorial details is but a gloss on what is being thought about it. The comedies and the histories contemplate evil as the loss of joy, the poems contemplate evil as horror, and in stylized and insulated expression acquaint us with the futility of the solutions thought offers.

Thus we see that the technique in these poems of concentration on a particular act in a particular relationship is enabling Shakespeare to approach catastrophe in a new way for him. It is not only that the world of nature and society is hardly more than a backdrop, character is simplified. There are as many unlit places in the feelings of these legendary beings as in their thought. The one complexity, such as it is, is in the range of their reasoning. The simplifications allow for this, and so the poems make as much as they can of the idea that all is intelligible, that not even in the passions are there powers that elude the codification of general truths. These bedevilled persons find themselves as deeply lost in a tangled wood as Richard and even more hopelessly, for in the poems much more than in the histories it is plainly fate that is at work ensuring the isolation of these creatures. When the issues of morality are so carefully identified with the activity of reason, solitude becomes all the more the appropriate condition for the representation of human life.

The perspective in *Venus and Adonis* reverses the usual manner in which we learn of the working of fate. All has proceeded apparently otherwise until Venus' prophecy at the very end—which is also a curse—in effect tells us that what we have been taking as Venus' free offering was the doomed way of passion at all times. We must even infer that Adonis' faith that he may come to know love at the right time, not blinded with lust, is wrong, and that murderous, bloody, full-to-blame rage is in all. This way of introducing at the very end of the poem the idea of the authority of fate at work within passion but decreed by divinity diminishes if it does not obliterate the affective power of the idea while it emphasizes the helplessness and isolation of humans now abandoned by Love.

Lucrece, as the poem proceeds, is isolated in her own mind

increasingly. At first, by the nature of the story, there is suspense in following the movements of Tarquin, but soon enough we are directing our attention to the matter of the debate that following the violation will become the explicit subject. This becomes so much the matter of chief interest that when Lucrece dies in the presence of her friends they seem hardly more than shadows bearing away a mere exemplar while we are left weighing an argument. The nature of the crime against Lucrece calls for a secret and lonely place, and the offence is felt most as a private one not to be known in its full evil except by the sufferer, perhaps the loneliest of all pains and indignities, and the more so because while not visible it is yet felt to be indelible. As Lucrece sees it, she is cut off from the right to share her life with others. There is the idea that terrifies her nearly as much, that nature, unless forestalled by another crime, will bring forth a criminally be-gotten child. There is no way to redeem pollution, and no way to prevent the increase of horror and yet remain in life.

Here, too, the narrative is so devised that we have almost none of the feelings that indications of impending doom occa-sion although there is a hint that Roman justice will work inde-flectibly in punishing Tarquin. Lucrece's curse, unlike Venus', calling for the torments of conscience, has less support than experience generally offers, and there is the annoying knowledge of how easily Tarquin got off.

Finally, the figures in these poems are as it were isolated because they have been taken out of the fully peopled world that is normally part of whatever Shakespeare's writing projects. They come out of non-Christian Rome, so far as ignorant of the humanity of God's plenteousness as Roman statuary, and even Nature, with all that the scene of hunting could have opened into, another Forest of Arden or a wood near Athens, is a mere property of the world, not unlike that woods in which Bassianus and Lavinia are murdered and mutilated.

However suggestively Plautus initiated Shakespeare into the formation of the *esprit critique* and the irony of humanism, Ovid and Livy and even more Boccaccio were introducing him into the savagely secular and the impious, to ways of dramatizing life as isolated from both human and divine communion. It is not the dehumanization of allegory that is controlling the manner of the poems, it is the exploration of the mentality of another civilization.

The style of *Venus and Adonis* is buoyant, the secondary bouncing rhythm often dominates the primary measure, and the frequent feminine endings contribute to an accent and a pace that somewhat endanger our interest in the narrative and deflect as well the sympathies that might have been heightened. The exuberance of the rhythms all but mocks the seriousness of the debate, the more so since the language itself often, and apparently deliberately, introduces ideas and feelings as disagreeable as they are inappropriate:

> With this she seizeth on his sweating palm,
> The precedent of pith and livelihood,
> And trembling in her passion, calls it balm,
> Earth's sovereign salve to do a goddess good. (25–8)

The style of *Lucrece* is more weighty, the rhythm steadier, otherwise exaggeration is even more dominating, the rhetoric so elaborate and so mannered we must believe we are being asked more to admire the harangues than to be moved by them.

In each poem the manner of the writing works against the growth of strong effects, against intensity either in feeling or in pursuing thought, the attention is more upon the outward aspects of the dramatic than upon the springs of action. The occasions of the poems—seduction bordering on brutality and an act of brutality—are intrinsically shocking, but here everything works successfully to avoid shock. One has only to compare the tremors we felt in contemplating the killing of Rutland or even in the thought of Proteus' violation of Silvia to see how successfully Shakespeare here has deadened such possibilities. He does this, I think, partly in humour, partly sardonically, partly in order to provide a most complex irony for morals so obviously simple and clear. Partly, too, he is exploiting the sense of the strangeness of the material, stories out of an alien civilization, and not only non-Christian and pagan, but in a character peculiarly characteristic of Rome, of a civilization given so deeply to the cultivation of decorum and so much more interested in effects than in processes and sensibility. It may even be that Shakespeare, in exploiting language and verse in these poems—elaborate, self-consciously ornate, exaggeratedly tempestuous—is by the contrasts mocking the ancient manner in its use of simple outline and thereby also reducing anything like intensity.

The suggestions of allegory were also obviously serviceable for just that result:

> 'Since thou art dead, lo here I prophesy,
> Sorrow on love hereafter shall attend.
> It shall be waited on with jealousy,
> Find sweet beginning, but unsavoury end.'
> *(Venus and Adonis,* 1135–8)

> She says her subjects with foul insurrection
> Have battered down her consecrated wall,
> And by their mortal fault brought in subjection
> Her immortality and made her thrall
> To living death and pain perpetual. *(Lucrece,* 722–6)

The continuous self-dramatizing is even more influential in preventing us from feeling for the troubled:

> 'O, thou dist kill me, kill me once again!
> Thy eyes' shrewd tutor, that hard heart of thine
> Hath taught them scornful tricks, and such disdain
> That they have murdered this poor heart of mine.'
> *(Venus and Adonis,* 499–502)

> 'I see what crosses my attempt will bring,
> I know what thorns the growing rose defends,

I think the honey guarded with a sting:
All this beforehand counsel comprehends.
But Will is deaf and hears no heedful friends.'

(*Lucrece*, 491–5)

Venus' concluding prophecy is elaborately staged, the words construct a universe of stars and planets for the playing out of endless misery, and Lucrece plans as elaborate a staging for her acquittal. These do in large what the figures of speech do in little, everything is dramatized, nothing is dramatic, a few stylized figures moving in a barely peopled scene.

One of the obvious results to this complex artifice is to emphasize the strangeness of the stories, of the esoteric in the ancient mythology and legend. Instead of bringing figures out of the ancient world into the life of the present with the vividness of actuality that is normally central to the imagination of humanists—so exquisitely done in *The Comedy of Errors* in that simple naming of a siren—the poems present us with half-heroic, half-barbarous figures deprived of grace.

This way of confounding the recognizably personal with the strange, the intimate with the public, the anguished with the stylized, is advanced into striking and sometimes repelling effects when grand, ambitiously elevated generalities are applied to low and disagreeable particulars:

'Call it not Love, for Love to heaven is fled
Since sweating Lust on earth usurped his name;
Under whose simple semblance he hath fed
Upon fresh beauty, blotting it with blame;
Which the hot tyrant stains and soon bereaves,
As caterpillars do the tender leaves.'

(*Venus and Adonis*, 793–8)

About the mourning and congealèd face
Of that black blood a watery rigol goes,
Which seems to weep upon the tainted place.

(*Lucrece*, 1744–6)

Add to the incongruity the humour—in Adonis' very situation, in the beauty of Lucrece's body in its sleeping ignorance, in—

> So from himself impiety hath wrought
> That for his prey to pray he doth begin—
> (*Lucrece*, 341–2)

and the very moral of it all is sapped.

But whatever Shakespeare's intent in all this, he is certainly exploiting artifice upon artifice, as we see him also doing in *Titus Andronicus*, and as he does not in the comedies even where he has such license to. Dealing with this ancient Roman matter he is drawn to concentrate on individuals as he had not done before, exploiting their isolation, pushing it so far that even nature is excluded from the representation of human crises. This manner so alien to Shakespeare's instinctive thinking gives him the opportunity for the sharpest and most limited focus, it leaves him free to manipulate a few elements in shaping a wholly new form. He seems to be working similarly in *Titus Andronicus*, dramatizing for the stage what in the poems may be better spoken of as posturing. Given this freedom to exclude the profoundly affecting he is able to devise an economy which in its own way will be as influential as the Plautine patterns in helping him work out the forms with which in time he will be communicating the full range of his thought and feeling.

At the very beginning of *Titus Andronicus* Titus determines that the son of the enemy queen must be sacrificed as amends for the death of his sons, and it is done:

> Alarbus' limbs are lopped,
> And entrails feed the sacrificing fire,
> Whose smoke like incense doth perfume the sky.
> (I, i, 143–5)

This is both a factual and a happy remark—no one, it appears, knows what it means to be squeamish about butchery. Then, as the horrors multiply, the time comes when a messenger brings Titus 'two heads and a hand' (III, i, 234), the heads of his sons and his own hand. Just as with Lavinia's stumps, it is the crime that is thought to offend, not the maiming and not even the pain. Lavinia, of course, cannot speak but she kisses Titus, and there is language enough to tell us as well as the deeds do that passions are at work—

When will this fearful slumber have an end? (III, i, 252)

But we have only to remember Macduff as he pulls his hat down over his brows on hearing of the murder of his sons and their mother to know that in this play no such effects are to be known. Nor, again, is the effect of the kind we know when Margaret brings in the head of Suffolk, kissing it. The play is not complicated by irony as the poems are, but the absence of sensibility is the same and it is this that makes it possible to manipulate artifice so freely. In the play the artifice is more elaborate because more persons are involved and because Shakespeare is here more free to tamper with his material. Something that has the standing of history he can alter vastly because his audience is not familiar with it, and in the plotting he is less constrained than when following Plautus and even Lyly. All these factors are enabling him to develop a new form for tragic material without the distraction of significant beliefs.

At the very beginning Shakespeare modified the pattern he had employed in commencing so many of the early plays, he began with a quarrel. This proceeds briefly and then a magnificent ceremonial affair—hopefully as *fastueux* as Rome itself—dominates the scene. Two men are rivals for the Emperorship, formal speeches are addressed to the Tribunes and Senators 'aloft', and among them is Marcus Andronicus holding the crown, ready to confer it on the one who is chosen. The speechmaking is formal and gracious, although it is clear that feelings are running high and each candidate is attended with followers bearing standards. But before the choice can be made, and before there is open fighting, Marcus urges the two sides to withdraw peaceably so that the Senate may do honour to the great general Titus Andronicus, returning from the wars.

'Sound drums and trumpets, and then enter two of Titus' sons, and then two men bearing a coffin covered with black, then two other sons, then Titus Andronicus, and then Tamora, the Queen of Goths, and her three sons, [Alarbus], Chiron, and Demetrius, with Aaron the Moor, and others as many as can be; then set down the coffin, and Titus speaks.' (I, i, following line 69)

The tomb bears the remains of twenty-five of Titus' sons. It is opened and those present look on in silence. A surviving brother then requests as amends that a son of the Queen of the Goths be taken and offered up in sacrifice, and this is done.

Not only is the spectacular ceremonial entry an interruption to what has already taken place upon the stage, it is, at the opening of the coffin, the immediate occasion for an act that will add to the strife that has been temporarily stilled. In *Henry VI* a funeral set the stage, here it causes the fires of violence to spread, it is itself pregnant with the violence that will soon overtake all Rome. Not even *Richard III* will begin so dramatically with an explosion, and, allowing for the differences between the complex play and the simpler narrative poems, the headlong manner of the beginning bears the same stamp.

Immediately Alarbus is carried off, the play now proceeds in a manner unlike that of any of the others, although soon in the manner of complication it will bear a close resemblance to *The Comedy of Errors*.

The sons of Titus return with their swords bloody, announcing the sacrifice of Alarbus; the coffin of Titus' dead sons is laid in the tomb, and Marcus and the rivals for the Emperor's crown—Saturninus and Bassianus—return. The choice is now to be made. Marcus asks that Titus agree to be a candidate, saying this is the people's will, but he pleads his age and already long service and asks the Tribunes to crown Saturninus Emperor. And as swiftly as words and deeds can come the action erupts.

Saturninus offers to take Titus' daughter Lavinia to wife, but on receiving Tamora as his personal prisoner he is smitten, and he begins to court her in dumb show. Bassianus, with the help of Titus' two sons, carries Lavinia off. A third son attempts to block the pursuit and Titus kills him.

And now the intrigues. Saturninus dismisses Titus. Bassianus and Lavinia return to confront Saturninus, but Tamora, now his queen, persuades him to make peace for the time until means can be found to get rid of all of them, including Titus. Then Aaron, Tamora's lover, contributes to the plot by inciting Tamora's two remaining sons to murder Bassianus and ravish Lavinia.

In the English history plays where strife and civil war were the matter, there were several plots sometimes formed in complicity with others, sometimes devised on the spur of the moment and for tangential purposes; here, in short order, a controlling intent is able to make use of all the occasion provides, and while what is to follow is by no means foreseen and there are to be consequences that cannot be forestalled, up to a point the game is being played perfectly.

York and then Richard mean to play for as high stakes and as relentlessly, but in the histories too many individuals are working at cross purposes and time takes longer to provide the appropriate circumstances. Moreover, there is a need to represent history in its expansiveness, to expatiate on all that can stand in the way of any policy. Above all else, there is the need to show that careers, however intimately interconnected, cannot be shown to demonstrate such complicity as we should see if it were certain that Providence were arranging matters. There is Henry's life, his early crowning, his marriage, his abdication, his murder; the fall of the Duchess of Gloucester; Gloucester's fall; the rise and fall of Suffolk; the rise and fall of Joan; the rise of Edward. All this, we might say in retrospect, was necessary if Richard and finally Richmond were to come to the throne, but much of the point to the series of plays is that one may not certainly perceive a principle at work in the ordering of the result. And the plotting in *Titus Andronicus*—of Saturninus and Tamora and Aaron and finally of Titus—illustrates a principle at work in the history itself, that revenge, in inspiring a policy of extermination, in its success provides the occasion for the destruction of its own agents.

The interest of the play goes quite beyond that to be comprehended in any point whatever, but such plays, like many comedies, are ordered to such an end. Meaning, import, morals even, may be inferred as governing much of the conception of the early histories, but their integrity is not formed within any such limits as that of *Titus Andronicus* or the narrative poems. To summarize roughly, one might say that the *Henry VI* plays show that at the centre of power many lives are lived out, some of these wholly involved in issues affecting the state, some only partly, and out of the welter of circumstance there comes into being for a while a stand-off among the aspirants for power when government is for a while effective. It is then possible for one man, it hardly signifies whether he is just or unjust, to keep affairs under control. In this everlasting flux only the idea of justice is inexpugnable.

As I see it, the modification of the form of the histories we see in *Titus Andronicus* is made possible by extending the conception of the poet as a manipulator of an idea, a moral idea, that is at work in the two poems. In part it is also effected through the control of an action by a plot that makes a point, not as the plots of *The Comedy of Errors* and *Love's Labour's Lost* are managed but as those of *The Taming of the Shrew* and *All's Well that Ends Well*, and many another that derives from narratives that followed upon the achievements of Boccaccio and the Italian satiric comedy.

Titus is in the highest position of honour, and his one-time captive, the Gothic Queen, suddenly finds herself able to bring him to his knees. As Lear later, in abdicating he counted on maintaining the prerogatives of power, but Saturninus proves to be as treacherous an heir as Goneril and Regan. There is, moreover, an established rivalry between Saturninus and Bassianus, and Tamora commences her work in taking advantage of this.

Aaron of course is her helper and he does not always wait for her to take the initiative, but up to a point it may be said of the plot of this play what has been said of that of *All's Well That Ends Well*, it is the plot of one of the persons in the drama—Helena improvising one move after another in pursuit of her aim, Tamora and Aaron arranging and overseeing a whole series of events in their single-minded fury. They play it as they would play a game, and since the rules are simple and clearly understood—that every offence calls for violence in retaliation—they are able to play it perfectly. But just short of the last trick the game is lost. Titus discovered that a game was being played, with him as both the pawn and the prize. He came to see what was going on because it was a game he knew very well himself although he had never been obliged to work at it so hard. He learned that what had so far happened had been a series of moves, he learns how they were masked, and so he begins countermoves, masking them, concealing from his opponents the fact that he has taken up the game and is setting out to reverse their success. He finds ways of keeping from them the last success of all, even as it seems to them more and more certainly in their grasp, and then, suddenly, he reveals to them that they have been trapped and he has inflicted greater losses upon them than they could ever have dreamed of.

The action is as perfectly articulated as in *The Comedy of Errors*, and the essential difference is that in the comedy the complications and the unwinding were largely in the power of circumstance and here they are determined in a matching of wits. In the *Comedy* it may be that circumstance is the implement of a mysterious power in life, and there will be plays in which that power will be seen performing in this way, as fate or Providence—but here all takes form in the minds of those for whom the relations between humans revert finally and lastingly to a single motivation. This is finally more the technique of the *Mandragola* than of the *Menaechmi*.

Differently than in the early plays, the number of persons is limited to those necessary for effecting the single action, and also

246

differently, the focus is upon one chief person. In the first half Titus is so to speak the object of the intrigue, in the second he becomes the chief intriguer. The audience, of course, comes to be interested in more the way the game is being played and especially in the raging and suffering of Titus. We discover that, as Shylock puts it, and Macduff, he feels as a man, and above all he feels the pain of injustice. So that when, beside himself, he sends messages and defies to the gods in the skies on the points of arrows, we have been so moved to horror, compounded with sympathy, that we are ready to accept the final killings as not only tolerable but as the only means of satisfying our concern that the wicked shall be punished and the tortured put out of their misery.

The probable source for the play—'A Noble Roman Historye of Tytus Andronicus', identified in an eighteenth-century printing as translated from the Italian—is a very well told story providing Shakespeare with a wealth of detail, and he made the fullest use of it. It gave him so much that one can see here better than almost anywhere else how and why he re-ordered source material. Apart, of course, from the opportunities for spectacle and any number of stage effects he was plainly engaged in relating the action representing a part of the history of Rome to the turmoil within a man and correlating the destruction within to a pattern of events. There will be almost none of the suggestions of allegory and of mythical analogy that give dignity to the story of Venus and Adonis, and very little of the philosophizing and the extended use of symbols we have in *Lucrece*, but there is the comparable manner of separating thought from feeling, or representing passion as gesture, and in the result expressing the idea of essential isolation.

Shakespeare appears to have held to a traditional conception of Roman character—self-reliant, severe, fixed in family obligations, public spirited, finding its ultimate satisfaction in contributing to the greatness of Rome. He was faithful to this view in *Coriolanus* as here, and in general his insight seems to have been so profound that it everywhere deserves what Jérome Carcopino has said in judging *Julius Caesar*: 'Car, enfin, n'est-ce point perdre son temps et sa peine que de pâlir, comme ils l'ont fait et continuent de le faire à longueur de journées, sur les documents dont la quête n'est jamais finie, d'en disséquer les textes, d'en peser les témoignages examinés à la loupe et retournés en tous sens, quand, d'un seul coup d'aile, le poète atteint les vérités essentielles dont ils ne s'approchent qu'en tâtonnant, et qu'ils ne se flattent jamais qu'avec hésitation d'avoir acquises après de si longues analyses et au prix de tant d'efforts.'[2]

In *Titus Andronicus* Shakespeare is intent upon a view of life as wholly of men's making, the men being war-like, adventurous, dedicated to Rome, and anxious to offer its enemies to her in sacrifice. In return for their success when it is greatest, Rome will give them glory. The language they use is frequently religious without taking on the mystical character appropriate to some military ideals, but the gods evidently keep their distance and the heroes appear never to count on their help. It may be that they never even ask for it. Much that they do the Romans do in the name of the gods but Tamora's cry cuts more ways than she intended—

O cruel, irreligious piety! (I, i, 130)

Nor is there any sign that the gods take notice of priests or suppliants in kindness or in doom. No sheeted-dead walk the streets, no all-devouring thunder-stroke smites the impious. No one ever supposes his life is lived out on anything but an empty stage. The barbarian Queen has some sense of tutelary spirits and of demons beneath the earth, but such sense as she has of them amounts to nothing in the face of Titus' mockery. As for his reproaches to Heaven, they are the empty taunts of a man half-mad, as vain as Joan's boasts, and he knows them to be vain.

Moreover, in this Rome not even the ties of blood are the ties of anything like the ties of corporate life. The great figure of speech that is at the centre of Shakespeare's thinking in *Coriolanus*—that life in society is of the order of the life in the body of humans—is absent from the thoughts of anyone in this play.

In *Titus Andronicus* the only ties that bind men to each other are the courtesy that the proud pay to the proud and the pity the helpless pay to the ruined.

In short, the interest in focusing upon individuals that we observe in *Venus and Adonis* and in *Lucrece* is here sustained and developed in drama, the drama itself confined within the limits set by the limits of characters conceived as individuals and nothing more, which is to say, in a society that has no other nourishment than resides in the accommodations with power. One may say that in this play Shakespeare is again applying the notion at the heart of the humanist undertaking, discovering and celebrating the common elements in mankind, this time pursuing it as undistractedly as if he were writing an allegory, but instead of treating with abstractions, applying a view to historical figures which must by the very terms of that view demonstrate the conclusions of tragedy. Without recourse to whatever lightened the implications of the early comedies and whatever gave perspective to the histories, he writes a play in which humans act as if they were powers unto themselves, and in what is therefore demonstrably folly they can only serve to illustrate the uninhibited authority of fate.

Hamlet and *Lear* may sustain tragic endings with the same import, but they will do so movingly because the terrible conclusions are being measured and sounded by Christian beliefs. These serve as opposition to the obvious completeness of the destruction of men's hopes and they therefore are used ironically to probe the reaches of thought. No reflection of such an endeavour even glimmers in *Titus Andronicus*, and the play is unique for Shakespeare in proceeding as drama without the help of irony. The humanist exercise is perfectly executed.

NOTES

[1] Once again I think it may be proper to illustrate the doctrine employed here as it is developed in Neo-Platonism:

'Vnde intimus in nobis præsidet iudex, inextinguibile rationis lumen, rectum ueri falsique et boni malique examen, ineuitabilis conscientiæ stimulus. Per hanc Deus infusam omnibus legem omnes ita fermè ad commune dirigit bonum, ut omnes flammas leuitate erigit ad superna. Ab hæc utique ingenita lege lex deinde scripta ducit originem. Quod quidem in ipso libri legum exordio Plato aperuit, dicens: non ab homine, sed ipso Deo leges initium habuisse. Sed ut ad præsentem Dialogum redeamus, subiungit Iouem per Mercurium condidisse legem, qua iubeantur omnes ciuilitatis participes, quippe cum hæc sola sit uinculum ciuitatis, ipsamque ciuitatem iustitia et pudore constantem ait ad omnes cœlitus demisisse, eo uidelicet pacte, ut quicunque posthac uirtutis huius omnino expers deprehensus fuerit, tanquam ciuitatis pestis ultime afficiatur supplicio. Quem uero primo appellauit pudorem, deinde temperantiam nominauit. Est enim pudor ingenitus temperantiæ fundamentum' (Marsilio Ficino, *Opera*, Basel, 1576, II, 1298–9 [*In Protagoram Epitome—Protagoras*, 322C]).

² *Recontres de l'Histoire et de la Littérature Romaines*, Paris, 1963, p. 271.

An Afterword

Shakespeare believed that a sustaining power holds men together. Life, a spirit, a need, however it was to be thought of,
nourished them—gave them guidance, bound them to each other
in families, directed them in ordering other attachments. It was
not a simple, single energy ordering families and societies but a
manifold power informing the understanding—but not equally
and not always—moving and even giving birth at times to the
affections, asserting itself at times intelligibly even in nature and
in fortune and in the larger universe. When, in the worlds of his
plays, to the men in them nothing could make sense of anything,
the plays themselves never enlist our subscription to mere point-
lessness. Even when the noblest go down in utmost wretchedness, or when the blindly selfish cut down the finest and best
with impunity, we are only permitted to conclude that darkness
has come over the world, and not, with Kent, that all is forever
dark. Light continues to be born, life to renew, faith and trust to
prove themselves sustaining. This power that sustains, that
illumines, that promises—and seems not to keep its promises, or
all of them—never vanishes into the abyss. It is never known
certainly as illusion.

We must think of this not merely as a feature of the different
works but as a belief of the writer, because every individual in
these works in reaching maturity bears witness to that maturity,
to that fulfilment, known as fulfilment, if not as 'a perfect man'
yet as a man, and every one of these creatures of an imagination
supposes his manhood is the effect of life advancing hand in hand

with truth. Each of them is always supposing he is acting freely, that he is choosing what is enabling him in love and power, and when they are the right choices they do. Even Gloucester, abandoning the thought of freedom, putting his trust in the beggar, is some little restored. Aaron and Iago and Lucio know that the fault was theirs. If it was ever otherwise, if the plays ever left us despairing and only despairing, then we should know that what once was a belief had been abandoned. But, as Jusserand said, beauty dominates it all, nothing is ugly and unformed, all is cherished.

If one attempts to refer this conviction of a sustaining life to a philosophy one is defeated. The Platonism of the early comedies, intrinsic to them, is yet matched and even confounded by the common sense of Launce and Speed, by the irreverent religiousness of unaccommodated men and women, by the mere staying power of 'obedient stones'. I think that in the early Platonism Shakespeare has absorbed an idea that will remain of vital consequence with him to the end, or at least he had found a way of thinking about a sense of purpose that always remained with him. But there are many other attitudes and interests that were lastingly important to him as well—the delight in society, in courtship and love-making, in wit, in flowers and storms and uproar—and I for my part have come to think that the principle sustaining this creating and the life in it we take to be so much like our own is the principle informing the delight in the variety of things, in the bounteousness of the world. It is because this unlimited variety is not confusion, because every part of it is a matter for delight—snails drawing back their tender horns in pain—but not only as the particulars poetry is always honouring and praising, but all the particulars in all their variety and abundance. This delight in infinite variety I take to be not merely the love of a mind for what comes into it but a response to the spirit in things themselves, in the existence that embraces them all. I hesitate to use the words harmony and nature and creation, although all these words even in metaphysical senses are drawn on in the plays, but applied to them they introduce the notions of systems that are sooner or later irrelevant. There is a phrase out of the Middle Ages, 'per charitatis concordiam', that for me comes nearest to expressing a comprehending conception that compromises least our sense of the play of Shakespeare's imagination, and that justifies us in believing that an idea of truth is at the centre of all the playing—'omnes sancti per charitatis concordiam quasi per diapason'[1]—all things made holy in concord of charity as it would be in the harmony of music—a little like Abraham Lincoln's God who must have loved the common people He made so many of them. Whatever Prospero has in mind in retiring, it is no such abandonment Henry VI contemplates or Valentine in the forest takes thought of, and no play ends in utter defeat.

The Platonic doctrine Shakespeare was always to make so much of and that indeed is one of the deepest wells of experience in the Renaissance, at the heart of if not all of most of the influential currents in humanism, at the heart of the Petrarchan explorations, the idea of the consultation of the principle of life and truth within the soul, was to show itself inadequate in the face of circumstance. No matter what Adonis holds to, the boar strikes him down. Whatever understanding illumines Valentine, it has no power to dispose of the lives of others. It may testify to an all-embracing mind or love or being, but wrong and evil assert their special destructive powers perennially, and the good and the true go down before them. None of the Shakespearean plays support Platonic solutions to the problem of evil.

Shakespeare was bound to test such solutions if for no other reason than that in the material he drew on for the early histories there were stories of men who cut themselves off from others, or who tried to, who meant to impose their individual wills upon others and upon what in themselves linked them to others, the claims of kind, men who did not acknowledge or else were truly ignorant of any other power than those of will and calculation and circumstance. Although in the end Richard and Aaron came to disaster, so did their foils, and the challenges they have made strike so deep that no facile opposition can outface them. If this imagined world of Shakespeare's is in the hands of, or includes another power than fortune and tetherless human will, there are many times when that does not make itself known to us, and even when we think we see its presence we are seldom persuaded it has anything but limited and evanescent authority—as elusive as a dream however enthralling even in the suggestion of it.

But one thing we do know, that the figures in this imagined world are caught up in the mesh of life, caught up in what embraces them with hoops of steel. How profoundly and comprehensive this force is we may see clearly when we compare the figures of the Shakespearean world with the great figures of antiquity Livy and Ovid and Plutarch told of. These were to offer him a view of greatness and goodness and civilization in which there was no expression of an embracing power that men might consult in the intimacy of their thoughts, assured that the truth of the soul was the reassurance of Providence. Whatever came to him through Plutarch or from his own age of the Stoic metaphysics, it did not come as part and parcel of Roman history and Roman drama and poetry.

If one were to pick out what distinguishes the conflicts between powerful persons in Shakespeare's works with those in the Roman histories, or with Petrarch's *Lives of Illustrious Men*—a kind of Bible for the humanist appreciation of antiquity—one would observe that no one in Shakespeare acts so freely, in so unconstrained a medium as these others. In the Rome of the ancient writers, and as Petrarch also sees it, there are of course obligations that are known to bind everyone, in family feeling, in law, in piety, in dedication, but so much more than in Shakespeare is thought to reside in mere will, in the almost unlimited capacity of brute force, in the capacity of wit and calculation and device to accomplish wonders. Quintus Fabius Maximus and Scipio and Tarquin and Caesar comes to us as colossi striding the world, and when defeated they are still themselves, thinking of themselves as freely subsiding, not like that other giant, Warwick, knowing that from the beginning he has been caught in the world's great snare. No one in Shakespeare, not even Iago, certainly not Enobarbus who had the longing, is ever such a master of himself as Hannibal or Xerxes or Caesar abandoning Capua, crossing the Athonite Gulf, or the Rubicon. They know demons and fevers and uncertainties as well as Shakespeare's heroes, they know, or think about, destiny and Providence and the wrath of the gods, yet they suppose in themselves a liberty and they possess an impudence Shakespeare never represents.

I think Coriolanus makes this certain. For once Shakespeare is almost literal in transporting an ancient into his world—the circumstances, the style of speech, come over into English as if English retained nothing of the life of the ages in which it had taken form and which so marvellously transformed Plautus' love of his vernacular. And the point of the ancient story, as it became moralized, would seem to prove that the Romans indeed understood that a man's life was as much in the possession of others as of himself, that the ties of family were the ties of nature, and these Romans could no more erase wife and mother and children from their thoughts and the very stirrings of their bodies than Lear could expunge Regan and Goneril from his blood. But it only seems alike, for although it is clear that in this play Shakespeare is giving full rein to the ambitions of a man to be wholly on his own, as it turns out Coriolanus is subdued to kin by more powerful and entangling bonds than Livy or even Plutarch knew of.

At the heart of the play, as is often remarked, is the figure of speech Menenius used in confronting the plebeians, the fable of the belly and the other members of the body. Menenius likens the Senate to the belly of a human body and the other parts of the state to the other parts of the body. His point was that the body politic was like the human body, the different organs have their functions, all depend upon the others, no one takes harm, only good, from the proper flourishing of the other. In this instance, the labouring classes must recognize their dependence upon those who provide them with work, and each class must perform its own duty in order for the whole body to prosper. The figure of speech came from antiquity—from a Greek sophist, from Euripides, from the Stoics—but it took on a new meaning in Saint Paul, who used it to affirm the Christian idea of the divinity present in the Creation: 'For as the body is one, and hath many members and all the members of that one body being many, are one body: so also is Christ. For by one Spirit we are all baptized into one body, whether we be Jews or Gentiles, whether we be bond or free: and have been all made to drink into one Spirit. . . . And whether one member suffer, all the members suffer with it: or one member be honoured, all the members rejoice with it.' (I *Corinthians* 12, 12–13, 26).

What Menenius would persuade the people of, Coriolanus would refute:

> I'll never
> Be such a gosling to obey instinct, but stand
> As if a man were author of himself
> And knew no other kin. (V, iii, 34–7)

He all but succeeded, but even in his negation his language revealed confusion. The idea of creation and a creator survived in it, and it was the idea of divorce that was beyond him. But this is much more than a provinciality of understanding, the rash ambition of a soldier not knowledgeable about the subtleties of relationship implied in the simplest affirmation, for when the tests were most demanding, he revealed an understanding of the seamlessness of the world into which he was born that is comparable in its sense of identity to the mysticism of Saint Paul. When he saw his wife looking at him silently, he spoke to her in words that Professor H. T. Price once called the most glorious expression of love in all Shakespeare, 'Best of my flesh' (V, iii, 42), thinking of himself incarnate in her as she in him. (This is, incidentally, a profound transformation of Suffolk's thought about his subjugation to Margaret.) And when he is finally overcome by his mother's appeal it is because, as he says, the gods scorn a division so 'unnatural' (V, iii, 184).

Venus and Adonis and *Lucrece*, poems centering on disastrous fortunes, provided the first opportunity of sounding the adequacy of the ancient view of human resources. What was at issue was the fullness of communication between individuals in two worlds, the poet in the civilization of the Christian dispensation and subjects from the pre-Christian world. In writing fancifully to Cicero Petrarch had said he felt such harmony between them that even though he knew his friend to be in Hell he knew as certainly that no one could ever more fully share his inmost thoughts. Shakespeare, on the other hand, does not read himself into the past, he re-creates it, he re-creates the beautiful and terrible figures in all their isolation. The poetry of the countryside is too much with him to be excluded from *Venus and Adonis*, but neither Venus nor Adonis are part of the natural world, they are not intricate with its life, they are aliens to it even in attempting vainly, both of them, to maintain an alliance with it. What Shakespeare does propose is that his ancients had a knowledge of their perfectibility as humans, that any human anywhere had, that the moral sense of Adonis and Lucrece testified to what would never fade from his thought, a certain sacredness to the person. This was what all people held in common, and if he himself would be choosing to translate this into philosophical conceptions less certainly universal, the main point would remain that for Livy and Ovid and the others as for himself, the defences against wrong and death were known to be inadequate. Once the resources of ancient heroism were sounded there would then be the need to test the value of the belief in a power sustaining men and nature and society. If *Coriolanus* provides that test, the answer is not ambiguous.

It is not necessary to pursue the argument further here, for the present point is simply that in these first plays we are seeing this most bounteous imagination bodying forth a plurality of worlds in which the humanist undertaking as such, the bringing into the present of a life long since gone, is a labour of criticism, both of the past and of the present. The issues are drawn from the start.

But there is still another respect in which these writings, in their very prodigality of language and beauty and the variousness of life are pursuing the ends of criticism to the limit. This is in part manifest in the enrichment of drama in the multiple actions and the range of character. It is in part in the lavishness Petrarch encouraged with his, one might almost call it, religion of amplification—not merely in the ringing of changes in similes and analogies but in the development of meaning through the very multiplicity of comparison. This is to say, the Renaissance style of elaboration, in the dramatic form and in the language, supported what Shakespeare might have been taking from his own Middle Ages, the fertility and richness of the imaginings not so much of medieval drama as of medieval ways generally. With help from both quarters, the currents of the Renaissance coming to him from Italy, and the medieval heritage, Shakespeare was developing his own art, measuring it against the classic accomplishments as they measured his.

NOTE

[1] Otleh de Saint Eméran (1032–1070), *Patrologia Latina* 146. *c.* 125, quoted by Edgar de Bruyne, *Etudes d'Esthétique Médiévale*, Brussels, 1946, II, 110.

INDEX

Index